Quantitative Financial Analysis (Course Slides)

Course Objectives

- Calculate cash flows and basic business economic indicators, including NPV, IRR, and other indicators, and understand the key input parameters in the model (interest rates, inflation rates, cost of money, and Weighted Average Cost of Capital).
- Describe the relationship of cash flow and economic indicators to the project decision-making process.
- Utilize a practical, user-oriented approach to project financial analysis.
- Model the financial and economic benefits of capital investment projects.
- Sensitivity analysis, scenario analysis, tornado analysis, risk-based Monte Carlo simulation, risk-based decision analytics, and analysis of alternatives.
- Project/program portfolio selection and optimal investment decisions in a portfolio with investment efficient frontiers.

COURSE SYLLABUS

Module 1: Project Economic Analysis

a. Course Objectives and Overview
b. Financial Management and Financial Environment
c. Corporate Life Cycle
d. Capital Allocation Process

Module 2: Time Value of Money

a. Time Value of Money
b. Present Value and Future Value
c. Multiple Cash Flows and Annuities
d. Amortization Models
e. Investment Analysis of Alternatives of Uneven Life-Cycle Projects
f. Discounting Conventions

Module 3: Interest Rates and Discount Rates

a. Cost of Money and General Economic Interest Rates
b. Cost of Capital: Using Discount Rates and Hurdle Rates
c. Weighted Average Cost of Capital (WACC)
d. Calculating the BETA and CAPM
e. Optimal Capital Structure

Module 4: Financial Statements Analysis

a. Financial Statement Analysis (Balance Sheets, Cash Flow Statements, Income Statements)
b. Financial Cash Flows
c. Operating Cash Flows
d. Project Valuation: Cost Approach, Income Approach, Market Approach
e. Creating a Financial Spreadsheet Model

Module 5: Decision Analysis and Project Valuation

a. Capital Budgeting Methods
b. Net Present value
c. Internal Rate of Return
d. Modified Internal Rate of Return
e. Return on Investment and Profitability Index
f. Payback and Discounted Payback Period
g. Risk and Return of Investments and Portfolio Analysis
h. Portfolio Optimization

Module 6: Advanced Decision Analytics, Monte Carlo Risk-Based Simulation, and Predictive Modeling

a. Integrated Risk Management
b. Tornado and Sensitivity Analysis
c. Scenario Analysis
d. Probability Distributions and Monte Carlo Simulation for Risk Analytics
e. Forecasting and Predictive Modeling

Module 7: Project Economics Analysis Toolkit (PEAT)

a. Introducing PEAT Methodology
b. Simulation, Sensitivity, Scenario
c. Portfolio Optimization and Project Selection

Module 8: Strategic Flexibility in Capital Investments and Real Options

a. Navigating Risk and Return Opportunities
b. Risk Mitigation and Risk Management Decisions
c. Case Studies and Example Industry Applications

Module 9: Stocks and Bonds

a. Technical Analysis vs. Fundamental Analysis
b. Contrarian, Momentum, Market Indicators View
c. Stock Valuation
d. Bond Valuation

Module 10: Derivatives (Options, Forwards, Futures, Swaps)

a. Financial Derivatives
b. Options, Options Payoffs, Option Valuation
c. Futures and Futures Valuation
d. Swaps (Interest and Forex Swaps)
e. Multinational Finance and Forex Forward Arbitrage

Additional Example Problems and Exercises

Definitions, Key Concepts, Equations, and Formulae

Course Professor

Dr. Johnathan Mun, *Ph.D., MBA, MS, BS, CRM, CQRM, CFC, FRM, MIFC*
Research Professor, Naval Postgraduate School
jcmun@nps.edu

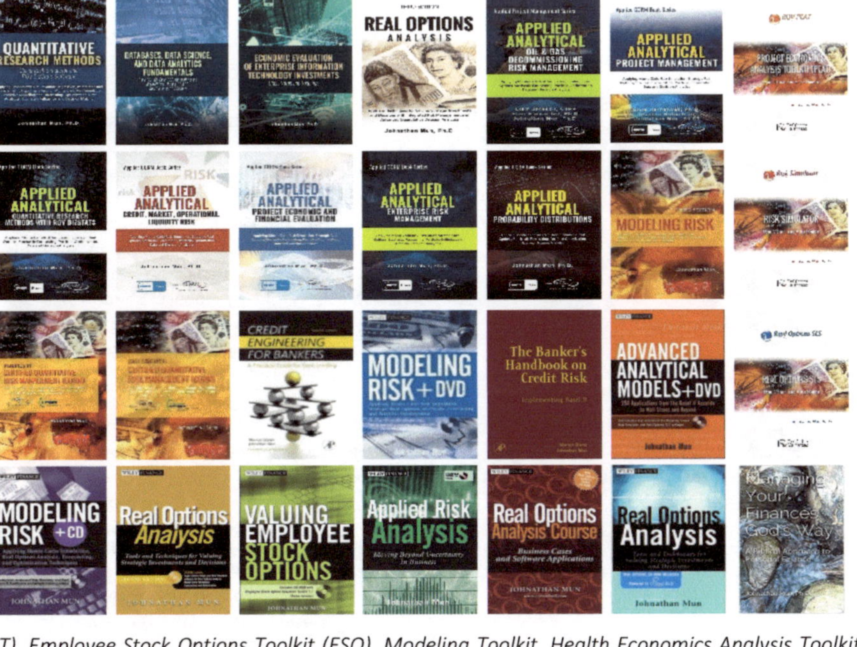

- ❖ Research Professor, Naval Postgraduate School. Formerly Professor in Finance, Economics, and Statistics at the Swiss School of Management (Switzerland), University of Applied Sciences (Germany), and Adjunct Professor at Golden Gate University (California), St. Mary's College (California), San Francisco State University (California).
- ❖ Founder and CEO, Real Options Valuation, Inc., and Chair, IIPER (International Institute of Professional Education and Research).
- ❖ Author of 28 books, including: *Quantitative Research Methods*, IIPER Press, 2018; *Modeling Risk: Applying Monte Carlo Risk Simulation, Strategic Real Options, Stochastic Forecasting and Portfolio Optimization,* First and Second Edition, Wiley 2006, 2010; Third Edition, Thomson-Shore, 2015; *Real Options Analysis: Tools and Techniques,* First and Second Edition Wiley 2002, 2005; *Credit Engineering*, Academic Press, 2010; *Advanced Analytical Models,* Wiley 2008; *Basel II Handbook on Credit Risk*, Elsevier Science, 2007-2008; *Real Options Analysis Course: Business Cases and Applications,* Wiley 2003; *Applied Risk Analysis: Moving Beyond Uncertainty,* Wiley 2003/2005; *Valuing Employee Stock Options 2004 FAS 123,* Wiley 2004.
- ❖ Holds 13 registered patents with another 10 patents pending
- ❖ Software Creator: *Risk Simulator, Real Options Super Lattice Solver, Project Economics Analysis Tool (PEAT), Employee Stock Options Toolkit (ESO), Modeling Toolkit, Health Economics Analysis Toolkit (HEAT), ROV Credit Market Operational Liquidity (CMOL), ROV BizStats, ROV Modeler, ROV Valuator, ROV Optimizer, ROV Visual Modeler, ROV Compiler, ROV Dashboard, Real Options Analysis Toolkit, etc.*
- ❖ Taught risk analytics, real options, simulation and optimization seminars worldwide (New York, San Francisco, Houston, Miami, Las Vegas, Tokyo, Singapore, Zurich, Ghana, London, Munich, Frankfurt, Paris, Colombia, Peru, Mexico, and many other locations).
- ❖ Currently CEO of Real Options Valuation, Inc. Formerly Vice President of Analytics at Decisioneering Crystal Ball, Inc., and worked for KPMG Consulting in Global Financial Strategies performing strategic valuation and developing real options and simulation applications. Headed a group in Financial and Economic Forecasting for FDX (FedEx) group of companies.
- ❖ Certified in Financial Consulting, Certified in Financial Risk Management, Charter Member of the Institute of Financial Consultants, Certified Risk Analyst, Certified in Quantitative Risk Management.
- ❖ Published dozens of academic journal articles in the *Global Finance Journal; Journal of Acquisitions Research; Neural Network Journal; Reliability and Systems Engineering' Advances in Quantitative Finance and Accounting; Journal of Financial Economics; Journal of International Finance, Institutions, and Money; Journal of the Society of Petroleum Engineers; American Institute of Physics; Defense Acquisition University; Expert Systems; Financial Engineering; Applied Energy Journal; NPS Acquisitions Symposium,* and others.

Module 1: Project Economic Analysis

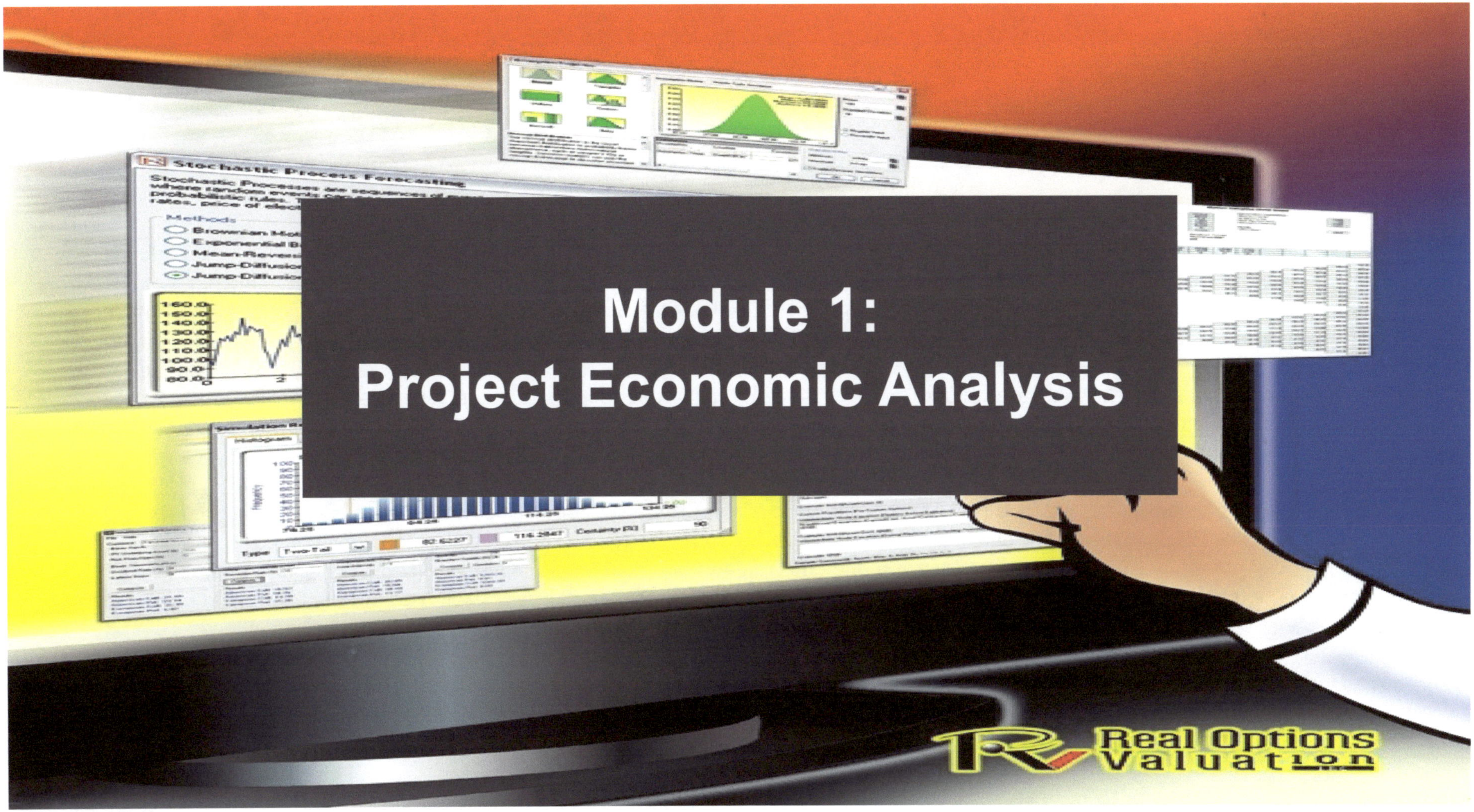

Financial Management

In this section, we provide a quick overview of financial management and the financial environment. We discuss the fundamental determinants of a firm's value, the nature of financial markets, the types of institutions that operate in these markets, and how interest rates are determined. The key concepts are:

- *Free cash flows* (FCF) are the cash flows available for distribution to all of a firm's investors (shareholders and creditors) after the firm has paid all expenses (including taxes) and made the required investments in operations to support growth.
  - FCF is the predominant determinant of a company's value or the value of any project within a company.
  - Three main factors determine free cash flows: sales revenues, operating costs (OPEX) and taxes, and required capital investments (CAPEX) in operations.
  - The value of a firm depends on the size of its free cash flows, the timing or speed of those cash flows, and their risk or uncertainty.
- The *Weighted Average Cost of Capital* (WACC) is the average return required by all of the firm's investors. It is determined by the firm's capital structure (the firm's relative amounts of debt and equity), interest rates, corporate taxes, and its risk, and the market's attitude toward risk.
- Probably one of the most important equations pertaining to financial management shows that the value of a firm, project, investment, or asset can be generalized to be the sum of the present value of free cash flows (FCF_t) at various points in time (t) discounted at some risk-adjusted discount rate (e.g., Weighted Average Cost of Capital or *WACC*, hurdle rate, required rate of return, corporate discount rate, and so forth):

$$Value = \frac{FCF_1}{(1+WACC)^1} + \frac{FCF_2}{(1+WACC)^2} + \ldots + \frac{FCF_N}{(1+WACC)^N} = \sum_{t=0}^{N} \frac{FCF_t}{(1+WACC)^t}$$

Financial Environment

- Capital is allocated through the pricing system—a price must be paid to borrow or "rent" money. Lenders charge *interest* on funds they lend, while equity investors receive *dividends and capital gains* in return for letting firms use their money.
- The *financial markets* bring together the lenders and borrowers. There are many different types of financial markets. Each market serves a different region or deals with a different type of security (e.g., physical exchanges like NYSE, NIKKEI, CAC, DAX, AMEX; over-the-counter *Electronic Communications Networks* using computers and telephone systems).
- Four fundamental factors affect the cost of money: production *opportunities*, *time* preferences for consumption, *risk*, and *inflation*.
- *Physical asset* markets, also called tangible or real asset markets, are those for such products as wheat, autos, and real estate.
- *Financial asset* markets deal with stocks, bonds, notes, mortgages, and other claims on real assets (e.g., mortgage-backed securities, credit derivatives, options, futures, forwards, swaps, swaptions, and other exotic option-embedded instruments).
- Financial securities are mainly classified as *Debt, Equity,* or *Derivatives* and are delineated by their maturity.
  - *Money markets* are the markets for debt securities with maturities of less than one year.
  - *Debt* instruments usually have a series of specified payments until maturity.
  - *Equity* instruments are ownership and have claim only to the *residual* value of a corporation.
  - *Derivatives* "derive" their value based on an underlying asset (derivatives by themselves do not have any value).
    - *Options*
    - *Forwards*
    - *Futures*
    - *Swaps*
    - *Exotics* (e.g., swaptions, options-embedded instruments)

Corporate Lifecycle

- The three main forms of business organization are *sole proprietorship*, *partnership*, and *corporation*. Although each form of organization offers advantages and disadvantages, corporations conduct most of the business in the world.
  - *Sole Proprietorship*. Positives: cheap and easy to form, few regulations, no corporate taxes (taxed as personal income). Negatives: unlimited personal liability, limited to the life of the owner, hard to raise large sums of capital.
  - *Partnership*. Positives: cheap and easy to form. Negatives: unlimited liability, limited life, hard to transfer ownership, hard to raise large sums of capital.
  - *Corporation*. Positives: unlimited or infinite life, easy stock ownership transfer, limited liability. Negatives: double taxation, lots of technical and legal filings (taxes, bylaws, charters, board meetings).
  - Hybrids. Combinations of the above.
    - *Limited Partnership*. Limited Partners (limited liability) and General Partners (unlimited liability).
    - *Limited Liability Partnership* (LLP/LLC). Limited liability for all partners.
    - *Professional Corporation* (PC/PA). Corporate protection but still exposed to professional malpractice liability (attorneys, doctors, accountants).
    - *S Corporations*. Similar to a regular corporation but owners are one or a few individuals and they choose to be taxed as a corporation.
- The primary objective of management should be to *maximize stockholders' wealth*, and it means *maximizing stock price*.
  - This further assumes a maximization of *intrinsic* or *fundamental* stock price with fair market value and an efficient market, as opposed to only market price maximization, which may be an incentive for short-term unethical gains.
  - Maximizing intrinsic value will also maximize value to society as customers, investors, owners, and employees are part of the society, and maximization of value means higher efficiency, lower price, competitive products, new innovations, and so forth.
- Corporations sometimes face issues such as the *Principal-Agent* problem and raising capital (from raising debt to initial public offerings or IPOs).

Capital Allocation

- *Securitized instruments* where the various security instruments are repackaged and sold in the market (e.g., MBS, CSO, CDO, etc.).
- *Spot Markets, futures, and forward markets* are terms that refer to whether the assets are bought or sold for "on-the-spot" delivery or for delivery at some future date.
- *Capital Markets* are the markets for *long-term debt and corporate stocks*, and *Money Markets* are for *short-term obligations* typically less than 1 year.
- *Primary markets* are the markets in which corporations raise new capital in an initial public offering (IPO).
- *Secondary markets* are the markets in which existing, already outstanding, securities are traded among investors (individuals purchasing stocks from stockbrokers or online accounts).
- Transfers of capital between borrowers and savers take place by *direct transfers* of money and securities (corporation sells directly to investors); by transfers through *investment banking houses*, which act as middlemen (primary and secondary markets); and by transfers through *financial intermediaries*, which create new securities (securitization, repackaging, mutual funds, index funds, and so forth).
- The major intermediaries include commercial banks, savings and loan associations, mutual savings banks, credit unions, pension funds, life insurance companies, and mutual funds.
- The stock market is an especially important market because this is where stock prices (which are used to "grade" managers' performances) are established.
- Sale and purchase orders from buyers and sellers can be matched in one of three ways: in an *open outcry auction*, through *dealers*, and automatically through an *electronic communications network* (ECN).

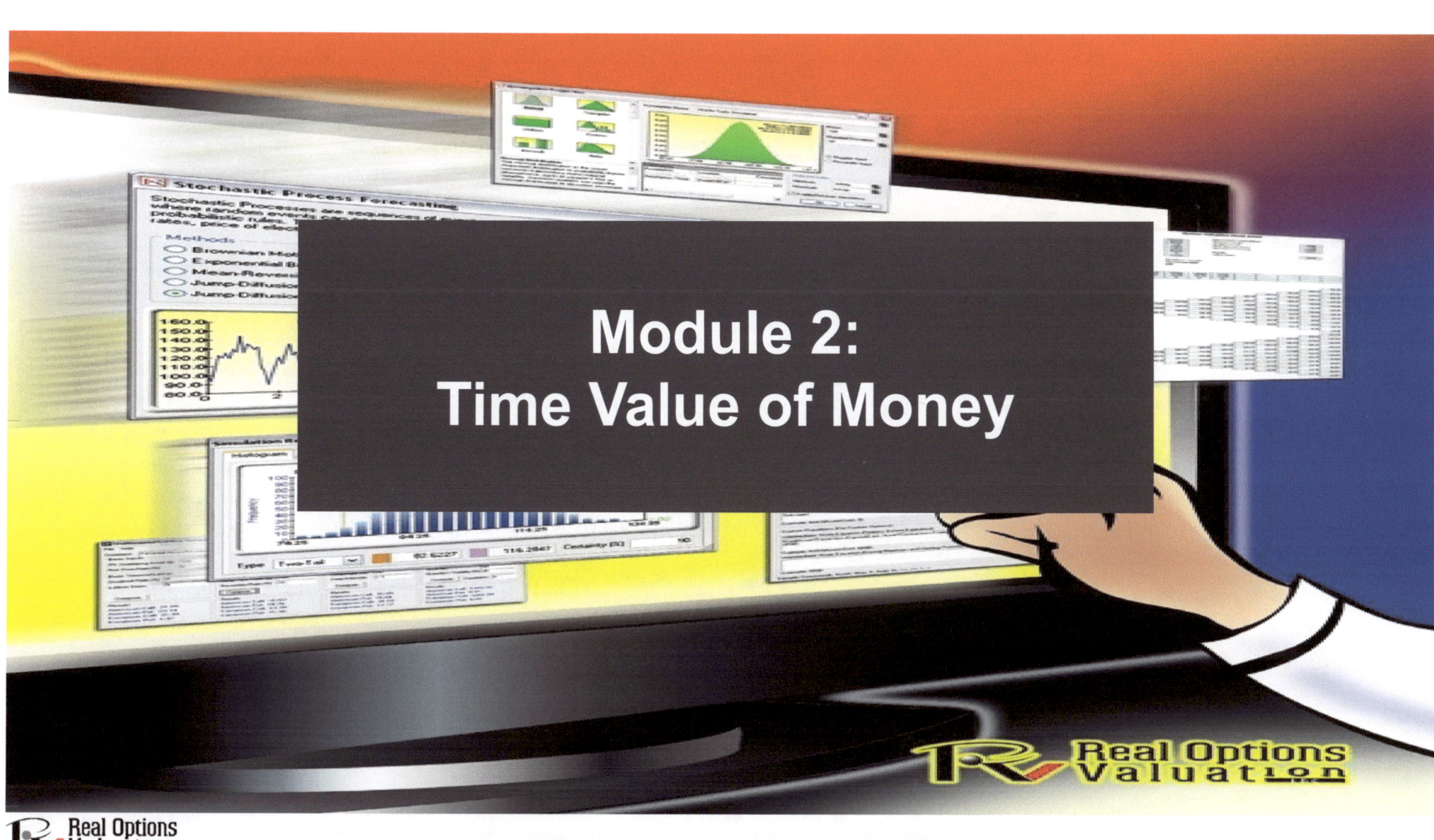
Module 2:
Time Value of Money
Stochastic Process Forecasting
Methods
Real Options Valuation

Time Value of Money

- Most financial decisions involve situations in which someone pays money at one point in time and receives money at some later time. The values of dollars paid or received at two different points in time are different; that is, the value of money changes over time. This difference in value is recognized and accounted for by *Time Value of Money* (TVM) analysis.
- *Compounding* is the process of determining the Future Value (FV) of a cash flow or a series of cash flows. The compounded amount, or future value, is equal to the beginning amount plus the interest earned.
- *Discounting* is the process of finding the Present Value (PV) of a future cash flow or a series of cash flows; it is the reciprocal, or reverse, of compounding.
- Future Value and Present Value are the basic building blocks.
- Given any three of the four (PV, FV, i, n) variables, you can solve for the missing variable. (Note that there will be a fifth variable, PMT, coming up shortly in the annuities section).

Time Value of Money II

- *Interest rate* is the price of money in the capital market system, and this cost of money is determined by multiple factors including supply and demand, perceived and actual market risk, inflation, economic conditions (gross domestic product, consumer and purchaser price index, federal budget deficit, recessionary periods), international economic conditions (exchange rate, imports/exports, flow of foreign investment funds), and monetary policy (e.g., US Federal Reserve expansionary/contractionary policies). To understand the effects of these economic variables on interest rate and cost of money, you need to think about the answers to the following questions:
  - *Why do interest rates rise with federal budget deficit?*
  - *Why do interest rates drop during recessionary periods?*
  - *Why do interest rates rise with an international trade deficit?*
  - *What about the effects of inflation, deflation, expansionary monetary policy, country risk, fiscal policy, war time, economic depression, and exchange rates?*
  - *What are the effects of interest rates (e.g., Treasury rates, Federal Funds Rate, Federal Reserve's Discount Rate) on the economic cycle in general?*
- *Compounding* is the process of determining the Future Value (FV) of a cash flow or a series of cash flows. The compounded amount, or future value, is equal to the beginning amount plus the interest earned.
- The idea of time value of money is that of an *implicit cost* or *opportunity cost*.
- TVM applies even if we have zero inflation. *Why?*
- TVM is solved using numerical methods (manual equations), financial tables (found at the back of a finance book, and we will create our own tables in a later exercise), financial calculators, and spreadsheets (we will be doing a lot of Microsoft Excel spreadsheet modeling).
- *Discounting* is the process of finding the Present Value (PV) of a future cash flow or a series of cash flows; it is the reciprocal, or reverse, of *compounding*

Future Value

As an example, if you saved \$100 today in a savings account yielding 5% a year, how much will you have at the end of 3 years?

DEFINITIONS:

- *FV*: Future Value amount (the amount you will have in the future, sometimes denoted with a subscript *n* to indicate n-periods into the future).
- *n*: Some time period *n* in the future. (This can be hours, days, months, quarters, years, etc., but to get started, we will simplify and use *years*. Later, we will run different compounding periods.)
- *i*: Interest rate or discount rate, the rate used to compound the value to the future, or to discount a future value to the present.
- *PV*: Present Value amount (the amount you currently have, sometimes denoted with a subscript *0* to indicate time zero, or now).
- *FVIF*: Future Value Interest Factor (usually for a combination of specific time *n* and interest rate *i* denoted as subscripts). This is the FV of one unit (\$1) of some present value for some time and interest rate.
- *PVIF*: Present Value Interest Factor (usually for a combination of specific time *n* and interest rate *i* denoted as subscripts). This is the PV of one unit (\$1) of some future value for some time and interest rate.

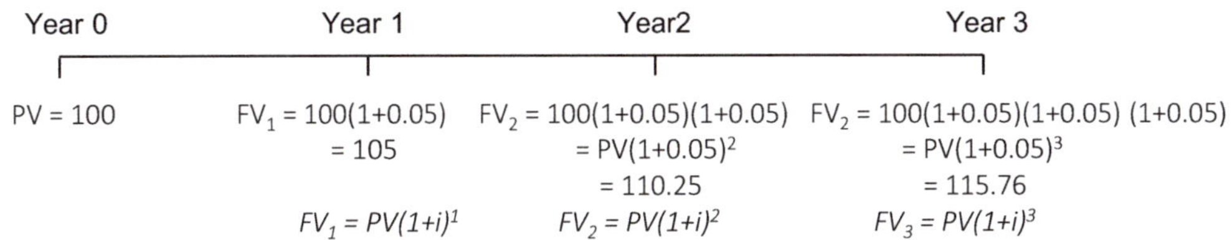

Year 0
Year 1
Year2
Year 3
PV = 100
FV1 = 100(1+0.05)
= 105
FV2 = 100(1+0.05)(1+0.05)
= PV(1+0.05)2
= 110.25
FV2 = 100(1+0.05)(1+0.05) (1+0.05)
= PV(1+0.05)3
= 115.76
FV1 = PV(1+i)1
FV2 = PV(1+i)2
FV3 = PV(1+i)3

$$FV_3 = FV_2(1+i)^1 = FV_1(1+i)^1(1+i)^1 = PV_0(1+i)^1(1+i)^1(1+i)^1 = PV_0(1+i)^3$$

This conforms to the equation: $FV_n = PV_0(1+i)^n = PV_0[FVIF_{i,n}]$

As another example, we can compute FV manually (using Excel, of course, but entering the equations manually) or using Excel's *FV* function:

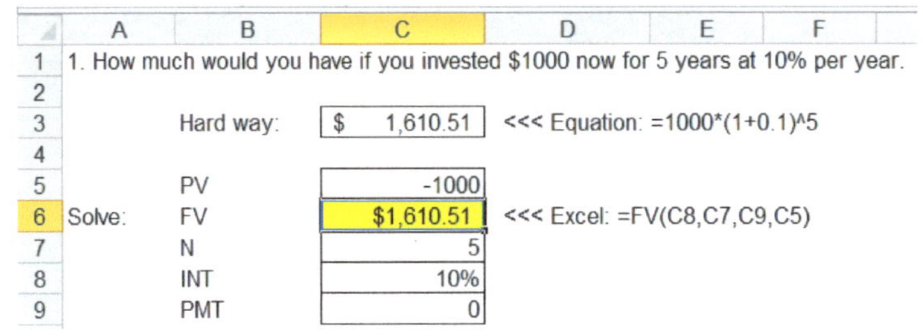

	A	B	C	D	E	F
1	1. How much would you have if you invested \$1000 now for 5 years at 10% per year.					
2						
3		Hard way:	\$ 1,610.51	<<< Equation: =1000*(1+0.1)^5		
4						
5		PV	-1000			
6	Solve:	FV	\$1,610.51	<<< Excel: =FV(C8,C7,C9,C5)		
7		N	5			
8		INT	10%			
9		PMT	0			

Open and Work on "A - Exercise - Time Value of Money"

Present Value

Similarly, we can compute the PV manually as well as by using Excel's *PV* function:

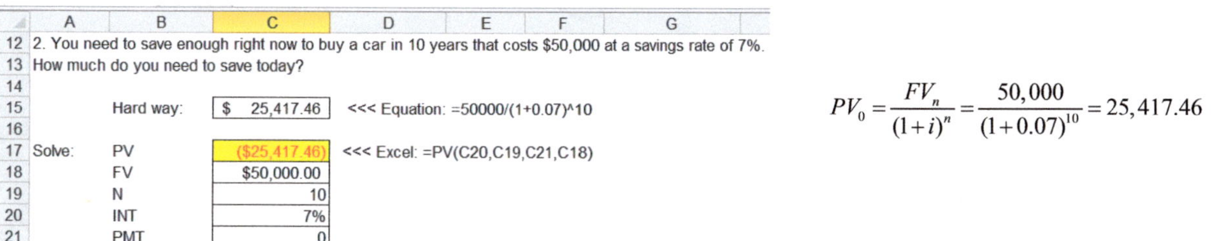

	A	B	C	D	E	F	G
12	2. You need to save enough right now to buy a car in 10 years that costs $50,000 at a savings rate of 7%.						
13	How much do you need to save today?						
14							
15		Hard way:	$ 25,417.46	<<< Equation: =50000/(1+0.07)^10			
16							
17	Solve:	PV	($25,417.46)	<<< Excel: =PV(C20,C19,C21,C18)			
18		FV	$50,000.00				
19		N	10				
20		INT	7%				
21		PMT	0				

$$PV_0 = \frac{FV_n}{(1+i)^n} = \frac{50,000}{(1+0.07)^{10}} = 25,417.46$$

Questions:

1. Why are cells C5 and C17 in the previous two figures negative values?
2. If we wanted the result to be positive (such that it matches the manual result and to have it make more sense), what do we need to do?
3. What is PMT?
4. Why is PMT set to 0 for the two examples above?

Open and Work on "A - Exercise - Time Value of Money"

Rate of Return and Interest Rates

As mentioned, given any four out of the five variables, we can compute the missing variable. The next example below shows how Interest Rate *i* can be computed.

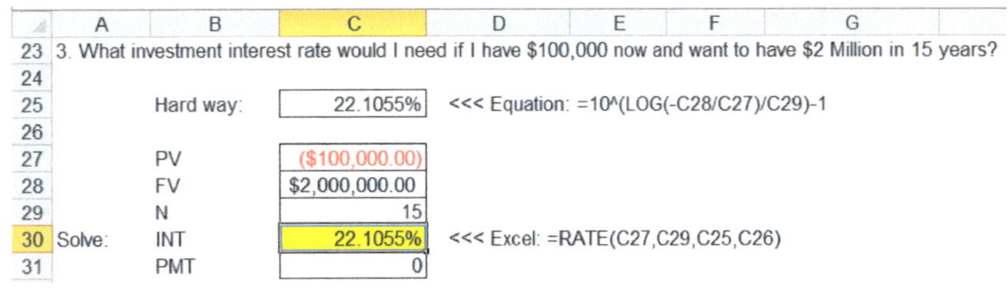

	A	B	C	D	E	F	G
23	3. What investment interest rate would I need if I have $100,000 now and want to have $2 Million in 15 years?						
24							
25		Hard way:	22.1055%	<<< Equation: =10^(LOG(-C28/C27)/C29)-1			
26							
27		PV	($100,000.00)				
28		FV	$2,000,000.00				
29		N	15				
30	Solve:	INT	22.1055%	<<< Excel: =RATE(C27,C29,C25,C26)			
31		PMT	0				

Now, how about doing this manually?

$FV = PV(1 + i)^n$

$2{,}000{,}000 = 100{,}000(1 + i)^{15}$

$20 = (1+i)^{15}$

$\log(20) = 15 \log(1 + i)$

$\log(20) / 15 = \log(1 + i) = 0.086735$

$10^{0.086735} = (1 + i) = 1.221055$

$i = 1.221055 - 1 = 0.221055 =$ **22.1055%**

This can be summarized as *=10^(LOG(-C28/C27)/C29)-1* as seen above.

$$i = 10^{\log\left[\frac{-FV_n}{PV_0}\right]/n} - 1$$

Open and Work on "A - Exercise - Time Value of Money"

Number of Investment Periods

Similarly, we can compute the n manually as well as by using Excel's *NPER* function:

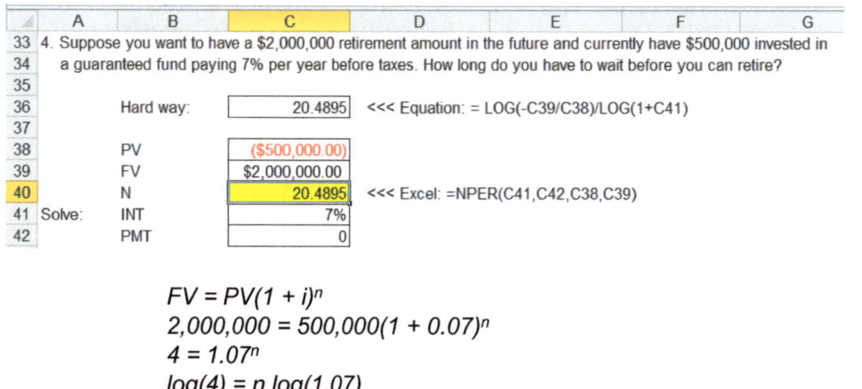

	A	B	C	D	E	F	G
33	4. Suppose you want to have a $2,000,000 retirement amount in the future and currently have $500,000 invested in						
34	a guaranteed fund paying 7% per year before taxes. How long do you have to wait before you can retire?						
35							
36		Hard way:	20.4895	<<< Equation: = LOG(-C39/C38)/LOG(1+C41)			
37							
38		PV	($500,000.00)				
39		FV	$2,000,000.00				
40		N	20.4895	<<< Excel: =NPER(C41,C42,C38,C39)			
41	Solve:	INT	7%				
42		PMT	0				

$FV = PV(1 + i)^n$
$2{,}000{,}000 = 500{,}000(1 + 0.07)^n$
$4 = 1.07^n$
$\log(4) = n \log(1.07)$
$n = \log(4) / \log(1.07) =$ ***20.4895 Years***

This can be summarized as = *LOG(–C39/C38)/LOG(1+C41)* as seen above.

$$n = \frac{\log\left[\frac{FV_n}{PV_0}\right]}{\log(1 + i)}$$

Open and Work on "A - Exercise - Time Value of Money"

Multiple Cash Flows and Annuities

- An annuity is defined as a series of equal periodic payments (PMT) for a specified number of periods. We can compute both the FV and PV of an annuity.
- An annuity whose payments occur at the end of each period is called an **ordinary** annuity.

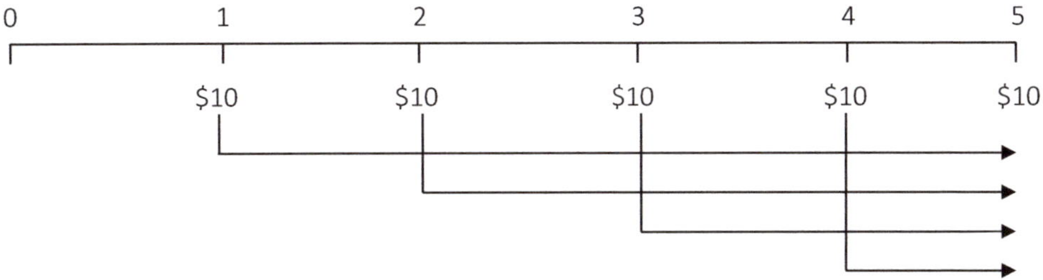

$$FVA_n = PMT_1(1+i)^4 + PMT_2(1+i)^3 + PMT_3(1+i)^2 + PMT_4(1+i)^1 + PMT_5(1+i)^0$$

Since this is an annuity, $PMT_1 = PMT_2 = PMT_3 = PMT_4 = PMT_5$

$$FVA_n = PMT\left[\sum_{t=1}^{n}(1+i)^{n-t}\right] = PMT\left[\frac{(1+i)^n}{i} - \frac{1}{i}\right] = PMT[FVIFA_{i,n}]$$

$$PVA_0 = \sum_{t=1}^{n}\frac{PMT}{(1+i)^t} = PMT\left(\frac{1}{i} - \frac{1}{i(1+i)^n}\right) = PMT[PVIFA_{i,n}]$$

Open and Work on "A - Exercise - Time Value of Money"

Multiple Cash Flows and Annuities

	A	B	C	D	E	F	G	H
44	5. I have a house mortgage loan of $300,000 at 7% per year. How much is my *monthly* payment for the next 30 years?							
45								
46		Hard way:	$1,995.91	<<<Equation: =C48/(1/C51-1/(C51*(1+C51)^C50))				
47								
48		PV	$300,000.00					
49		FV	$0.00					
50		N	360					
51		INT	0.58%					
52	Solve:	PMT	($1,995.91)	<<< Excel: =PMT(C49,C48,C46,C47)				

Questions:

1. How do we use the PMT function in Excel? What did we need to modify in terms of periodic inputs (for this "monthly" mortgage payment) compared to previous examples with annual periodicities?
2. Explain the manual computations performed in the example above. That is, which equation was used and modified?
3. Why do we usually use PVA instead of FVA to compute a periodic loan payment such as a mortgage in the example above?

Open and Work on "A - Exercise - Time Value of Money"

Real Options
Valuation

Amortization Model Calculation

You decide to open your own fast-food restaurant. You decide to borrow $48,040 from a local bank charging you annual interest at 11.9959%. How much do you have to pay a year assuming you want to pay off the loan in 3 years? Show the amortization table.

Step 1: Calculate the recurring payment necessary:

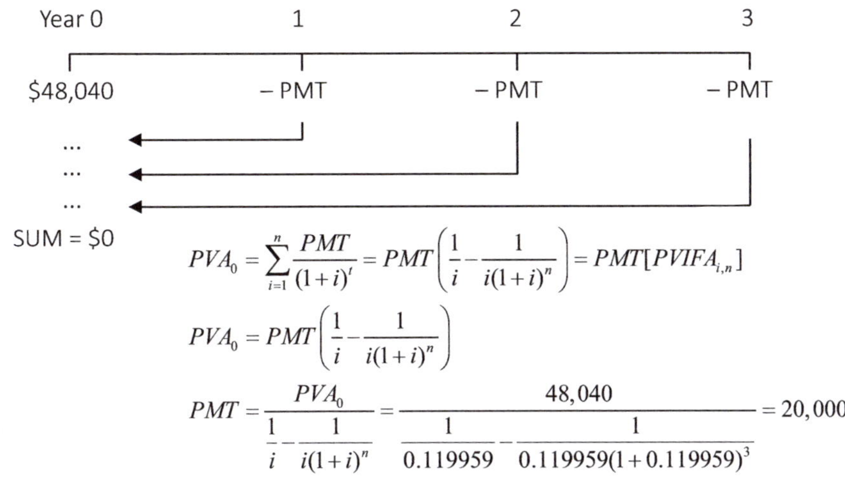

Amortization Table					
	SUM::	$ 718,526.69	$ 418,526.69	$ 300,000.00	
Period	Starting	Payment	Interest	Principal	Remaining
1	$ 300,000.00	$1,995.91	$ 1,750.00	$245.91	$ 299,754.09
2	$ 299,754.09	$1,995.91	$ 1,748.57	$247.34	$ 299,506.75
3	$ 299,506.75	$1,995.91	$ 1,747.12	$248.78	$ 299,257.97
4	$ 299,257.97	$1,995.91	$ 1,745.67	$250.24	$ 299,007.73
5	$ 299,007.73	$1,995.91	$ 1,744.21	$251.70	$ 298,756.03
6	$ 298,756.03	$1,995.91	$ 1,742.74	$253.16	$ 298,502.87
7	$ 298,502.87	$1,995.91	$ 1,741.27	$254.64	$ 298,248.23
355	$ 11,734.70	$1,995.91	$ 68.45	$1,927.46	$ 9,807.25
356	$ 9,807.25	$1,995.91	$ 57.21	$1,938.70	$ 7,868.55
357	$ 7,868.55	$1,995.91	$ 45.90	$1,950.01	$ 5,918.54
358	$ 5,918.54	$1,995.91	$ 34.52	$1,961.38	$ 3,957.16
359	$ 3,957.16	$1,995.91	$ 23.08	$1,972.82	$ 1,984.33
360	$ 1,984.33	$1,995.91	$ 11.58	$1,984.33	$ 0.00

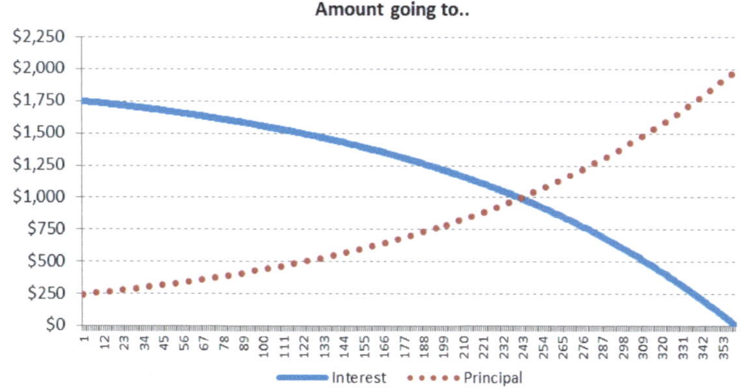

Excel's PMT function: PMT (*Rate, N, PV, FV*): PMT (0.119959, 3, 48040, 0)

Step 2: Set up the amortization schedule (replicate this yourself, use a rounded 12% interest):

Year	*Payment*	=	*Interest*	+	*Principal*	*Balance*
1	*20,000*		*5,764.80*		*14,235.20*	*33,804.80*
2	*20,000*		*4,056.58*		*15,943.42*	*17,861.38*
3	*20,000*		*2,143.37*		*17,861.38*	*0*

Interest is computed by 12% (48,040), 12% (33,804), 12% (17,861.38)

Last payment of 20,000 is distributed: 2,143.37 Interest and 17,861.38 Principal

Multiple Compounding Periods

- Thus far in this section we have assumed that payments are made, and interest is earned, annually. However, many contracts call for more frequent payments; for example, mortgage and auto loans call for monthly payments, or most bonds pay interest semiannually. Similarly, most banks compute interest daily. When compounding occurs more frequently than once a year, we must compute the equivalent or effective interest rates by adjusting the interest rate by the compounding periodicity.
- If we are comparing the costs of loans that require payments more than once a year, or the rates of return on investments that pay interest more frequently, then the comparisons should be based on equivalent (or effective) rates of return.

$$n \times p$$

$$i \div p$$

where p is the periodicity of compounding per year, n is the number of years, and i is the annual interest rate.

Compounding Periodicity Example

Calculate the future value of $50 today in two years if the annual rate of interest is 8% compounding annually, semiannually, monthly, and daily.

$$FV_2(annually) = 50[1 + (0.08 \div 1)]^{1\times 2} = \$58.32$$
$$FV_2(semiannually) = 50[1 + (0.08 \div 2)]^{2\times 2} = \$58.49$$
$$FV_2(monthly) = 50[1 + (0.08 \div 12)]^{12\times 2} = \$58.64$$
$$FV_2(daily) = 50[1 + (0.08 \div 365)]^{365\times 2} = \$58.67$$
$$FV_2(continuous) = 50e^{0.08\times 2} = \$58.67$$

Effective Annual Rate (EAR) Using Multiple Compounding Periods

$$EAR = \left[1 + \frac{i}{p}\right]^p - 1$$

where *p* is the periodicity of compounding and *i* is the nominal quoted interest rate. As an example, suppose you get a credit card offering an introductory rate of 1% a month. What is the annual percentage rate (APR)? What is the effective annual rate (EAR) if interest is compounded annually, monthly, and daily? What is the relationship between APR and EAR?

APR = nominal rate = quoted rate = 1% x 12 = 12%
This is the stated rate on the brochure or offer letter.

EAR (annual) = APR because the EAR (annual) = $[1 + (0.12 \div 1)]^1 - 1 = 12.00\%$
EAR (monthly) = $[1 + (0.12 \div 12)]^{12} - 1 = 12.68\%$
EAR (daily) = $[1 + (0.12 \div 365)]^{365} - 1 = 12.75\%$
The daily compounded EAR is $e^{0.12} - 1 = 12.75\%$

Extensions and Applications

Annuities Due

If each payment occurs at the beginning of the period rather than at the end, then we have an *annuity due*. The PV of each payment would be larger, because each payment would be discounted back less a year, so the PV of the annuity would also be larger. Similarly, the FV of the annuity due would also be larger because each payment would be compounded for an extra year.

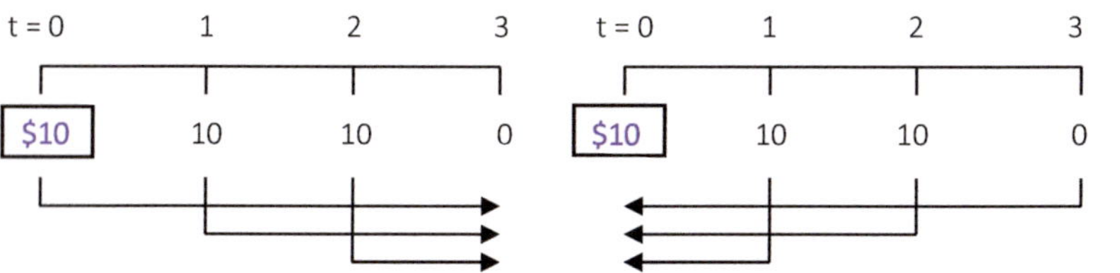

$$PVA_0 = \left[\sum_{t=1}^{n} \frac{PMT}{(1+i)^t}\right](1+i) = PMT\left(\frac{1}{i} - \frac{1}{i(1+i)^n}\right)(1+i) = PMT[PVIFA_{i,n}](1+i)$$

$$FVA_n = PMT\left[\sum_{t=1}^{n}(1+i)^{n-t}\right](1+i) = PMT\left[\frac{(1+i)^n}{i} - \frac{1}{i}\right](1+i) = PMT[FVIFA_{i,n}](1+i)$$

	A	B	C	D	E	F	G	H
54	6. I am 35 years old now, and my brother is 45. If we start investing today at $10,000 and put in $10,000 per year after that,							
55	and we both want to retire at age 65, how much money will we both have at retirement? If our life expectancy is 90, how much							
56	money will I have each year in retirement payment back to me if we assume the same 10% annual interest rate indefinitely?							
57	How much will my brother have in comparison?							
58			Me	Brother			Me	Brother
59		PV	($10,000.00)	($10,000.00)		PV	($1,819,434.25)	($640,024.99)
60	Solve:	FV	$1,819,434.25	$640,024.99		FV	$0.00	$0.00
61		N	30	20		N	25	25
62		INT	10.00%	10.00%		INT	10.00%	10.00%
63		PMT	($10,000.00)	($10,000.00)	Solve:	PMT	$200,443.56	$70,510.32

Perpetuities

If the timeline were extended out forever so that the annuity payments went on forever, we would have a *perpetuity*. The sum of the present values of these perpetual annuity values is:

$$PV_0 = \frac{PMT}{i}$$

This is because the geometric sum of

$$\frac{1}{(1+i)^n} \text{ as } n \to \infty \text{ becomes } \frac{1}{i}$$

Extensions and Applications

Uneven Cash Flow

To find the PV or FV of an uneven series, find the PV or FV of each individual cash flow and then sum them. Note, though, that if some of the cash flows constitute an annuity, then the annuity formula can be used to calculate the present value of that part of the cash flow stream. Financial calculators have built-in programs that perform all of the operations discussed in this section. It would be useful for you to buy such a calculator and to learn how to use it. However, we will focus on using Excel spreadsheets, which are useful for problems with many uneven cash flows and for large free cash flow models, the same ones that real-life projects tend to have. They are also very useful if you want to solve a problem repeatedly with different inputs, or to run scenarios, sensitivity analysis, and risk simulations.

Net Present Value as Sum of Present Values

Now things get interesting. As a preview of *capital budgeting* (the analysis of capital investments in projects, project selection, investment decisions, and valuation of a project), we see an example below where there is a simple cash flow model of three investment choices:

	A	B	C	D	E	F	G	H	I
65	7. You are choosing to invest in three different projects where the interest rate is assumed to be 10%. Which project is the best?								
66	The cash flows or net income are listed below. What is the NPV, IRR and ROI?								
67			Year 0	Year 1	Year 2	Year 3	NPV	IRR	ROI
68		Sardenia	($1,000.00)	$300.00	$300.00	$300.00	($253.94)	-5.09%	-25.39%
69		Costa S.	($1,100.00)	$290.00	$350.00	$320.00	($306.69)	-6.42%	-27.88%
70		Salzburg	($500.00)	$150.00	$250.00	$300.00	$68.37	16.79%	13.67%
71									
72		Example of Sardenia's calculations:			$NPV = CF_0 + \frac{CF_1}{(1+k)^1} + \frac{CF_2}{(1+k)^2} + \ldots + \frac{CF_N}{(1+k)^N} = \sum_{t=0}^{N} \frac{CF_t}{(1+k)^t}$				
73									
74		Year	0	1	2	3			
75		Cash Flow	($1,000.00)	$300.00	$300.00	$300.00			
76		PV Cash Flow	($1,000.00)	$272.73	$247.93	$225.39			
77		Equations::	=C75/(1+0.1)^C74	=D75/(1+0.1)^D74	=E75/(1+0.1)^E74	=F75/(1+0.1)^F74			
78		SUM PV	($253.94)						

Discounting Conventions

- In using discounted cash flow analysis, there are several conventions that require consideration: continuous versus periodic discrete discounting, full-year versus midyear convention, and end-of-period versus beginning-of-period discounting.
- The discounting convention is important when performing a discounted cash flow analysis. Using the same compounding period principle, future cash flows can be discounted using the effective annualized discount rate. For instance, suppose an annualized discount rate of 30% is used on a $100 cash flow. Depending on the compounding periodicity, the calculated present values and future values differ, as noted below.

Periodicity	Periods/Year	Interest Factor	Future Value	Present Value
Annual	1	30.00%	$130.00	$76.92
Quarterly	4	33.55%	$133.55	$74.88
Monthly	12	34.49%	$134.49	$74.36
Daily	365	34.97%	$134.97	$74.09
Continuous	∞	34.99%	$134.99	$74.08

Full Year vs. Mid-Year Discounting

In the conventional discounted cash flow approach, cash flows occurring in the future are discounted back to the present value and summed to obtain the net present value of a project. These cash flows are usually attached to a particular period in the future, commonly measured in years, quarters, or months. The timeline below illustrates a sample series of cash flows over the next five years, with an assumed 20% discount rate. Because the cash flows are attached to an annual timeline, they are usually assumed to occur at the end of each year. That is, $500 will be recognized at the end of the first full year, $600 at the end of the second year, and so forth. This is termed the full-year discounting convention.

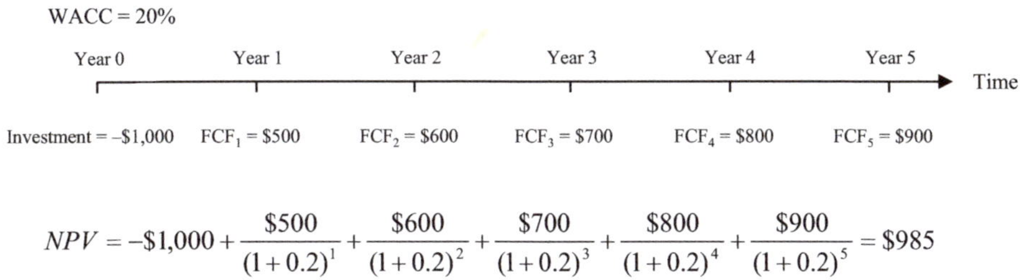

However, under usual business conditions, cash flows tend to accrue throughout the entire year and do not arrive in a single lump sum at the end of the year. Instead, the midyear convention may be applied. That is, the $500 cash flow gets accrued over the entire first year and should be discounted at 0.5 years, rather than 1.0 years. Using this midpoint supposes that the $500 cash flow comes in equally over the entire year.

$$NPV = -\$1{,}000 + \frac{\$500}{(1+0.2)^{0.5}} + \frac{\$600}{(1+0.2)^{1.5}} + \frac{\$700}{(1+0.2)^{2.5}} + \frac{\$800}{(1+0.2)^{3.5}} + \frac{\$900}{(1+0.2)^{4.5}} = \$1{,}175$$

End-of-Period vs. Beginning-of-Period Discounting

Another key issue in discounting involves the use of end-of-period versus beginning-of-period discounting. Suppose the cash flow series is generated on a timeline such as:

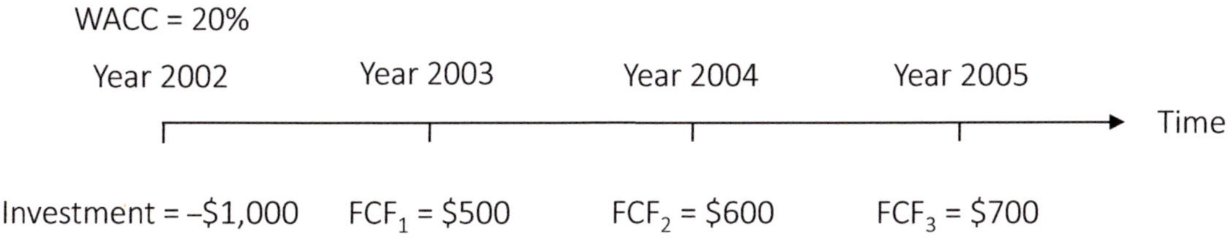

Further suppose that the valuation date is January 1, 2002. The $500 cash flow can occur either at the beginning of the first year (January 1, 2003) or at the end of the first year (December 31, 2003). The former requires the discounting of one year, and the latter, the discounting of two years. If the cash flows are assumed to roll in equally over the year, that is, from January 1, 2002, to January 1, 2003, the discounting should only be for 0.5 years.

In retrospect, suppose that the valuation date is December 31, 2002, and the cash flow series occurs at January 1, 2003, or December 31, 2003. The former requires no discounting, while the latter requires a one-year discounting using an end-of-year discounting convention. In the midyear convention, the cash flow occurring on December 31, 2003, should be discounted at 0.5 years.

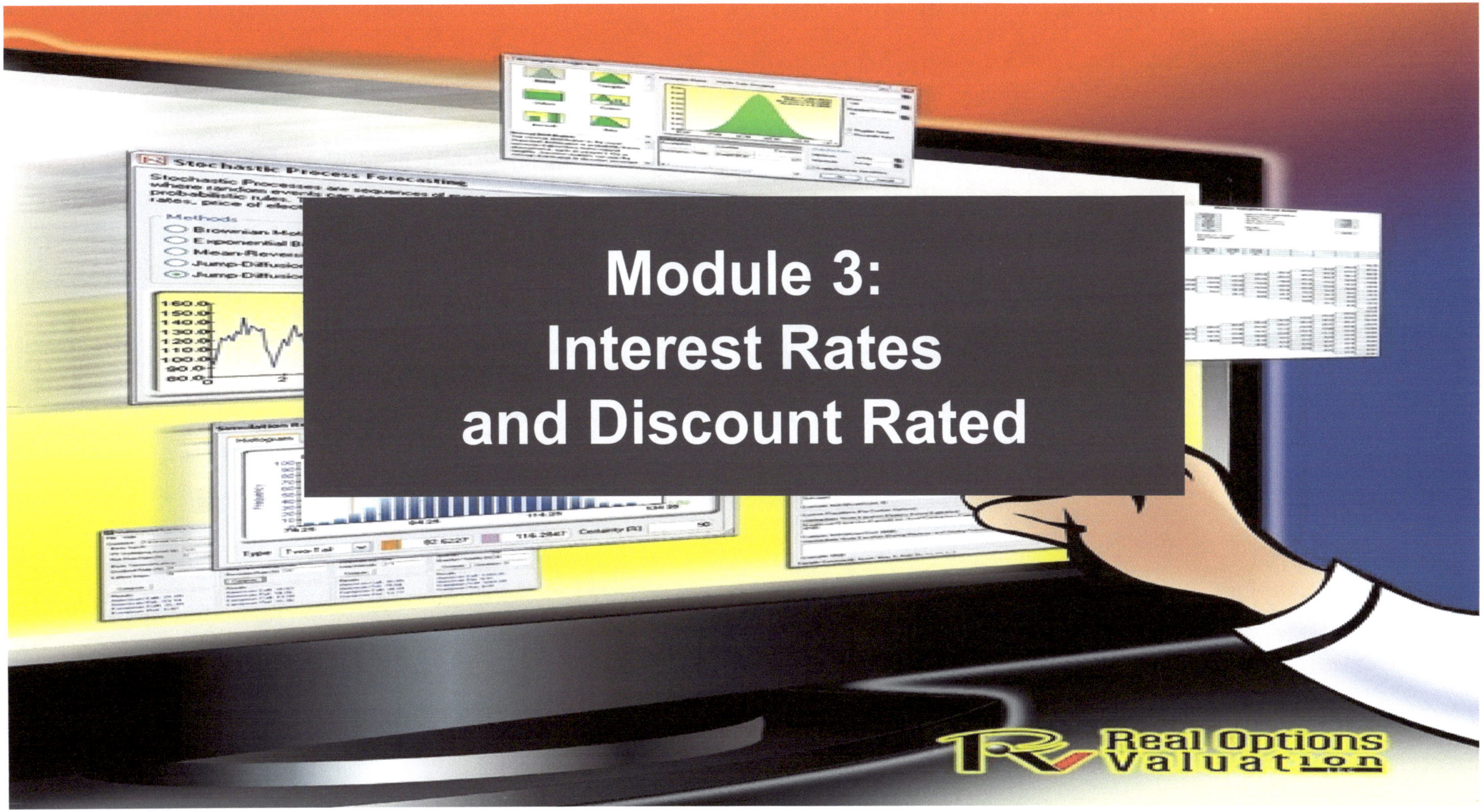

Module 3: Interest Rates and Discount Rated

Weighted Average Cost of Capital

The Weighted Average Cost of Capital (WACC) of issuing debt, preferred stock, and common equity is:

$$WACC = \omega_d k_d(1-\tau) + \omega_p k_p + \omega_e k_e$$

Cost of Debt

Use the after-tax cost of debt since interest paid on debt is tax deductible. We need to include this tax shield. If the company has issued debt in the past, the Yield to Maturity (YTM) or Yield to Call (YTC) can be used as an estimate of the cost of debt. A comparable company's debt YTM or YTC or borrowing interest rate can also be used as a proxy of the marginal cost of debt if the company does not have any previously issued debt.

Cost of Debt = Interest Paid – Taxes Saved (Tax Shield)

$$\text{Cost of Debt} = k_d - \tau k_d = k_d(1-\tau)$$

Cost of Preferred Stock

Similar to a perpetual stock valuation, P_{net} is the preferred stock price net of any flotation (F) costs or $P_{net} = Pps\,(1-F)$. No tax adjustments are made as preferred dividends paid are not tax deductible.

$$k_p = \frac{D_p}{P_{net}}$$

Weighted Average Cost of Capital

The Weighted Average Cost of Capital (WACC) of issuing debt, preferred stock, and common equity is: $WACC = \omega_d k_d (1-\tau) + \omega_p k_p + \omega_e k_e$

Cost of Common Equity

There are three ways to compute the cost of equity, typically raised by reinvested earnings (retained earnings or internal equity, and the cost is k_s) or raised through issuing new shares (external equity, and the cost is k_e):

CAPM approach: $k_s = k_{rf} + \beta_i (k_m - k_{rf})$

Discounted Cash Flow (Gordon Growth Model)

$$k_s = \frac{D_0(1+g)}{P_0} + g$$

$$k_e = \frac{D_0(1+g)}{P_0(1-F)} + g = \frac{D_1}{P_{net}} + g$$

The growth rate g = *Retention Rate x ROE = (1 – Payout Rate) x ROE*

Risk Premium over Bond Yield

k_s = *bond yield + subjective estimate of risk premium*

Securities Market Line (SML) or Capital Asset Pricing Model (CAPM)

$$k_i = k_{rf} + [k_m - k_{rf}]\beta_i$$

$$\beta_p = w_1\beta_1 + w_2\beta_2 + \ldots + w_n\beta_n$$

k_i = required return on stock *i*
k_{rf} = risk-free rate
$[k_m - k_{rf}]$ = market risk premium = market return – risk-free rate
b_i = the Beta relative risk coefficient for a particular stock

Risk Premium for a Stock: $RP_i = (MRP)b_i$, where *MRP* is the market risk premium

Regression Analysis Report

Regression Statistics		
R-Squared (Coefficient of Determination)	0.5260	This is the R-square tracking coefficient
Adjusted R-Squared	0.5231	
Multiple R (Multiple Correlation Coefficient)	0.7253	
Standard Error of the Estimates (SEy)	0.0082	
Number of Observations	165	

The R-Squared or Coefficient of Determination indicates that 0.53 of the variation in the dependent variable can be explained and accounted for by the independent variables in this regression analysis. However, in a multiple regression, the Adjusted R-Squared takes into account the existence of additional independent variables or regressors and adjusts this R-Squared value to a more accurate view of the regression's explanatory power. Hence, only 0.52 of the variation in the dependent variable can be explained by the regressors.

The Multiple Correlation Coefficient (Multiple R) measures the correlation between the actual dependent variable (Y) and the estimated or fitted (Y) based on the regression equation. This is also the square root of the Coefficient of Determination (R-Squared).

The Standard Error of the Estimates (SEy) describes the dispersion of data points above and below the regression line or plane. This value is used as part of the calculation to obtain the confidence interval of the estimates later.

Regression Results	Intercept	SP500	
Coefficients	-0.0003	0.8987	This is the Beta Coefficient
Standard Error	0.0006	0.0668	
t-Statistic	-0.5355	13.4499	
p-Value	0.5930	0.0000	
Lower 5%	-0.0016	0.7667	
Upper 95%	0.0009	1.0306	

$SML: k_i = k_{rf} + (k_m - k_{rf})\beta_i$

Notes:
$y = a + mx$
$y = intercept + slope * x$
$y = k_i \text{ and } x = \beta_i$
$slope = \Delta y/\Delta x = (k_m - k_{rf})/1.0$

Real Options Valuation

BETA, CAPM, APT, MAPM

The CAPM was developed in a hypothetical world with the following assumptions about investors and opportunity sets:

1. Investors are risk-averse individuals who maximize the expected utility of their end-of-period wealth
2. Investors are price takers and have homogeneous beliefs and expectations about asset returns
3. There exists a risk-free asset and the investors may borrow or lend unlimited amounts at the risk-free rate
4. The quantities of assets are fixed, and all assets are marketable and perfectly divisible
5. Asset markets are frictionless, and information is costless and available to all investors
6. There are no market imperfections like taxes, regulations, or restrictions on short sales

CAPM requires that in equilibrium the market portfolio be efficient. It must lie on the upper half of the minimum variance opportunity set ($MRS = MRT$). The efficiency can be established based on homogeneous expectation assumptions. Given this, consumers will all perceive the same minimum variance opportunity set. The market portfolio must hence be efficient since the market is simply the sum of all holdings, and all individual holdings are efficient. Given market efficiency, the market portfolio M where all assets are held according to their market value weights by simple algebraic manipulation, i.e., equating the slope of the capital market line with the slope of the opportunity set, we can derive the following expression: $E(RI) = Rrf + [E(Rm) - Rrf]\,(sim/s^2{}_m)$. This CAPM model can also be derived using the $MRT = MRS$ convention, where a linear programming method is used to solve for the minimum variance opportunity set and the maximum expected return efficiency set.

BETA, CAPM, APT, MAPM II

The APT is based on similar, but more general, intuitions. It assumes that any rate of return on any security is a linear function of *k* factors: $R_i = E(R_i) + \beta_{i1}F_1 + \ldots + \beta_{ik}F_k + \varepsilon_i$ or simplified as $E(R_i) = R_f + [\delta_k - R_f]\, \beta_{ik}$

Another alternative is to use a multifactor model that adequately captures the systematic risks experienced by the firm. Other researchers have tested the CAPM and found that a single factor, Beta, does not sufficiently explain expected returns. Their empirical research finds support for the inclusion of both size (measured using market value) and leverage variables. The two leverage variables found to be significant were the book-to-market ratio and the price-to-earnings ratio. However, when used together, the book-to-market ratio and size variable absorb the effects of the price-to-earnings ratio. With empirical support that Beta alone is insufficient to capture risk, their model relies on the addition of the natural logarithm of both the book-to-market ratio and the size of the firm's market equity as

$$E[R_{i,t}] - R_{f,t} = \beta_{i,t}\left(E[R_{m,t}] - R_{f,t}\right) + \delta_{i,t}\ln(BME_{i,t}) + \gamma_{i,t}\ln(ME_{i,t})$$

$$E[R_{i,t}] - R_{f,t} = \beta_{i,t}\left(E[R_{m,t}] - R_{f,t}\right) + \xi_{i,t}\ln(SMB_{i,t}) + \psi_{i,t}\ln(HML_{i,t})$$

where $R_{i,t}$, $R_{m,t}$, and $R_{f,t}$ are the individual expected return for firm *i*, the expected market return, and the risk-free rate of return at time *t*, respectively. $BME_{i,t}$ and $ME_{i,t}$ are the book-to-market ratio and the size of the total market equity value for firm *i* at time *t*, respectively in the first equation, and for the second equation, $SMB_{i,t}$ is the time-series of differences in average returns from the smallest and largest capitalization stocks. $HML_{i,t}$ is the time-series of differences in average returns from the highest to the lowest book-to-market ratios, after ranking the market portfolios into differing quartiles.

BETA

- A stock's Beta coefficient, β, is a measure of its relative market risk.
- Beta measures the extent to which the stock's returns move relative to the market.
- Beta can be defined simply as the undiversifiable, systematic risk of a financial asset.
- The Beta concept is made famous through the CAPM, where a higher Beta means a higher risk, which, in turn, requires a higher expected return on the asset.
- A high-Beta stock is more volatile than an average stock, while a low-Beta stock is less volatile than an average stock. An average stock (the market portfolio) has $\beta = 1.0$.
- The Beta of a portfolio is a weighted average of the Betas of the individual securities in the portfolio.
- The Securities Market Line (SML) equation shows the relationship between a security's market risk and its required rate of return. The return required for any security i is equal to the risk-free rate plus the market risk premium times the security's Beta. The CAPM is also known as the SML.
- Even though the expected rate of return on a stock is generally equal to its required return, a number of things can happen to cause the required rate of return to change: the risk-free rate can change because of changes in either real rates or anticipated inflation; a stock's Beta (β) can change; and investors' aversion to risk can change.
- Other ways of measuring beta risk:
  - Pure-Play Method: Find firms specializing in certain projects and calculate their average Beta.
  - Accounting Beta Method: Regress $ROA_i = \alpha + \beta_i ROA^*$ where ROA* is the average ROA for a large set of companies.
- A stock's Beta can be computed as the slope of a regression model with the stock's historical returns on the y-axis and the market's returns on the x-axis, for the same time period with the same periodic frequency (daily, weekly, or monthly returns). Be careful here as the Beta is NOT the slope of the SML. The slope of the SML is the market risk premium!

BETA II

- Beta can, hence, be seen as a risk measure using the relationship between a stock's movements and the movements of the overall stock market. As mentioned, it is the slope of a regression line by regressing the stock's historical returns to the market's historical returns or can be similarly calculated as:

  $$\beta_i = \frac{\text{cov}(i,m)}{\text{var}(m)} = \frac{\rho_{i,m}\sigma_i\sigma_m}{\sigma_m^2}$$

- In the regression equation, remember that we are using *stock returns* and not stock prices.
- The SML shows the relationship between risk as measured by Beta and the required rate of return for an individual security: $k_i = k_{rf} + [k_m - k_{rf}]\beta_i$
- As discussed previously, k_i is the required return on stock *i*, k_{rf} is the risk-free rate, k_m is the market rate of return, and β_i is the Beta for a particular stock.
- The $[k_m - k_{rf}]$ portion is the *market risk premium* (MRP) computed as the market rate of return less the risk-free rate.
- This MRP measures the additional return over the risk-free rate that is required to compensate investors for the added risk inherent in the stock. And this premium can be larger or smaller than the premium required on an average stock (Beta of 1 for the entire stock market), depending on the riskiness of the stock in relationship with the overall market as measured by the Beta coefficient. Additional risk premiums can be added to the risk-free rate, such as inflation risk, or other types of risk such as maturity risk, default risk, and others, which we will discuss in a later section.
- Market Beta = 1.0. This means Beta > 1.0 stocks are more volatile than the market on average, and Beta < 1.0 stocks are less volatile than the market on average.

Discount Rates, Hurdle Rates, Required Rates of Return

- The most important (and most difficult) step in analyzing a capital budgeting project is estimating the incremental after-tax cash flows the project will produce. The cash flows generated will, of course, need to be discounted in the *Time Value of Money* fashion, typically using a Weighted Average Cost of Capital (WACC).
- The *cost of capital* used in capital budgeting is a weighted average of the types of capital the firm uses—typically *debt*, *preferred stock*, and *common equity*—and is known as the *Weighted Average Cost of Capital* (WACC).
- Each firm has a *target capital structure*, defined as that mix of debt, preferred stock, and common equity that *minimizes its WACC*, which will in turn *maximize stock price*. The WACC is the weighted average cost of capital of the various components of issuing debt, preferred stock, and common equity and is calculated by $WACC = \omega_d k_d (1-\tau) + \omega_p k_p + \omega_e k_e$ where ω represents the respective weights, τ is the corporate effective tax rate, and k are the costs corresponding to debt d, preferred stocks p, and common equity e.
- The component cost of debt is the after-tax cost of new debt. It is found by multiplying the cost of new debt k_d by $(1-\tau)$ where τ is the firm's marginal tax rate. Therefore, the weighted component of the cost of new debt is $\omega_d k_d(1-\tau)$.
- The component cost of preferred stock is calculated as the preferred dividend divided by the net issuing price, where the net issuing price is the price the firm receives after deducting flotation costs: $k_p = \frac{D_p}{P_{net}}$ This equation is essentially the inverse of a perpetuity valuation.
- The cost of common equity (common stock), k_s, is also called the cost of common stock. It is the rate of return required by the firm's stockholders, and it can be estimated by three methods: the CAPM approach; the dividend-yield-plus-growth rate, or DCF, approach; and the bond-yield-plus-risk-premium approach.

Discount Rates, Hurdle Rates, Required Rates of Return II

- To use the CAPM approach, first estimate the firm's Beta, then multiply this Beta by the market risk premium to determine the firm's risk premium, and, finally, add the firm's risk premium to the risk-free rate to obtain the cost of common stock:

  $k_s = k_{rf} + \beta_i(k_m - k_{rf})$ where the Market Risk Premium = $k_m - k_{rf}$

- The best proxy for the risk-free rate is the yield on long-term Treasury-bonds or country-specific government bonds with the maturity comparable to that of the project.
- To use the dividend-yield-plus-growth-rate approach, which is also called the discounted cash flow (DCF) approach, add the firm's expected growth rate to its expected dividend yield: $k_e = \frac{D_0(1+g)}{P_0(1-F)} + g = \frac{D_1}{P_{net}} + g$
- The growth rate can be estimated from historical earnings and dividends or by use of the retention growth model, the growth rate

  g = ROE(1–Payout), or it can be based on analysts' forecasts *(Payout = 1 – Retention Rate)*.

- The bond-yield-plus-risk-premium approach calls for adding a risk premium of 3 to 5 percentage points to the firm's interest rate on long-term debt: k_s = *Bond Yield + Risk Premium*.
- Various factors affect a firm's cost of capital. Some of these factors are determined by the financial environment, but the firm influences others through its financing, investment, and dividend policies.
- Ideally, the cost of capital for each project should reflect the risk of the project itself, not the risks associated with the firm's average project as reflected in its composite WACC.
- Failing to adjust for differences in project risk would lead a firm to accept too many value-destroying risky projects and reject too many value-adding safe ones. Over time, the firm becomes riskier, its WACC would increase, and its shareholder value would decline.

Discount Rates, Hurdle Rates, Required Rates of Return III

- A project's *stand-alone risk* is the risk the project would have if it were the firm's only asset and if stockholders held only that one stock. Stand-alone risk is measured by the variability of the asset's expected returns.
- *Corporate,* or *within-firm, risk* reflects the effects of a project on the firm's risk, and it is measured by the project's effect on the firm's earnings variability.
- *Market,* or *Beta, risk* reflects the effects of a project on the riskiness of stockholders, assuming they hold diversified portfolios. Market risk is measured by the project's effect on the firm's Beta coefficient.
- Most decision makers consider all three risk measures in a judgmental manner and then classify projects into subjective risk categories. Using the composite WACC as a starting point, risk-adjusted costs of capital are developed for each category. The risk-adjusted cost of capital is the cost of capital appropriate for a given project, given the riskiness of that project. The greater the risk, the higher the cost of capital.
- Firms may be able to use the CAPM to estimate the cost of capital for specific projects or divisions. However, estimating Betas for projects is difficult.
- The *pure play* and *accounting Beta methods* can sometimes be used to estimate Betas for large projects or for divisions.
- In Risk Simulation, we can also use a combination of risk simulated volatility estimates and cross-correlations among projects to compute an internal risk Beta coefficient and apply that to the internal CAPM model.
- Companies generally hire an investment banker to assist them when they issue common stock, preferred stock, or bonds. In return for a fee, the investment banker helps the company with the terms, price, and sale of the issue. The banker's fees are often referred to as *flotation costs*. The total cost of capital should include not only the required return paid to investors but also the flotation fees paid to the investment banker for marketing the issue.
- When calculating the cost of new common stock, the DCF approach can be adapted to account for flotation costs. For a constant growth stock, this cost can be expressed as $k_e = \frac{D_0(1+g)}{P_0(1-F)} + g = \frac{D_1}{P_{net}} + g$
- Note that flotation costs cause k_e to be greater than k_s. We can add this differential to the CAPM estimate of k_s in order to obtain the CAPM estimate of k_e. These two rates are identical if the flotation cost is zero.

Discount Rates, Hurdle Rates, Required Rates of Return IV

- Flotation cost adjustments can also be made for debt. The bond's issue price is reduced for flotation expenses and then used to solve for the after-tax yield to maturity.
- The three equity cost estimating techniques discussed in this section have serious limitations when applied to small firms, thus increasing the need for the small-business manager to use judgment.
- Project cash flow is different from accounting income. Project cash flow reflects cash outlays for fixed assets, the tax shield provided by depreciation, and cash flows due to changes in net operating working capital. Project cash flow does not include interest payments.
    - *Noncash Expenses.* Noncash expenses such as *depreciation* and *amortization* are deducted in accounting income for tax shield purposes, but in financial cash flow analysis, these are added back as they are not cash expenses (they are typically capital expenses that will be amortized over the allowed tax-life of the machine or asset).
    - *Changes in Net Operating Working Capital.* The difference between the required increase in current assets and the spontaneous increase in current liabilities means additional financing is required.
    - *Interest Expenses.* Project cash flow is cash flow available to all investors, so interest expense is usually not deducted, whereas accounting income does take interest payments into account to compute net income. For instance, *NOPAT* is *EBIT(1 – Tax Rate)*, which bypasses interest payments.
    - *Cost of Fixed Assets.* The costs of fixed assets are amortized and deducted slowly over time in accounting income, but they are actual cash outflows and shown as negative cash flows.
- In determining incremental cash flows, *opportunity costs* (the cash flows forgone by using an asset) must be included, but *sunk costs* (cash outlays that have been made and that cannot be recouped) are not included. Any *externalities* (effects of a project on other parts of the firm) should also be reflected in the analysis.
- Capital projects often require additional investments in net operating working capital (NOWC).
- The incremental cash flows from a typical project can be classified into three categories, and for each year of the project's economic life, the net cash flow is determined as the sum of the cash flows from each of these three categories:
    - Initial investment outlay
    - Operating cash flows over the project's life
    - Terminal year cash flows
- Inflation effects must be considered in project analysis. The best procedure is to build expected inflation into the cash flow estimates.

Optimal Capital Structure

- The optimal level of capital is the crossover between *Marginal Cost of Capital* (MCC) and *Investment Opportunity Schedule* (IOS). This concept is fraught with multiple problems.
- MCC is the cost schedule of raising an additional dollar of capital. It is essentially the WACC showing the break points in retained earnings.
- IOS ranks returns from highest to lowest.
- Threshold Debt Level is the level above which bankruptcy costs matter.
- Optimal capital structure is where the marginal tax shelter benefits = marginal bankruptcy costs at D/A* where the value of the firm and stocks are at the maximum.
- The cost of capital needs to be adjusted based on the project- and market-related risks. Some of these risks pertain to:
    - *Project-specific risks* (these can be adjusted for using Beta in the CAPM model, for risk simulation using volatility estimates, or modified using some other proxy for risk such as Value at Risk or probability of failure, etc.)
    - *Market risks* (competitive landscape, go-to market risks, pricing risks, demand risks)
    - *Economic risks* (interest rate fluctuations, economic cycles)
    - *Liquidity risks* (whether the project brings in cash flow quickly or can be divested quickly in the event of catastrophic failure)
    - *Maturity risks* (longer maturity projects with longer payback period tend to have higher liquidity risks)
    - *Inflation risks* (cost of money and purchasing power parity risks)

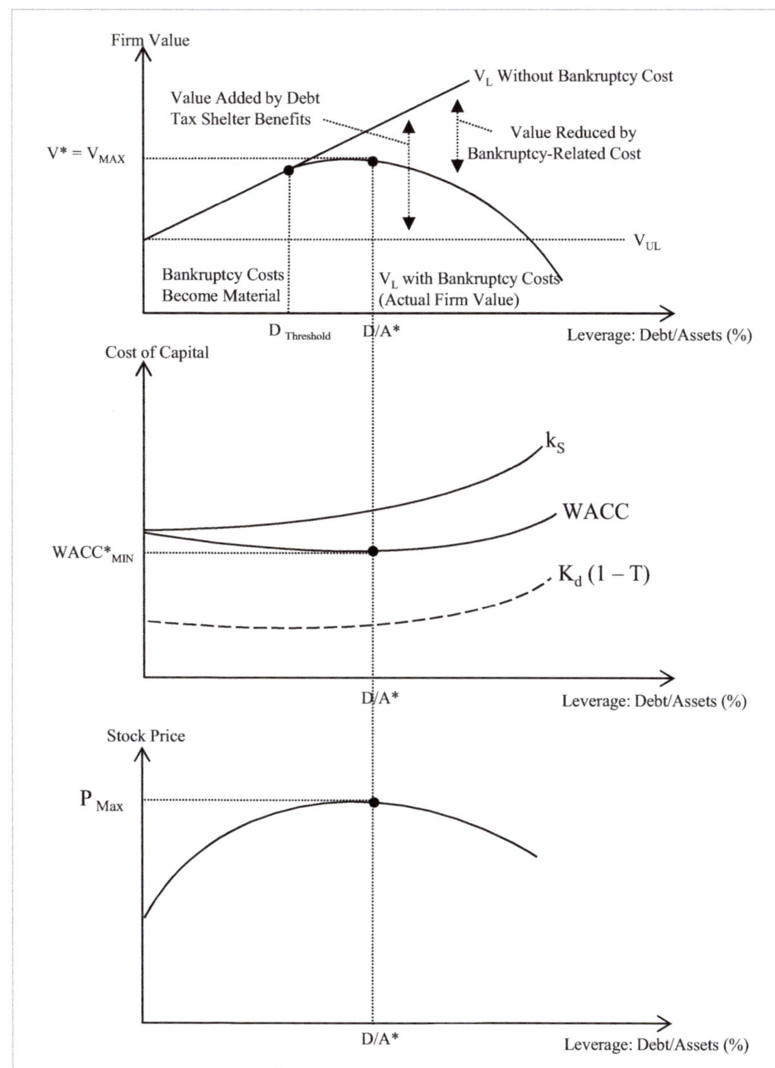

3. INTEREST AND DISCOUNT RATE

Factors Affecting the Cost of Capital

Generally, the weighted average cost of capital (WACC) would be used as the discount rate for the cash flow series. The only mitigating circumstance is when the firm wishes to use a hurdle rate that exceeds the WACC to compensate for the additional uncertainty, risks, and opportunity costs the firm believes it will face by investing in a particular project. As we will see, the use of a WACC is problematic, and in the real options world, the input is, instead, a US Treasury spot rate of return with its maturity corresponding to the economic life of the project under scrutiny. However, multiple other factors affect the cost of capital that need to be considered, including:

- The company's *capital structure* used to calculate the relevant WACC discount rate may be inadequate because project-specific risks are usually not the same as the overall company's risk structure, or the company may change its capital structure by increasing or decreasing its proportion of debt to equity ratio.
- The current and future general *interest rates* in the economy may be higher or lower, thus bond coupon rates may change in order to raise the capital based on fluctuations in the general interest rate. Therefore, an interest-rate-bootstrapping methodology should be applied to infer the future spot interest rates using forward interest rates.
- *Tax law changes* over time may affect the tax shield enjoyed by debt repayments. Furthermore, different tax jurisdictions in different countries have different tax law applications of tax shields.
- The firm's capital structure policy may have specific *long-term debt to equity targets* and weights that do not agree with the current structure, and the firm may find itself moving toward that optimal structure over time.
- *Payout versus retention rate* policy may change the dividend policy and thereby change the projected dividend growth rate necessary to calculate the cost of equity.

Factors Affecting the Cost of Capital II

- Additional items that may affect capital structure:
  - Investment policy of the firm, including the minimum required rate of return and risk profile.
  - Dynamic considerations in the economy and industry both ex post and ex ante, such as changes in credit availability in the market, cost of debt rising, and so forth.
  - Measurement problems on specific security cost structure.
  - Small business problems making it difficult to measure costs correctly.
  - Depreciation-generated funds and off-balance sheet items are generally not included.
  - Geometric averages and not simple arithmetic averages should be used for intra-year WACC rates.
  - Market value versus book value weightings in calculating the WACC.
  - CAPM is flawed, and other models such as APT, MAPT, or other well-researched methods may be more applicable.

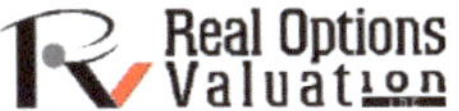

Inflation Rates, Interest Rates, and Expectations Theory

- Understand the differences among the quoted or nominal interest rate, real risk-free rate, and nominal risk-free rates and their interrelationships

$$k_{RF} = k^* + IP \text{ (Fisher Effect)}$$
$$k = k_{RF} + DRP + LP + MRP$$
$$k = k^* + IP + DRP + LP + MRP$$

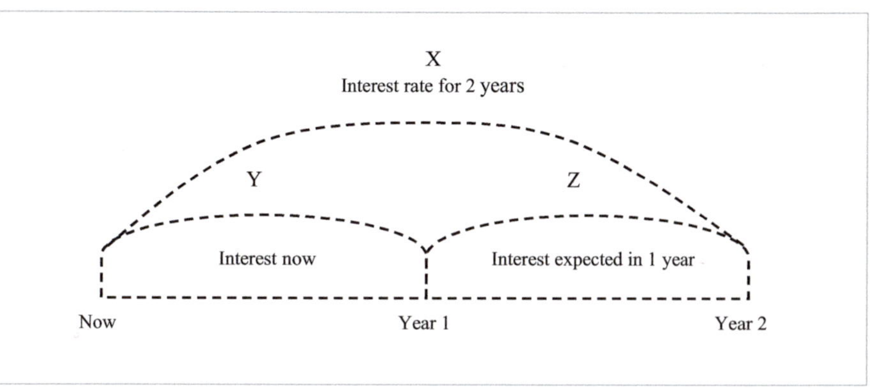

k = quoted or nominal interest rate (+IP)
k = <u>real</u> risk-free interest rate*
k_{RF} = quoted or <u>nominal</u> risk-free rate
IP = inflation premium
DRP = default risk premium
LP = liquidity premium (fast cash)
MRP = maturity risk premium
DRP = US Corp. Bond – US Treasury bond (same maturity/marketability)
MRP = reinvestment rate risk and interest rate risk

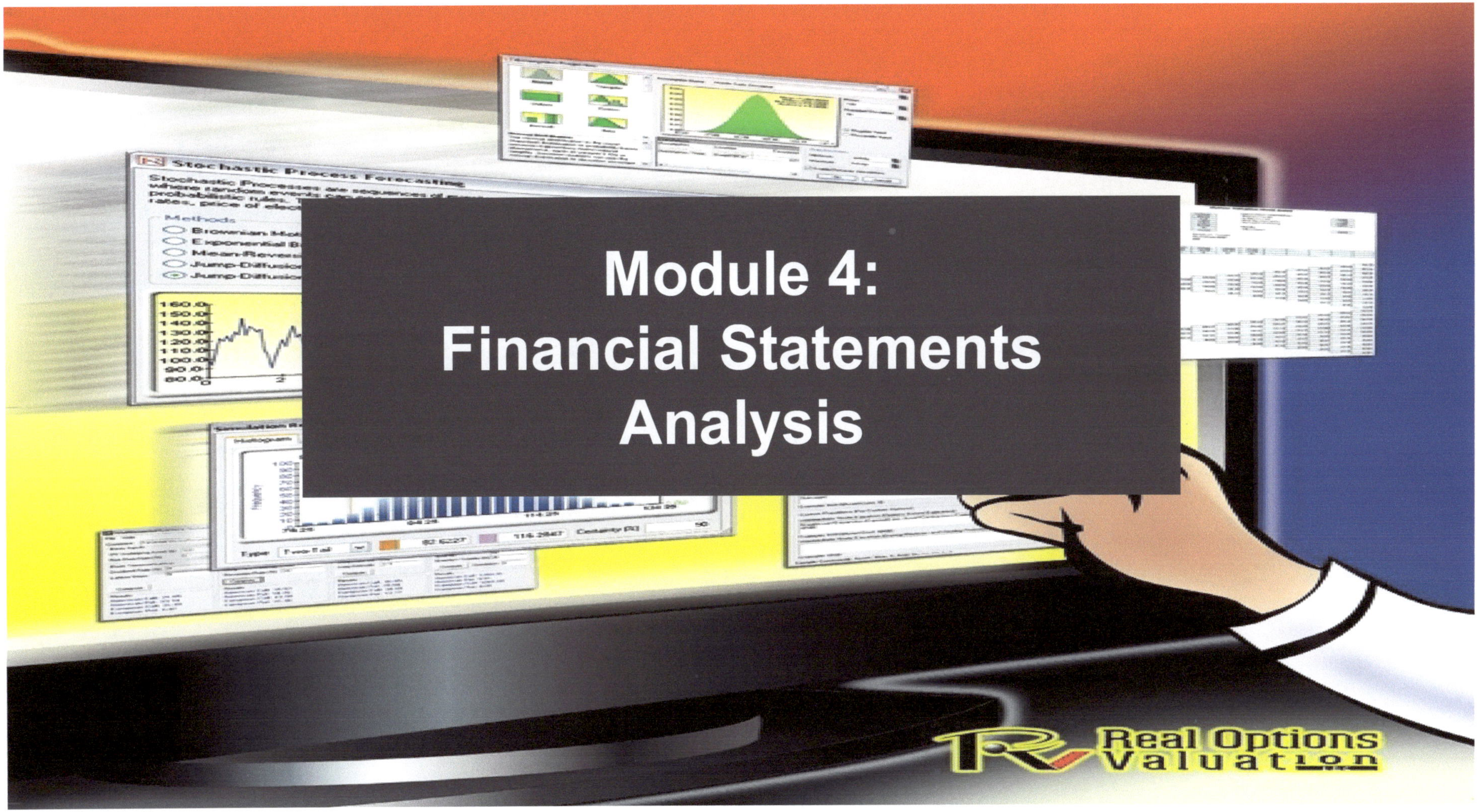

Module 4: Financial Statements Analysis

Financial Statement Analysis

The primary purpose of this section includes providing a description of the basic financial statements, background information on cash flows, and an overview of the income tax system.

The key concepts covered are:

- The four basic statements contained in the annual report are the *balance sheet*, the *income statement*, the *statement of retained earnings*, and the *statement of cash flows*. Investors use the information provided in these statements to form expectations about the future levels of earnings and dividends, and about the firm's riskiness.
- The *balance sheet* shows assets on the left-hand side and liabilities and equity, or claims against assets (listed in order of liquidity), on the right-hand side (listed in the order in which they must be paid). Sometimes assets are shown at the top and claims at the bottom of the balance sheet. The balance sheet may be thought of as a snapshot of the firm's financial position at a particular point in time.
- The typical equation for a balance sheet is *Asset – Liabilities – Preferred Stock = Common Stockholder's Equity (Net Worth).* The Common Equity section comprises common stock and retained earnings of the company.
- The *income statement* reports the results of operations over a period of time, and it shows earnings per share as its "bottom line."
- The *statement of retained earnings,* or statement of shareholder's equity, shows the change in retained earnings between balance sheet dates. Retained earnings represent a claim against assets, not assets per se.
- The *statement of cash flows* reports the effects of operating, investing, and financing activities on cash flows over an accounting period.

1.6.3 Balance Sheet

	2016		2015	
ASSETS				
01 CASH	$7,282		$57,600	L15 [Cash Flow Statement]
02 ACCOUNTS RECEIVABLE	632,160	–	351,200	= 280,960
03 INVENTORIES	1,287,360	–	715,200	= 572,160
04 TOTAL CURRENT ASSETS	**$1,926,802**		**$1,124,000**	
05 GROSS FIXED ASSETS	1,202,950	–	491,000	= 711,950
06 LESS ACCUMULATED DEPRECIATION	263,160	–	146,200	= 116,960
07 NET FIXED ASSETS	$ 939,790		$ 344,800	
08 TOTAL ASSETS	**$2,866,592**		**$1,468,800**	
LIABILITIES AND EQUITY				
09 ACCOUNTS PAYABLE	$ 524,160	–	$145,600	= 378,560
10 NOTES PAYABLE	720,000		200,000	= 520,000
11 ACCRUALS	489,600	–	136,000	= 353,600
12 TOTAL CURRENT LIABILITIES	**$1,733,760**		**$481,600**	
13 LONG-TERM DEBT	1,000,000	–	323,432	= 676,568
14 COMMON STOCK (100,000 SHARES)	460,000		460,000	
15 RETAINED EARNINGS	(327,168)		203,768	L4 [Retained Earnings]
16 TOTAL EQUITY	$132,832		$663,768	
17 TOTAL LIABILITIES & EQUITY	**$2,866,592**		**$1,468,800**	

1.6.4 Income Statement

	2016	2015	
01 SALES	$5,834,400	$3,432,000	
02 COST OF GOODS SOLD	5,728,000	2,864,000	
Gross Profit	***106,400***	***568,000***	
03 OTHER EXPENSES	680,000	340,000	
04 DEPRECIATION	116,960	18,900	ΔL6 [Balance Sheet]
Total Operating Costs	***$6,524,960***	***$3,222,900***	L2+L3+L4
05 EBIT ***Operating Income***	($690,560)	$209,100	L1-L2-L3-L4
06 INTEREST EXPENSE	176,000	62,500	
07 EBT	($866,560)	$146,600	L5-L6
08 TAXES (40%)	(346,624)	58,640	L7 x 40%
09 NET INCOME	($519,936)	$87,960	L7-L8
10 EPS	($5.19)	$0.88	L9 ÷ L14
11 DPS	$0.110	$0.220	L3 [Retained Earnings] ÷ L14
12 BOOK VALUE PER SHARE	$1.328	$6.638	L16 [Balance Sheet] ÷ L14
13 STOCK PRICE	$2.25	$8.50	Market Price of Stock
14 SHARES OUTSTANDING	100,000	100,000	
15 TAX RATE	40.00%	40.00%	

1.6.5 Statement of Retained Earnings

01 BALANCE OF RETAINED EARNINGS, 12/31/11	$203,768	L15 [Balance Sheet]
02 ADD: NET INCOME	(519,936)	L09 [Income Statement]
03 LESS: DIVIDENDS PAID	(11,000)	L11xL14 [Income Statement]
04 BALANCE OF RETAINED EARNINGS, 12/31/12	($327,168)	L1+L2+L3

1.6.6 Statement of Cash Flow

OPERATING ACTIVITIES		
01 NET INCOME	($ 519,936)	L9 [Income Statement]
ADDITIONS (SOURCES OF CASH)		
02 DEPRECIATION	116,960	ΔL6 [Balance Sheet]
03 INCREASE IN ACCOUNTS PAYABLE	378,560	ΔL9 [Balance Sheet]
04 INCREASE IN ACCRUALS	353,600	ΔL11 [Balance Sheet]
SUBTRACTIONS (USES OF CASH)		
05 INCREASE IN ACCOUNTS RECEIVABLE	(280,960)	ΔL2 [Balance Sheet]
06 INCREASE IN INVENTORIES	(572,160)	ΔL3 [Balance Sheet]
07 NET CASH PROVIDED BY OPERATING ACTIVITIES	($523,936)	1+2+3+4-5-6
LONG-TERM INVESTING ACTIVITIES		
08 CASH USED TO ACQUIRE FIXED ASSETS	($ 711,950)	L5 [Balance Sheet]
FINANCING ACTIVITIES		
09 INCREASE IN NOTES PAYABLE	$520,000	ΔL10 [Balance Sheet]
10 INCREASE IN LONG-TERM DEBT	676,568	ΔL13 [Balance Sheet]
11 PAYMENT OF CASH DIVIDENDS	(11,000)	L3 [Retained Earnings]
12 NET CASH PROVIDED BY FINANCING ACTIVITIES	$1,185,568	9+10+11
13 SUM: NET DECREASE IN CASH	($50,318)	7+8+12
14 PLUS: CASH AT BEGINNING OF YEAR	57,600	L1 [Balance Sheet]
15 CASH AT END OF YEAR [To B/Sheet]	$7,282	13+14

FINANCIAL CASH FLOW	OPERATIONAL CASH FLOW	CASH FLOW TO INVESTORS
+ Revenues	+ Revenues	+ Revenues
– Direct Cost of Goods Sold (COGS)	– Direct Cost of Goods Sold (COGS)	– Direct Cost of Goods Sold (COGS)
= GROSS PROFIT	= GROSS PROFIT	= GROSS PROFIT
– Indirect Expenses	– Indirect Expenses	– Indirect Expenses
= EBITDA	= EBITDA	= EBITDA
– Depreciation	– Depreciation	– Depreciation
– Amortization	– Amortization	– Amortization
= EBIT (OPER. INCOME)	= EBIT (OPER. INCOME)	= EBIT (OPER. INCOME)
– Interest		
= EBT		
– Tax	– Tax	– Tax
= Net Income (NI)	= NOPAT	= NOPAT
+ Depreciation	+ Depreciation	+ Depreciation
+ Amortization	+ Amortization	+ Amortization
+ Noncash Expenses	+ Noncash Expenses	– Total Gross Invested Oper. Capital
= Net Cash Flow (NCF)	= Operational Cash Flow (OCF)	= Free Cash Flow (FCF)
	– Interest (After Tax): [INT (1-T)]	
	= Net Cash Flow (NCF)	

Equations and Calculations

1. Earnings Before Interest, Taxes, Depreciation, and Amortization (EBITDA) = Revenue – Operating Expenses (OPEX)
2. Earnings Before Interest and Taxes (EBIT) = EBITDA – Depreciation – Amortization
3. Net Income = (EBIT – Interest) (1 – Tax Rate)
4. Net Cash Flow (NCF) = Net Income + Depreciation + Amortization
5. Net Cash Flow (NCF) = Operating Cash Flow – (Interest Charges)(1 – Tax Rate)
6. Net Operating Profit After Taxes (NOPAT) = EBIT(1 – Tax Rate)
7. Operating Cash Flow (OCF) = EBIT(1 – Tax Rate) + Depreciation + Amortization
8. Operating Cash Flow = NOPAT + Depreciation + Amortization
9. Free Cash Flow (FCF) = NOPAT – Net Investment in Operating Capital
10. Free Cash Flow (FCF) = Operating Cash Flow – Gross Investment in Operating Capital
11. Net Investment in Operating Capital (NET IOC) = Change in Net Operating Capital Year Over Year
12. Gross Investment in Operating Capital = Net Investment in Operating Capital + Depreciation + Amortization
13. Return on Invested Capital (ROIC) = NOPAT ÷ Total Net Operating Capital
14. Economic Value Added (EVA) = NOPAT – After Tax Cost of Capital
15. Economic Value Added (EVA) = EBIT(1 –Tax Rate) – (Total Net Operating Capital)(WACC)
16. Economic Value Added (EVA) = Total Net Operating Capital (ROIC – WACC)

Be careful to not confuse NET IOC with NOWC and EVA with MVA

- Net Operating Working Capital (NOWC) = Current Assets – Current Liabilities
- Current Assets = Cash + Accounts Receivables + Inventories
- Current Liabilities = Accounts Payable + Accruals + Wages Payable
- Net Operating Capital = NOWC + Operating Long – Term Assets
- Market Value Added (MVA) = Market Value of Stock – Equity Capital Supplied
- Market Value Added (MVA) = (Shares Outstanding)(Stock Price) – Total Common Equity
- Market Value Added (MVA) = Total Market Value – Investor Supplied Capital
- Market Value Added (MVA) = MV Stock + MV Debt – Investor Supplied Capital

Financial Statement Notes

- *Net Cash Flow* differs from accounting profit because some of the revenues and expenses reflected in accounting profits may not have been received or paid out in cash during the year. Depreciation is typically the largest noncash item, so net cash flow is often expressed as net income plus depreciation. Investors are at least as interested in a firm's projected net cash flow as in reported earnings because it is cash, not paper profit that is paid out as dividends and plowed back into the business to produce growth.
- *Operating Current Assets* are the current assets that are used to support operations, such as cash, inventory, and accounts receivable. They do not include short-term investments.
- *Operating Current Liabilities* are the current liabilities that occur as a natural consequence of operations, such as accounts payable and accruals. They do not include notes payable or any other short-term debts that charge interest.
- *Net Operating Working Capital* (NOWC) is the difference between operating current assets and operating current liabilities. Thus, it is the working capital acquired with investor-supplied funds. NOWC can be seen as current assets used in operations (operating working capital) less accounts payable and accruals.
- *Operating Long-term Assets* are the long-term assets used to support operations, such as net plant and equipment. They do not include any long-term investments that pay interest or dividends.
- *Total Net Operating Capital* (operating capital and net operating assets) is the sum of net operating working capital and operating long-term assets. It is the total amount of capital needed to run the business.
- *NOPAT* or *Net Operating Profit After Taxes*, or EBIT (1 – Tax Rate). It is the after-tax profit a company would have if it had no debt and no investments in nonoperating assets. Because it excludes the effects of financial decisions, it is a better measure of operating performance than is net income.
- *Free Cash Flow* (FCF) is the amount of cash flow remaining after a company makes the asset investments necessary to support operations. In other words, FCF is the amount of cash flow available for distribution to investors, *so the value of a company is directly related to its ability to generate free cash flow*. It is defined as NOPAT – Net Investment in Operating Capital. It is also defined as Operating Cash Flow – Gross Investment in Operating Capital.

Financial Statement Notes II

- *Market Value Added* (MVA) represents the Total Market Value of a Firm – Total Amount of Investor-supplied Capital. If the market values of debt and preferred stock equal their values as reported on the financial statements, then MVA is the difference between the market value of a firm's stock and the amount of equity its shareholders have supplied.
- *Economic Value Added* (EVA) is After-tax Operating Profit – Total Dollar Cost of Capital, including the cost of equity capital. EVA is an estimate of the value created by management (a measure of management performance) during the year, and it differs substantially from accounting profit because no charge for the use of equity capital is reflected in accounting profit. It is also defined as NOPAT – After-tax Cost of Capital, which is the same as saying EBIT (1 – Tax Rate) – Operating Capital (After-tax Percentage Cost) or Capital (ROIC – WACC).
- The value of any asset depends on the stream of after-tax cash flows it produces. Tax rates and other aspects of our tax system are changed by the legislature every year or so.
- Interest income received by a corporation is taxed as ordinary income; however, 70% of the dividends received by one corporation from another are excluded from taxable income.
- Because interest paid by a corporation is a deductible expense while dividends are not, a country's tax system usually favors debt over equity financing (e.g., US).
- Ordinary corporate operating losses can be carried back to each of the preceding 2 years and forward for the next 20 years and used to offset taxable income in those years.
- *Return on Invested Capital* (ROIC) = NOPAT/Capital, which is the rate of return a company generates on its capital.
- *Weighted Average Cost of Capital* (WACC) is the rate of return that the company must generate to satisfy its investors because this is the average cost of raising capital for the firm.
- Assets such as stocks, bonds, and real estate are defined as *capital assets*. If a capital asset is sold for more than its cost, the profit is called a *capital gain*. If the asset is sold for a loss, it is called a *capital loss*. Assets held for more than a year provide long-term gains or losses.

Limitations of Financial Statement Analysis

Limitations of Financial Statement Analysis

- Comparison with industry averages is difficult if the firm operates many different divisions.
- Average performance is not necessarily good performance.
- Inflation distorts firms' balance sheets.
- Seasonal factors can distort ratios.
- "Window dressing" can make statements and ratios look better than reality.
- Different operating and accounting practices distort comparisons.
- Determining if a particular ratio is good or bad is difficult.
- Determining if a particular firm's ratios are, on balance, good or bad is difficult.

Qualitative Factors

- Are the company's revenues tied to one key customer and to what extent?
- To what extent does one company rely on a single supplier?
- Overseas and foreign businesses? If so, what percentage?
- Competition
- Future prospects
- Legal and regulatory environments

Project and Valuation Approaches

Value is defined as the single time-value discounted number that is representative of all future net profitability. In retrospect, the market price of an asset may or may not be identical to its value. (The terms assets, projects, and strategies are used interchangeably). For instance, when an asset is sold at a significant bargain, its price may be somewhat lower than its value, and one would surmise that the purchaser has obtained a significant amount of value. The idea of valuation in creating a fair market value is to determine the price that closely resembles the true value of an asset. This true value comes from the physical aspects of the asset as well as the nonphysical, intrinsic, or intangible aspect of the asset. Both aspects have the capabilities of generating extrinsic monetary or intrinsic strategic value. Traditionally, there are three mainstream approaches to valuation, namely, the market approach, the income approach, and the cost approach.

Market Approach

The market approach looks at comparable assets in the marketplace and their corresponding prices and assumes that market forces will tend to move the market price to an equilibrium level. It is further assumed that the market price is also the fair market value after adjusting for transaction costs and risk differentials. Sometimes a market-, industry- or firm-specific adjustment is warranted to bring the comparables closer to the operating structure of the firm whose asset is being valued. These approaches could include common-sizing the comparable firms, performing quantitative screening using criteria that closely resemble the firm's industry, operations, size, revenues, functions, profitability levels, operational efficiency, competition, market, and risks.

Project and Valuation Approaches II

Income Approach

The income approach looks at the future potential profit or free cash flow-generating potential of the asset and attempts to quantify, forecast, and discount these net free cash flows to a present value. The cost of implementation, acquisition, and development of the asset is then deducted from this present value of cash flows to generate a net present value. Often, the cash flow stream is discounted at a firm-specified hurdle rate, at the weighted average cost of capital, or at a risk-adjusted discount rate based on the perceived project-specific risk, historical firm risk, or overall business risk.

Cost Approach

The cost approach looks at the cost a firm would incur if it were to replace or reproduce the asset's future profitability potential, including the cost of its strategic intangibles, if the asset were to be created from the ground up. Although the financial theories underlying these approaches are sound in the more traditional deterministic view, they cannot be reasonably used in isolation when analyzing the true strategic flexibility value of a firm, project, or asset.

Project and Valuation Approaches III

Other Approaches

Other approaches used in valuation, more appropriately applied to the valuation of intangibles, rely on quantifying the economic viability and economic gains the asset brings to the firm. There are several well-known methodologies to intangible-asset valuation, particularly in valuing trademarks and brand names. These methodologies apply the combination of the market, income, and cost approaches described above.

The first method compares pricing strategies and assumes that by having some dominant market position by virtue of a strong trademark or brand recognition—for instance, Coca-Cola—the firm can charge a premium price for its product. Hence, if we can find market comparables producing similar products, in similar markets, performing similar functions, facing similar market uncertainties and risks, the price differential would then pertain exclusively to the brand name. These comparables are generally adjusted to account for the different conditions under which the firms operate. This price premium per unit is then multiplied by the projected quantity of sales, and the outcome after performing a discounted cash flow analysis will be the residual profits allocated to the intangible. A similar argument can be set forth in using operating profit margin in lieu of price per unit. Operating profit before taxes is used instead of net profit after taxes because it avoids the problems of comparables having different capital structure policies or carry-forward net operating losses and other tax-shield implications.

Another method uses a common-size analysis of the profit and loss statements between the firm holding the asset and market comparables. This takes into account any advantage from economies of scale and economies of scope. The idea here is to convert the income statement items as a percentage of sales, and balance sheet items as a percentage of total assets. In addition, to increase comparability, the ratio of operating profit to sales of the comparable firm is then multiplied by the asset-holding firm's projected revenue structure, thereby eliminating the potential problem of having to account for differences in economies of scale and scope. This approach uses a percentage of sales, return on investment, or return on asset ratio as the common-size variable.

Financial Spreadsheet Model in Excel

Discounted Cash Flow / ROI Model

Base Year	*2017*	*Sum PV Net Benefits*	***$4,762.09***	*Discount Type*	Discrete End-of-Year Discounting
Start Year	*2017*	*Sum PV Investments*	***$1,634.22***		
Market Risk-Adjusted Discount Rate	*15.00%*	*Net Present Value*	***$3,127.87***	*Model :*	Include Terminal Valuation
Private-Risk Discount Rate	*5.00%*	*Internal Rate of Return*	***55.68%***		
Terminal Period Growth Rate	*2.00%*	*Return on Investment*	***191.40%***		
Effective Tax Rate	*40.00%*	*Profitability Index*	***2.91***		

	2017	2018	2019	2020	2021	2022	2023	2024	2025	2026
Product A Avg Price/Unit	$10.00	$10.50	$11.00	$11.50	$12.00	$12.50	$13.00	$13.50	$14.00	$14.50
Product B Avg Price/Unit	$12.25	$12.50	$12.75	$13.00	$13.25	$13.50	$13.75	$14.00	$14.25	$14.50
Product C Avg Price/Unit	$15.15	$15.30	$15.45	$15.60	$15.75	$15.90	$16.05	$16.20	$16.35	$16.50
Product A Sale Quantity ('000s)	50	50	50	50	50	50	50	50	50	50
Product B Sale Quantity ('000s)	35	35	35	35	35	35	35	35	35	35
Product C Sale Quantity ('000s)	20	20	20	20	20	20	20	20	20	20
Total Revenues	***$1,231.75***	***$1,268.50***	***$1,305.25***	***$1,342.00***	***$1,378.75***	***$1,415.50***	***$1,452.25***	***$1,489.00***	***$1,525.75***	***$1,562.50***
Direct Cost of Goods Sold	$184.76	$190.28	$195.79	$201.30	$206.81	$212.33	$217.84	$223.35	$228.86	$234.38
Gross Profit	***$1,046.99***	***$1,078.23***	***$1,109.46***	***$1,140.70***	***$1,171.94***	***$1,203.18***	***$1,234.41***	***$1,265.65***	***$1,296.89***	***$1,328.13***
Operating Expenses	$157.50	$157.50	$157.50	$157.50	$157.50	$157.50	$157.50	$157.50	$157.50	$157.50
Sales, General and Admin. Costs	$15.75	$15.75	$15.75	$15.75	$15.75	$15.75	$15.75	$15.75	$15.75	$15.75
Operating Income (EBITDA)	***$873.74***	***$904.98***	***$936.21***	***$967.45***	***$998.69***	***$1,029.93***	***$1,061.16***	***$1,092.40***	***$1,123.64***	***$1,154.88***
Depreciation	$10.00	$10.00	$10.00	$10.00	$10.00	$10.00	$10.00	$10.00	$10.00	$10.00
Amortization	$3.00	$3.00	$3.00	$3.00	$3.00	$3.00	$3.00	$3.00	$3.00	$3.00
EBIT	***$860.74***	***$891.98***	***$923.21***	***$954.45***	***$985.69***	***$1,016.93***	***$1,048.16***	***$1,079.40***	***$1,110.64***	***$1,141.88***
Interest Payments	$2.00	$2.00	$2.00	$2.00	$2.00	$3.00	$4.00	$5.00	$6.00	$7.00
EBT	***$858.74***	***$889.98***	***$921.21***	***$952.45***	***$983.69***	***$1,013.93***	***$1,044.16***	***$1,074.40***	***$1,104.64***	***$1,134.88***
Taxes	$343.50	$355.99	$368.49	$380.98	$393.48	$405.57	$417.67	$429.76	$441.86	$453.95
Net Income	***$515.24***	***$533.99***	***$552.73***	***$571.47***	***$590.21***	***$608.36***	***$626.50***	***$644.64***	***$662.78***	***$680.93***
Noncash: Depreciation Amortization	$13.00	$13.00	$13.00	$13.00	$13.00	$13.00	$13.00	$13.00	$13.00	$13.00
Noncash: Change in Net Working Capital	$0.00	$0.00	$0.00	$0.00	$0.00	$0.00	$0.00	$0.00	$0.00	$0.00
Noncash: Capital Expenditures	$0.00	$0.00	$0.00	$0.00	$0.00	$0.00	$0.00	$0.00	$0.00	$0.00
Free Cash Flow	***$528.24***	***$546.99***	***$565.73***	***$584.47***	***$603.21***	***$621.36***	***$639.50***	***$657.64***	***$675.78***	***$5,444.64***
Investment Outlay	***$500.00***		***$1,500.00***							
Net Free Cash Flow	***($1,105.97)***	***$546.99***	***$565.73***	***$584.47***	***$603.21***	***$621.36***	***$639.50***	***$657.64***	***$675.78***	***$5,444.64***
Financial Analysis										
Present Value of Free Cash Flow	***$528.24***	***$475.64***	***$427.77***	***$384.30***	***$344.89***	***$308.92***	***$276.47***	***$247.23***	***$220.91***	***$1,547.71***
Present Value of Investment Outlay	***$500.00***	***$0.00***	***$1,134.22***	***$0.00***	***$0.00***	***$0.00***	***$0.00***	***$0.00***	***$0.00***	***$0.00***
Discounted Payback Period	***3.47 Years***									

Price-to-Earning (PE) Ratios

Related concepts in valuation include the uses of market multiples. An example is using the price-to-earnings multiple, which is a simple derivation of the constant growth model shown above, breaking it down into dividends per share *(DPS)* and earnings per share *(EPS)* components. The derivation starts with the constant growth model: $P_0 = \frac{DPS_0(1+g_n)}{k_e - g_n} = \frac{DPS_1}{k_e - g_n}$

We then use the fact that the dividend per share next period (DPS_1) is the earnings per share current period multiplied by the payout ratio (*PR*), defined as the ratio of dividends per share to earnings per share, which is assumed to be constant, multiplied by one plus the growth rate (*1+ g*) of earnings:

$$DPS_1 = EPS_0[PR](1+g_n)$$

$$PR = \frac{DPS_1}{EPS_0(1+g_n)}$$

The earnings per share the following period is the same as the earnings per share this period multiplied by one plus the growth rate: $EPS_1 = EPS_0(1+g_n)$

Substituting the earnings per share model for the dividends per share in the constant growth model, we get the pricing relationship: $P_0 = \frac{EPS_0[PR](1+g_n)}{k_e - g_n}$

Because we are using price-to-earnings ratios, we can divide the pricing relationship by earnings per share to obtain an approximation of the price-to-earnings ratio (PE): $\frac{P_0}{EPS_1} = \frac{[PR](1+g_n)}{k_e - g_n} \approx PE_1$

$$P_0 \approx EPS_1(PE_1)$$

One of the issues that arises when using PE ratios is the fact that PE ratios change across different markets. If a firm serves multiple markets, it is difficult to find an adequate weighted average PE ratio. PE ratios may not be stable through time and are most certainly not stable across firms. If more efficient firms are added to less efficiently run firms, the average PE ratio may be skewed. In addition, market overreaction and speculation, particularly among high-growth firms, provide an overinflated PE ratio. Furthermore, not all firms are publicly held, some firms may not have a PE ratio, and if valuation of individual projects is required, PE ratios may not be adequate because it is difficult to isolate a specific investment's profitability and its corresponding PE ratio. Similar approaches include using other proxy multiples including Business Enterprise Value to Earnings, Price to Book, Price to Sales, and so forth, with similar methods and applications.

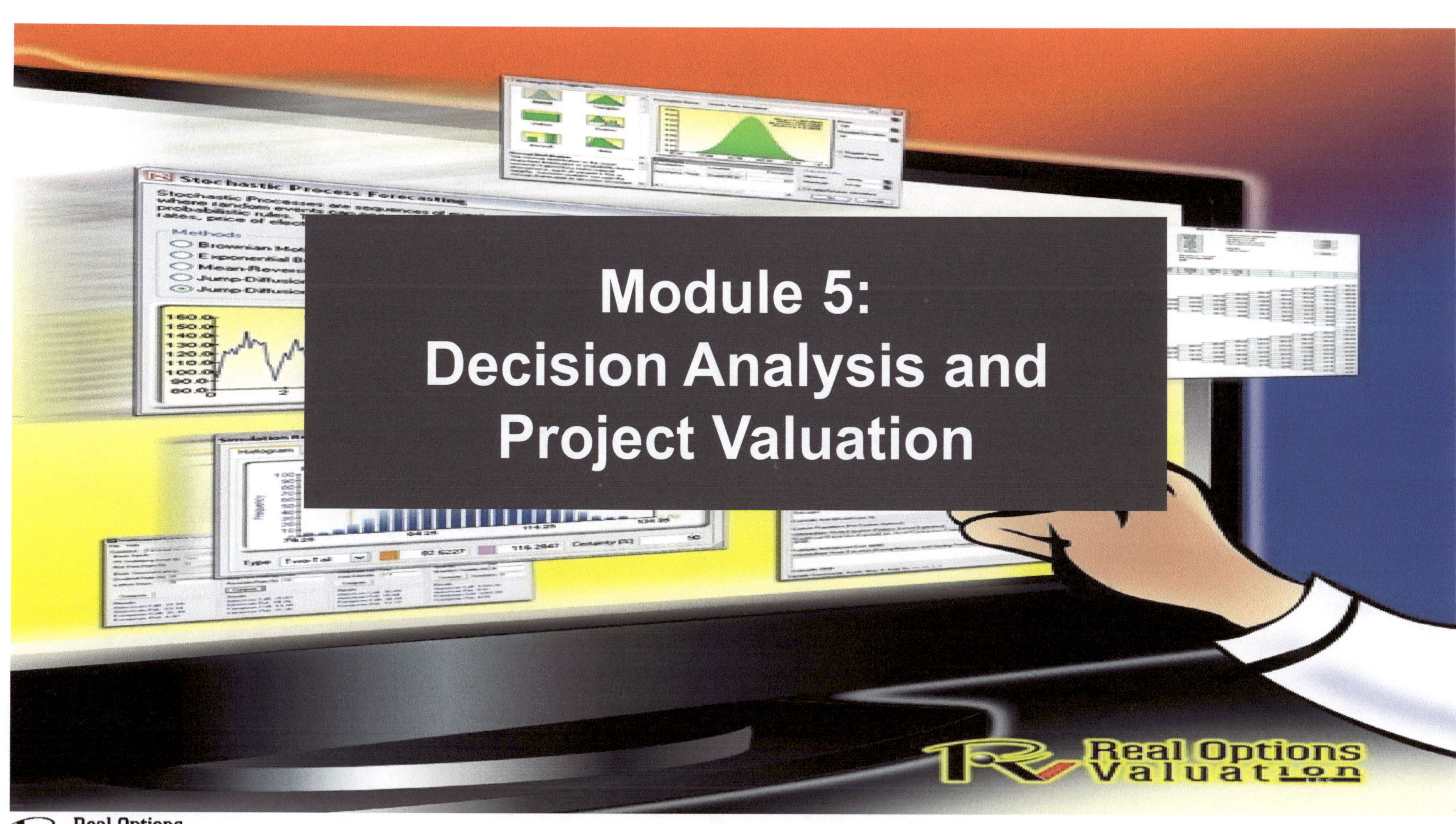

Real Options Valuation

Capital Budgeting

- Capital budgeting is the process of analyzing potential projects. Capital budgeting decisions are probably the most important ones managers must make, which helps decision makers to decide if a company should replace worn out/damaged equipment, or replace or add to existing equipment to reduce cost; undergo expansion; or invest in a new project or equipment. At its most general, the capital budgeting process involves simply choosing the best project from among several alternatives.
- Once a potential capital budgeting project is identified, its evaluation usually requires the determination of project investment cost, project cash flow estimation, riskiness of the project, and cost of capital adjusting for riskiness of the project, as well as a determination of the six key economic indicators (NPV, IRR, MIRR, ROI and PI, PP, DPP).
- The payback period is defined as the number of years required to recover a project's cost. The regular payback period method ignores cash flows beyond the payback period, and it does not consider the time value of money. The payback does, however, provide an indication of a project's risk and liquidity, because it shows how long the invested capital will be "at risk."
- The discounted payback method is similar to the regular payback method except that it discounts cash flows at the project's cost of capital. It considers the time value of money, but it ignores cash flows beyond the payback period.
- The net present value (NPV) method discounts all cash flows at the project's cost of capital and then sums those cash flows. The project should be accepted if the NPV is positive.
- The internal rate of return (IRR) is defined as the discount rate that forces a project's NPV to equal zero. The project should be accepted if the IRR is greater than the cost of capital.
- The NPV and IRR methods make the same accept/reject decisions for independent projects, but if projects are mutually exclusive, ranking conflicts can arise. If conflicts arise, the NPV method should be used. The NPV and IRR methods are both superior to the payback method, but NPV is superior to IRR.
- The NPV method assumes that cash flows will be reinvested at the firm's cost of capital, while the IRR method assumes reinvestment at the project's IRR. Reinvestment at the cost of capital is generally a better assumption because it is closer to reality.

Capital Budgeting II

- The NPV method assumes that cash flows will be reinvested at the firm's cost of capital, while the IRR method assumes reinvestment at the project's IRR. Reinvestment at the cost of capital is generally a better assumption because it is closer to reality.
- The modified IRR (MIRR) method corrects some of the problems with the regular IRR. MIRR involves finding the terminal value (TV) of the cash inflows, compounded at the firm's cost of capital, and then determining the discount rate that forces the present value of the TV to equal the present value of the outflows.
- The profitability index (PI) shows the dollars of present value divided by the initial cost, so it measures relative profitability.
- Sophisticated managers consider all of the project evaluation measures because each measure provides a useful piece of information.
- Payback measures liquidity, NPV measures direct dollar benefit, IRR measures percentage return with a safety margin built in, MIRR measures a percentage return considering a better reinvestment rate, and PI measures bang for the buck.
- The post-audit is a key element of capital budgeting. By comparing actual results with predicted results and then determining why differences occurred, decision makers can improve both their operations and their forecasts of projects' outcomes.
- Small firms tend to use the payback method rather than a discounted cash flow method. This may be rational because (1) the cost of conducting a Discounted Cash Flow analysis may outweigh the benefits for the project being considered, (2) the firm's cost of capital cannot be estimated accurately, or (3) the small-business owner may be considering nonmonetary goals.
- If mutually exclusive projects have unequal lives, it may be necessary to adjust the analysis to put the projects on an equal-life basis. This can be done using the replacement chain (common life) approach, covered later in this module.
- A project's true value may be greater than the NPV based on its physical life if it can be terminated at the end of its economic life.
- Flotation costs and increased riskiness associated with unusually large expansion programs can cause the marginal cost of capital to rise as the size of the capital budget increases.
- Capital rationing occurs when management places a constraint on the size of the firm's capital budget during a particular period.

Payback Period

Simple but ineffective by itself, the payback period method calculates the time necessary to pay back the initial cost (i.e., a breakeven analysis). It does not take into account time valuation of money, does not consider different life spans after the initial payback breakpoint and ignores the cost of capital. The payback period approach helps identify the project's *liquidity* in determining how long funds will be tied up in the project.

Payback = Year before full recovery + [unrecovered cost ÷ Cash Flow at time t]

Suppose you are to choose between two projects, A and B. Project A costs $442 but pays back $200 for the next 3 years, while B costs $718 and pays back $250, $575, and $100 for the next 3 years.

Payback A = 2 + [42/200] = 2.21 years.

Payback B = 1 + [(718–250)/575] = 1.81 years.

Disadvantages:

Neglects time value of money and neglects cash flows after the payback period.

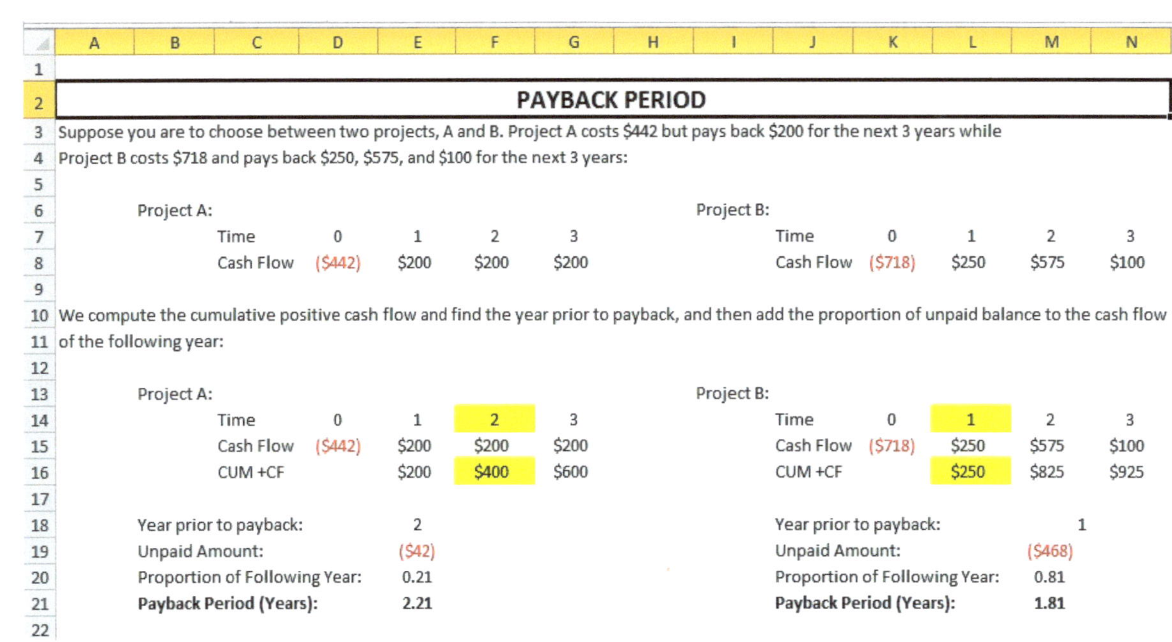

PAYBACK PERIOD

Suppose you are to choose between two projects, A and B. Project A costs $442 but pays back $200 for the next 3 years while Project B costs $718 and pays back $250, $575, and $100 for the next 3 years:

Project A:

Time	0	1	2	3
Cash Flow	($442)	$200	$200	$200

Project B:

Time	0	1	2	3
Cash Flow	($718)	$250	$575	$100

We compute the cumulative positive cash flow and find the year prior to payback, and then add the proportion of unpaid balance to the cash flow of the following year:

Project A:

Time	0	1	2	3
Cash Flow	($442)	$200	$200	$200
CUM +CF		$200	$400	$600

Year prior to payback:	2
Unpaid Amount:	($42)
Proportion of Following Year:	0.21
Payback Period (Years):	**2.21**

Project B:

Time	0	1	2	3
Cash Flow	($718)	$250	$575	$100
CUM +CF		$250	$825	$925

Year prior to payback:	1
Unpaid Amount:	($468)
Proportion of Following Year:	0.81
Payback Period (Years):	**1.81**

Disadvantage of Payback Period

- *Neglects time value of money.* To solve this, use present values instead of cash flows, that is, use a discounted payback period instead. This means that in the example above, the $200, or $250, $575, and $100 cash flows are first discounted to present values. (See the Discounted Payback Period example next.)
- *Cash flows and length of time remaining are left out after the payback period.* As an example, suppose we have two new projects, X and Y with cash flows shown below. Both have identical payback periods but clearly, project Y is superior as it has additional cash flows. These cash flows post payback period are ignored.

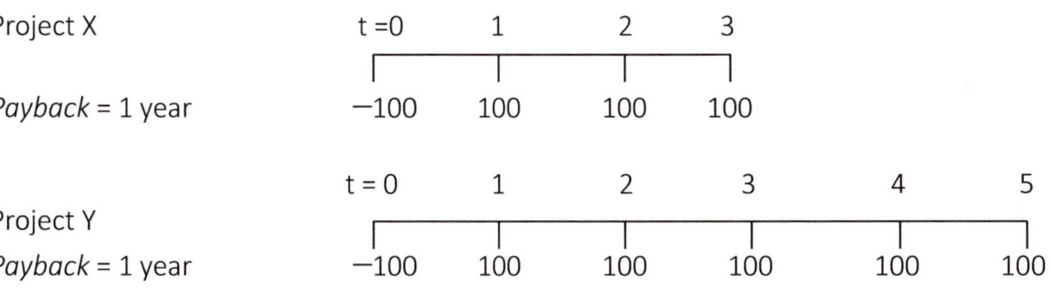

Discounted Payback Period

The discounted payback period method is similar to the payback period method but the cash flows used are in present values. This solves the issue of cost of capital, but the disadvantage of ignoring cash flows beyond the payback period still remains.

Discounted Payback = Year before full recovery + [unrecovered cost ÷ PV Cash Flow at time t]

Suppose you are to choose between two projects, A and B. Project A costs $442 but pays back $200 for the next 3 years, while B costs $718 and pays back $250, $575, and $100 for the next 3 years. Further suppose that the WACC discount rate is 12%.

Discounted Payback A =

2 + [(442–338.0)/142.4] = 2.73 years.

Discounted Payback B =

2 + [(718-681.6) – 71.2] = 2.51 years.

DISCOUNTED PAYBACK PERIOD

Suppose you are to choose between two projects, A and B. Project A costs $442 but pays back $200 for the next 3 years while Project B costs $718 and pays back $250, $575, and $100 for the next 3 years. Now suppose the WACC discount rate is 12%.

Project A:					Project B:				
Time	0	1	2	3	Time	0	1	2	3
Cash Flow	($442)	$200	$200	$200	Cash Flow	($718)	$250	$575	$100

We compute the cumulative positive cash flow and find the year prior to payback, and then add the proportion of unpaid balance to the cash flow of the following year:

Project A:					Project B:				
Time	0	1	2	3	Time	0	1	2	3
Cash Flow	($442)	$200	$200	$200	Cash Flow	($718)	$250	$575	$100
PV Cash Flow	($442)	$178.6	$159.4	$142.4	PV Cash Flow	($718)	$223.2	$458.4	$71.2
CUM +CF		$178.6	$338.0	$480.4	CUM +CF		$223.2	$681.6	$752.8
Year prior to payback:		2			Year prior to payback:			2	
Unpaid Amount:		($104)			Unpaid Amount:			($36)	
Proportion of Following Year:		0.73			Proportion of Following Year:			0.51	
Payback Period (Years):		**2.73**			**Payback Period (Years):**			**2.51**	

Net Present Value

The net present value (NPV) method is simple and powerful: *All future cash flows are discounted at the project's cost of capital and then summed.* Be aware that CF_0 is usually a negative number as this may be an initial capital investment in the project. Complications include differing life spans and different rankings using IRR. The general rule is if NPV > 0, accept the project; if NPV < 0, reject the project; if NPV = 0, you are indifferent (other qualitative variables need to be considered). The NPV is the sum of cash flows (*CF*) from time zero (*t* = 0) to the final cash flow period (*N*) discounted as some discount rate (*k*), which is typically the WACC. NPV has a direct relationship between economic value added (EVA) and market value added (MVA). It is equal to the present value of the project's future EVA, and, hence, a positive NPV usually implies a positive EVA and MVA.

$$NPV = CF_0 + \frac{CF_1}{(1+k)^1} + \frac{CF_2}{(1+k)^2} + \ldots + \frac{CF_N}{(1+k)^N} = \sum_{t=0}^{N} \frac{CF_t}{(1+k)^t}$$

$$NPV = CF_0 + \frac{CF_1}{(1+WACC)^1} + \frac{CF_2}{(1+WACC)^2} + \ldots + \frac{CF_N}{(1+WACC)^N} = \sum_{t=0}^{N} \frac{CF_t}{(1+WACC)^t}$$

Comparing A and B, A has a higher NPV, therefore A should be chosen before B although both projects should be undertaken if sufficient funds exist, otherwise, only undertake project A. Rank remains the same but NPV values differ using different discount rates.

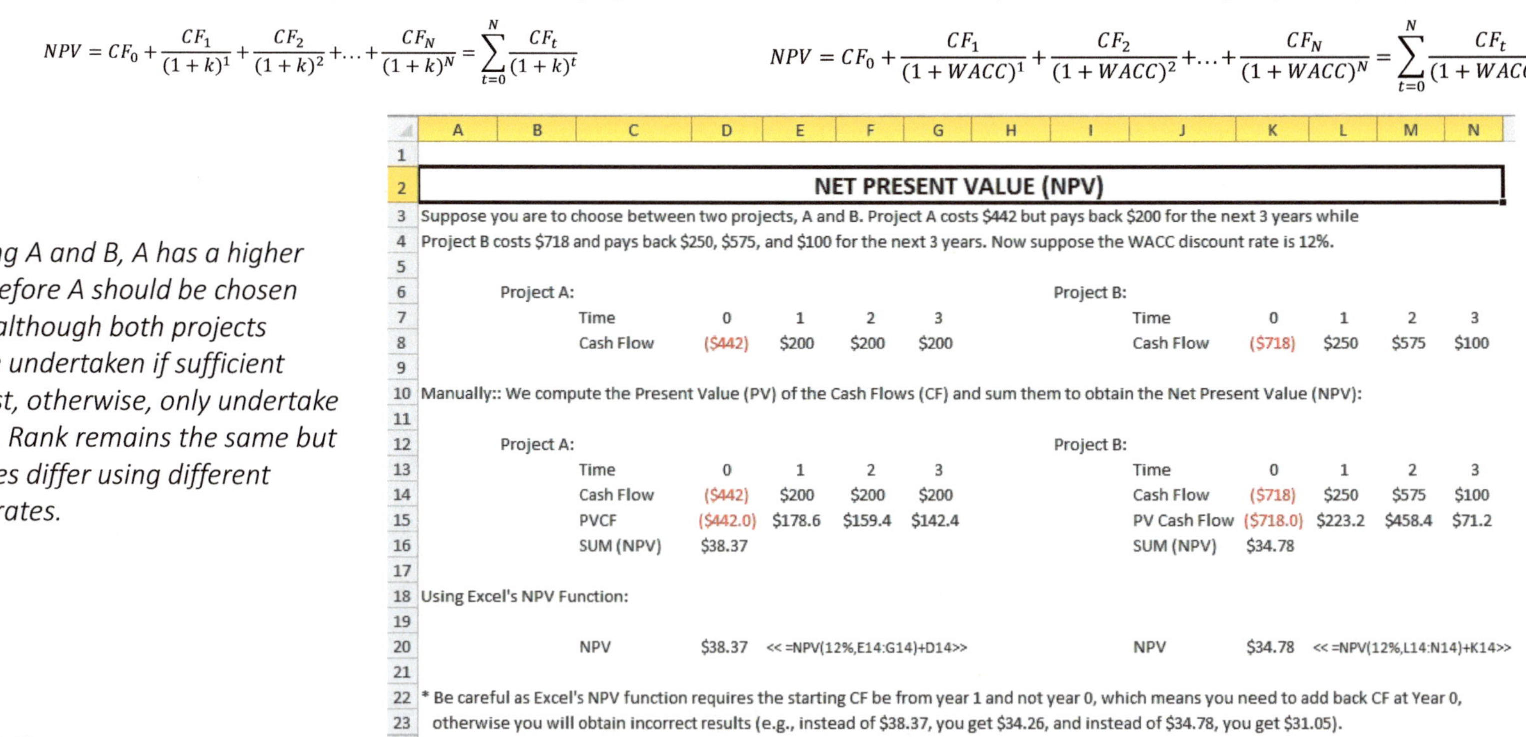

Row	A–C		D	E	F	G	H–I	J	K	L	M	N
1												
2	**NET PRESENT VALUE (NPV)**											
3	Suppose you are to choose between two projects, A and B. Project A costs $442 but pays back $200 for the next 3 years while											
4	Project B costs $718 and pays back $250, $575, and $100 for the next 3 years. Now suppose the WACC discount rate is 12%.											
5												
6	Project A:						Project B:					
7		Time	0	1	2	3		Time	0	1	2	3
8		Cash Flow	($442)	$200	$200	$200		Cash Flow	($718)	$250	$575	$100
9												
10	Manually:: We compute the Present Value (PV) of the Cash Flows (CF) and sum them to obtain the Net Present Value (NPV):											
11												
12	Project A:						Project B:					
13		Time	0	1	2	3		Time	0	1	2	3
14		Cash Flow	($442)	$200	$200	$200		Cash Flow	($718)	$250	$575	$100
15		PVCF	($442.0)	$178.6	$159.4	$142.4		PV Cash Flow	($718.0)	$223.2	$458.4	$71.2
16		SUM (NPV)	$38.37					SUM (NPV)	$34.78			
17												
18	Using Excel's NPV Function:											
19												
20		NPV	$38.37	<< =NPV(12%,E14:G14)+D14>>				NPV	$34.78	<< =NPV(12%,L14:N14)+K14>>		
21												
22	* Be careful as Excel's NPV function requires the starting CF be from year 1 and not year 0, which means you need to add back CF at Year 0,											
23	otherwise you will obtain incorrect results (e.g., instead of $38.37, you get $34.26, and instead of $34.78, you get $31.05).											

Internal Rate of Return

Internal rate of return (IRR) is the discount rate that equates the project's cost to the sum of the present cash flow of the project. That is, setting NPV = 0 and solving for k in the NPV equation, where k is now called IRR. Note that there may exist multiple IRRs when the cash flow stream is erratic. Also, the IRR and NPV rankings may be dissimilar. The general rule is that when IRR > required rate of return or hurdle rate or cost of capital, accept the project. That is, if the IRR exceeds the cost of capital required to finance and pay for the project, a surplus remains after paying for the project, which is passed on to the shareholders. The NPV and IRR methods make the same accept/reject decisions for independent projects, but if projects are mutually exclusive, ranking conflicts can arise. If conflicts arise, the NPV method should be used. The NPV and IRR methods are both superior to the payback, but NPV is superior to IRR. Conflicts may arise when the cash flow timing (most of the cash flows come in during the early years compared to later years in another project) and amounts (the cost of one project is significantly larger than another) are vastly different from one project to another. Finally, there sometimes can arise multiple IRR solutions in erratic cash flow streams such as large cash outflows occurring during or at the end of a project's life. In such situations, the NPV provides a more robust and accurate assessment of the project's value.

$$NPV = \sum_{t=0}^{N} \frac{CF_t}{(1+IRR)^t} = 0$$

Using the same scenario described in the Excel model (see right), calculate the IRR for projects A and B assuming a 12% WACC discount rate (this will now be used as the hurdle rate). Should we accept both projects again and which project is better? *Choose Project A over B as it has a higher return (IRR) and IRR > k for both.*

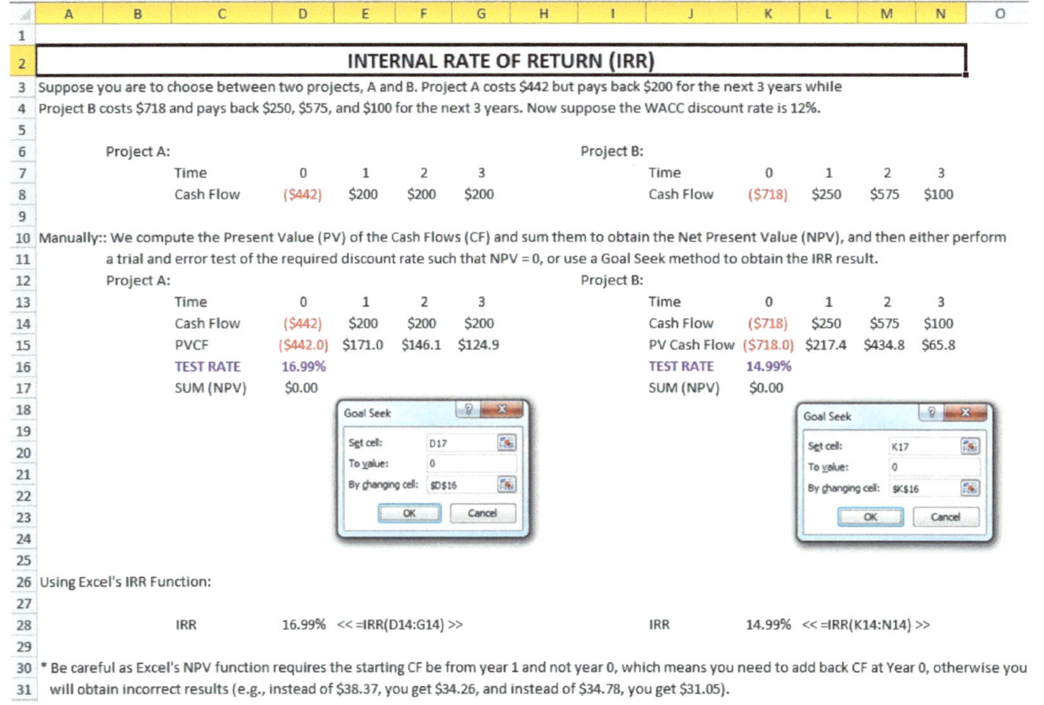

INTERNAL RATE OF RETURN (IRR)

Suppose you are to choose between two projects, A and B. Project A costs $442 but pays back $200 for the next 3 years while Project B costs $718 and pays back $250, $575, and $100 for the next 3 years. Now suppose the WACC discount rate is 12%.

Project A:					Project B:				
Time	0	1	2	3	Time	0	1	2	3
Cash Flow	($442)	$200	$200	$200	Cash Flow	($718)	$250	$575	$100

Manually:: We compute the Present Value (PV) of the Cash Flows (CF) and sum them to obtain the Net Present Value (NPV), and then either perform a trial and error test of the required discount rate such that NPV = 0, or use a Goal Seek method to obtain the IRR result.

Project A:					Project B:				
Time	0	1	2	3	Time	0	1	2	3
Cash Flow	($442)	$200	$200	$200	Cash Flow	($718)	$250	$575	$100
PVCF	($442.0)	$171.0	$146.1	$124.9	PV Cash Flow	($718.0)	$217.4	$434.8	$65.8
TEST RATE	16.99%				TEST RATE	14.99%			
SUM (NPV)	$0.00				SUM (NPV)	$0.00			

Using Excel's IRR Function:

IRR	16.99%	<< =IRR(D14:G14) >>	IRR	14.99%	<< =IRR(K14:N14) >>

* Be careful as Excel's NPV function requires the starting CF be from year 1 and not year 0, which means you need to add back CF at Year 0, otherwise you will obtain incorrect results (e.g., instead of $38.37, you get $34.26, and instead of $34.78, you get $31.05).

Disadvantages of Internal Rate of Return

- Multiple IRR can sometimes occur in cash flows that fluctuate significantly up and down over time.
- Non-negative cash flows at time 0 mean IRR cannot be computed, and shifting cash flows or costs over time to compensate for this will not work either.

When cash flows are both + and –, there may exist multiple IRRs. For instance, consider a project costing –$1.6M with returns of +$10M in the first year and a loss of –$10M in the second year. What is the project's IRR?

$$NPV = -1.6M + [10 \div (1+IRR)^1] - [10 \div (1+IRR)^2] \text{ yields } IRR = 25\% \text{ and } 400\%$$

	A	B	C	D	E	F	G	H	I	J	K	L	M	N	O
1															
2	**MULTIPLE IRR ERROR EXAMPLE**														
3	When cash flows are both + and –, there may exist multiple IRRs. For instance, consider a project costing –$1.6M and returns +$10M in the first year														
4	and a loss of –$10M in the second year. What is the project's IRR?														
5															
6		Result 1:							Result 2:						
7			Time	0	1	2				Time	0	1	2		
8			Cash Flow	($1.6)	$10.0	($10.0)				Cash Flow	($1.6)	$10.0	($10.0)		
9															
10	Manually:: We compute the Present Value (PV) of the Cash Flows (CF) and sum them to obtain the Net Present Value (NPV), and then either perform														
11		a trial and error test of the required discount rate such that NPV = 0, or use a Goal Seek method to obtain the IRR result.													
12		Result 1:							Result 2:						
13			Time	0	1	2				Time	0	1	2		
14			Cash Flow	($1.6)	$10.0	($10.0)				Cash Flow	($1.6)	$10.0	($10.0)		
15			PVCF	($1.6)	$8.0	($6.4)				PV Cash Flow	($1.6)	$2.0	($0.4)		
16			TEST RATE	25.0%						TEST RATE	400.0%				
17			SUM (NPV)	$0.00						SUM (NPV)	$0.00				

Modified Internal Rate of Return

The NPV method assumes that the project cash flows are reinvested at the cost of capital, whereas the IRR method assumes project cash flows are reinvested at the project's own IRR. The reinvestment rate at the cost of capital is the more correct approach in that this is the firm's opportunity cost of money (if funds were not available, then capital is raised at this cost).

The modified internal rate of return (MIRR) method is intended to overcome two IRR shortcomings by setting the cash flows to be reinvested at the cost of capital and not its own IRR, as well as preventing the occurrence of multiple IRRs, because only a single MIRR will exist for all cash flow scenarios. Also, NPV and MIRR will usually result in the same project selection when projects are of equal size (significant scale differences might still result in a conflict between MIRR and NPV ranking).

The MIRR is the discount rate that forces the present value of costs of cash outflows (COF) to be equal to the present value of the terminal value (the future value of cash inflows, or CIF, compounded at the project's cost of capital, k).

$$\sum_{t=0}^{n}\frac{COF_t}{(1+k)^t}=\sum_{t=0}^{n}\frac{CIF_t(1+k)^{n-t}}{(1+MIRR)^n}$$

$$\sum_{t=0}^{n}\frac{COF_t}{(1+WACC)^t}=\sum_{t=0}^{n}\frac{CIF_t(1+WACC)^{n-t}}{(1+MIRR)^n}$$

$$PV\ Costs=\frac{\text{Terminal Value}}{(1+MIRR)^n}$$

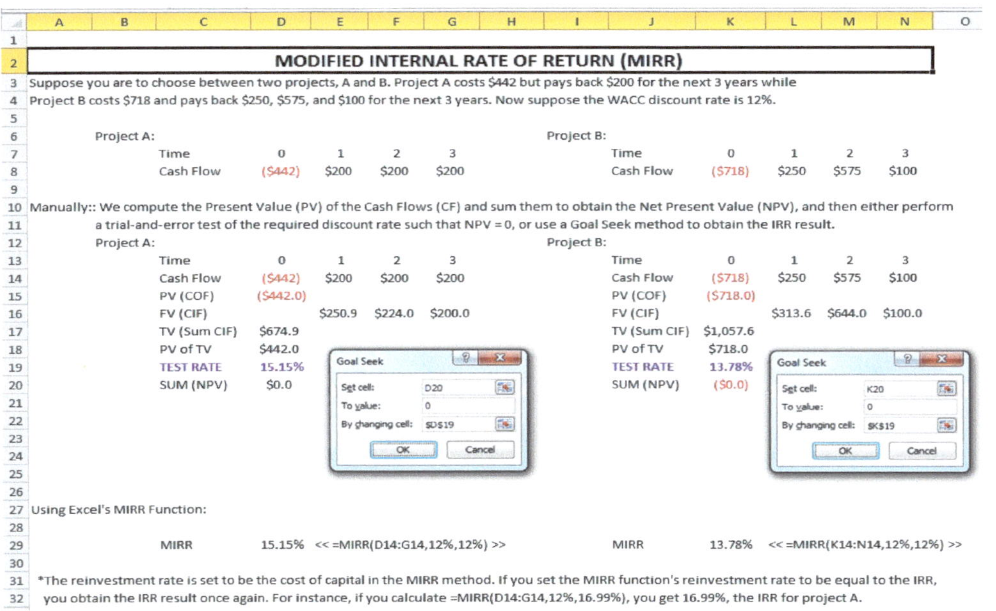

MODIFIED INTERNAL RATE OF RETURN (MIRR)

Suppose you are to choose between two projects, A and B. Project A costs $442 but pays back $200 for the next 3 years while Project B costs $718 and pays back $250, $575, and $100 for the next 3 years. Now suppose the WACC discount rate is 12%.

Project A:					Project B:				
Time	0	1	2	3	Time	0	1	2	3
Cash Flow	($442)	$200	$200	$200	Cash Flow	($718)	$250	$575	$100

Manually:: We compute the Present Value (PV) of the Cash Flows (CF) and sum them to obtain the Net Present Value (NPV), and then either perform a trial-and-error test of the required discount rate such that NPV = 0, or use a Goal Seek method to obtain the IRR result.

Project A:					Project B:				
Time	0	1	2	3	Time	0	1	2	3
Cash Flow	($442)	$200	$200	$200	Cash Flow	($718)	$250	$575	$100
PV (COF)	($442.0)				PV (COF)	($718.0)			
FV (CIF)		$250.9	$224.0	$200.0	FV (CIF)		$313.6	$644.0	$100.0
TV (Sum CIF)	$674.9				TV (Sum CIF)	$1,057.6			
PV of TV	$442.0				PV of TV	$718.0			
TEST RATE	15.15%				TEST RATE	13.78%			
SUM (NPV)	$0.0				SUM (NPV)	($0.0)			

Goal Seek
Set cell: D20
To value: 0
By changing cell: D19
OK Cancel

Goal Seek
Set cell: K20
To value: 0
By changing cell: K19
OK Cancel

Using Excel's MIRR Function:

MIRR	15.15%	<< =MIRR(D14:G14,12%,12%) >>	MIRR	13.78%	<< =MIRR(K14:N14,12%,12%) >>

*The reinvestment rate is set to be the cost of capital in the MIRR method. If you set the MIRR function's reinvestment rate to be equal to the IRR, you obtain the IRR result once again. For instance, if you calculate =MIRR(D14:G14,12%,16.99%), you get 16.99%, the IRR for project A.

Return on Investment (ROI) and Profitability Index (PI)

The profitability index (PI) is the ratio of the sum of the present value of cash flows to the initial cost of the project, which measures its relative profitability. A project is acceptable if PI > 1, and the higher the PI, the higher the project ranks. PI is mathematically very similar to return on investment (ROI). PI is a relative measure whereas ROI is an absolute measure. PI returns a ratio (the ratio is an absolute value, ignoring the negative investment cost) while ROI is usually described as a percentage.

Mathematically, NPV, IRR, MIRR, and PI should provide similar rankings although conflicts may sometimes arise, and all methods should be considered as each provides a different set of relevant information.

$$PI = \frac{\sum_{t=1}^{n} \frac{CF_t}{(1+k)^t}}{CF_0} = \frac{Benefit}{Cost} = \frac{PV\ Cash\ Flows}{Initial\ Cost}$$

$$ROI = \frac{\sum_{t=1}^{n} \frac{CF_t}{(1+k)^t} - CF_0}{CF_0} = \frac{Benefit - Cost}{Cost} = PI - 1$$

PROFITABILITY INDEX (PI) AND RETURN ON INVESTMENT (ROI)

Suppose you are to choose between two projects, A and B. Project A costs $442 but pays back $200 for the next 3 years while Project B costs $718 and pays back $250, $575, and $100 for the next 3 years. Now suppose the WACC discount rate is 12%.

Project A:					Project B:				
Time	0	1	2	3	Time	0	1	2	3
Cash Flow	($442)	$200	$200	$200	Cash Flow	($718)	$250	$575	$100

Manually:: We compute the Present Value (PV) of the Cash Flows (CF) for the negative CF (investment cost) and positive CF:

Project A:					Project B:				
Time	0	1	2	3	Time	0	1	2	3
Cash Flow	($442)	$200	$200	$200	Cash Flow	($718)	$250	$575	$100
PVCF	($442.0)	$178.6	$159.4	$142.4	PV Cash Flow	($718.0)	$223.2	$458.4	$71.2
ABS(CF(0)) Cost	$442.0	<< =ABS(D15) >>			ABS(CF(0)) Cost	$718.0	<< =ABS(K15) >>		
SUM CF(i)	$480.4	<< =SUM(E15:G15) >>			SUM CF(i)	$752.8	<< =SUM(L15:N15) >>		
Profitability Index (PI)	1.086801	<< =D17/D16 >>			Profitability Index (PI)	1.04844	<< =K17/K16 >>		
Return on Investment (ROI	8.68%	<< =(D17-D16)/D16 >>			Return on Investment (ROI)	4.84%	<< =(K17-K16)/K16 >>		

* We usually convert the initial investment cost (a negative value) into a positive absolute value to simplify the calculations, otherwise it is difficult to keep in mind which values are positive and which are negative. The *ROI* value is simply *PI - 1* in percent.

Advanced Concept: Cash Flows

Free Cash Flow to a Firm

An alternative version of the free cash flow for an unlevered firm can be defined as:

Free Cash Flow = Earnings Before Interest and Taxes [1 – Effective Tax Rate] + Depreciation + Amortization – Capital Expenditures ± Change in Net Working Capital

Levered Free Cash Flow

For a levered firm, the free cash flow becomes:

Free Cash Flow = Net Income + α[Depreciation + Amortization] ± α[Change in Net Working Capital] – α[Capital Expenditures] – Principal Repayments + New Debt Proceeds – Preferred Debt Dividends

where α is the equity-to-total-capital ratio and (1 – α) is the debt ratio.

Inflation Adjustment

The adjustments below show an inflationary adjustment for free cash flows and discount rates from nominal to real conditions:

$$Real\ CF = \frac{Nominal\ CF}{(1+\mathrm{E}[\pi])} \qquad Real\ k = \frac{1+Nominal\ k}{(1+\mathrm{E}[\pi])}-1$$

where *CF* is the cash flow series, *p* is the inflation rate, *E[p]* is the expected inflation rate, and *k* is the discount rate.

Advanced Concept: Terminal Value

The following are commonly accepted ways of getting terminal free cash flows under zero growth, constant growth, and supernormal growth assumptions:

Zero Growth Perpetuity: $$\sum_{t=1}^{\infty}\frac{FCF_t}{[1+WACC]^t}=\frac{FCF_T}{WACC}$$

Constant Growth: $$\sum_{t=1}^{\infty}\frac{FCF_{t-1}(1+g_t)}{[1+WACC]^t}=\frac{FCF_{T-1}(1+g_T)}{WACC-g_T}=\frac{FCF_T}{WACC-g_T}$$

Punctuated Growth: $$\sum_{t=1}^{N}\frac{FCF_t}{[1+WACC]^t}+\frac{\left[\frac{FCF_N(1+g_N)}{[WACC-g_N]}\right]}{[1+WACC]^N}$$

Weighted Average Cost of Capital (WACC): $$WACC=\omega_e k_e+\omega_d k_d(1-\tau)+\omega_{pe}k_{pe}$$

WACC is the weighted average cost of capital
FCF is the free cash flow series
g is the growth rate of free cash flows
t is the individual time periods
T is the terminal time at which a forecast is available
N is the time when a punctuated growth rate occurs
w is the respective weights on each capital component
k_e is the cost of common equity
k_d is the cost of debt
k_{pe} is the cost of preferred equity
τ is the effective tax rate

Advanced Concept: Uneven Lifecycle Projects

When comparing projects with unequal lives, we can use the *Replacement Chain* approach or the *Equivalent Annual Annuities* approach. Suppose we are comparing two different projects A and B below with the following cash flows and parameters:

Project A

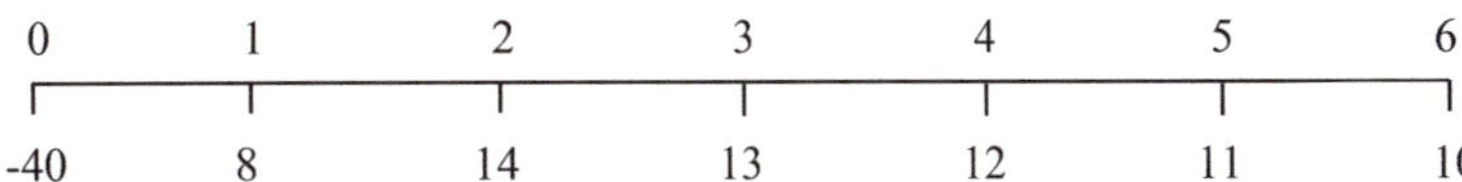

Using WACC (k) = 12%, NPV = 6.49 and IRR = 17.47%

Project B

Using WACC (k) = 12%, NPV = 5.15 and IRR = 25.2%

Notice the conflict between IRR and NPV!

We can make these two comparable using the Replacement Chain Approach and Equivalent Annuities Approach

Advanced Concept: Uneven Lifecycle Projects II

Replacement Chain Approach

One or both projects are extended until an equal life is achieved. For instance, in the example above, we have two projects, one with a 6-year life and another a 3-year life. We simply extend the project with a 3-year life to 6 years:

Project B becomes:

0	1	2	3	4	5	6
–20	7	13	12 –20 –8	7	13	12

Using WACC (k) = 12%, NPV = 8.82 and IRR = 25.20%

In another example, suppose the two projects have a 2-year and 3-year life, respectively. We simply extend both projects to an equal 6-year term and replicate the same analysis above.

Equivalent Annuities Approach (EAA)

The EAA converts each project's NPV into a stream of annuities having the same NPV.

Project A: N = 6, NPV = PV = 6.49, I = 12, FV = 0, we obtain PMT = 1.58
Project B: N = 3, NPV = PV = 5.15, I = 12, FV = 0, we obtain PMT = 2.14

Both the replacement chain and EAA methods favor Project B over Project A.

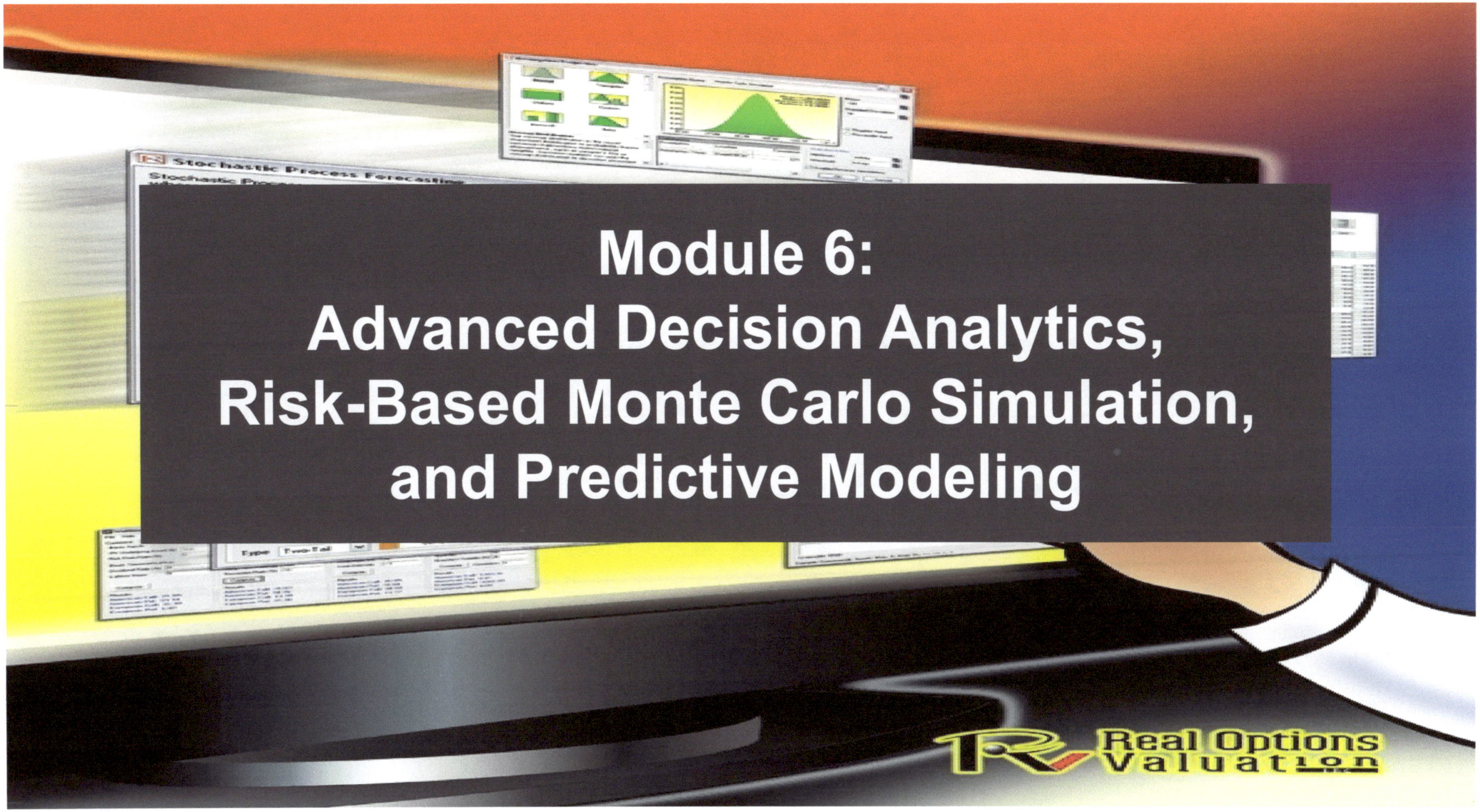

Module 6: Advanced Decision Analytics, Risk-Based Monte Carlo Simulation, and Predictive Modeling

Integrated Risk Management

1 QUALITATIVE MANAGEMENT SCREENING

RISK IDENTIFICATION

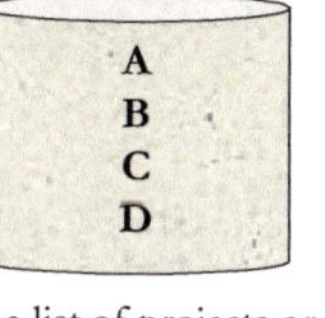

Start with a list of projects or strategies to be evaluated that have already been through qualitative screening…

2 FORECAST PREDICTION MODELING

RISK PREDICTION

Back-fitting, Forecasting and Scenario Analysis

ARIMA, GARCH, Fuzzy Logic, Markov Chains, Time Series Models…

…with the assistance of forecasting algorithms, future outcomes can be predicted...

3 BASE CASE STATIC MODELS

RISK MODELING

Traditional analysis stops here!

…create traditional static base case financial or economic models for each project…

4 DYNAMIC MONTE CARLO RISK SIMULATION

RISK ANALYSIS

Simulate thousands of scenario outcomes

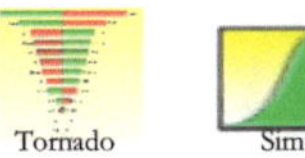

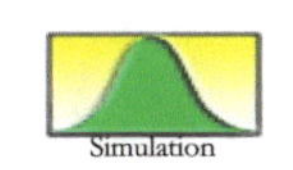

…Tornado analysis identifies critical success factors, then dynamic sensitivities and Monte Carlo risk simulations are run…

5 REAL OPTIONS PROBLEM FRAMING

RISK MITIGATION

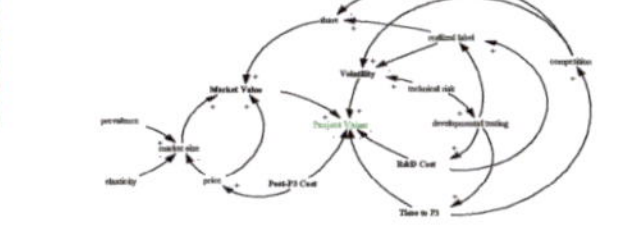

…strategic real options are framed to hedge and mitigate downside risks and take advantage of upside potential…

6 REAL OPTIONS VALUATION AND MODELING

RISK HEDGING

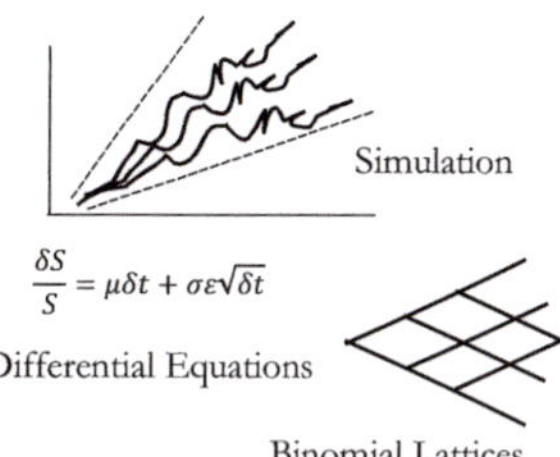

$$\frac{\delta S}{S} = \mu\delta t + \sigma\varepsilon\sqrt{\delta t}$$

…the real options are valued using binomial lattices and closed-form partial-differential models with simulation…

7 PORTFOLIO AND RESOURCE OPTIMIZATION

RISK DIVERSIFICATION

Efficient Frontier

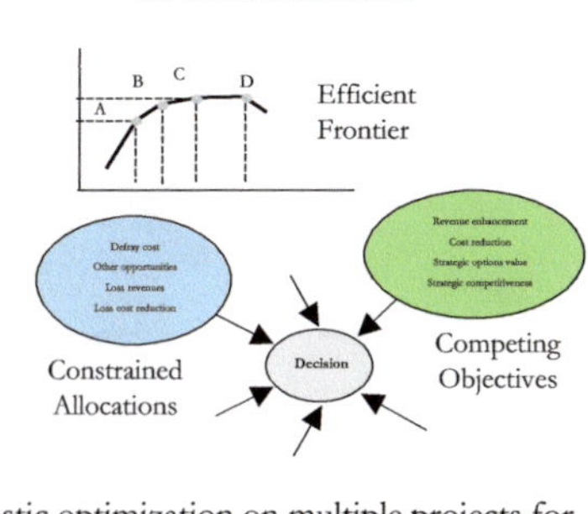

…stochastic optimization on multiple projects for efficient asset allocation subject to resource constraints…

8 REPORTS, PRESENTATION, AND UPDATES

RISK MANAGEMENT

…create reports, make decisions, and update analysis iteratively when uncertainty is resolved over time…

Monte Carlo Risk Simulation

COMMONLY USED DISTRIBUTIONS

TRIANGULAR
Looks like a triangle, continuous values, tails end at min and max with most likely as its peak. Can be skewed or symmetrical, with negative excess kurtosis (truncated tails). Examples: sales forecasts, subject matter estimates, management assumptions.

NORMAL
Continuous bell curve, a.k.a. Gaussian distribution, infinite tails on both ends, requires mean and standard deviation as inputs. Symmetrical with zero skew and zero excess kurtosis. Examples: stock returns, height, weight, IQ (most are truncated normal with limits).

UNIFORM
Flat continuous area with equal probability of occurrence at any point between the minimum and maximum. Symmetrical with zero skew and negative excess kurtosis (fixed end points). Examples: business forecasts and economic forecasts.

BINOMIAL
Discrete events with two mutually exclusive and independent outcomes with fixed probability of success at each successive trial. Symmetrical and approaches normal distribution with high number of trials. Example: tossing a coin multiple times.

POISSON
Discrete events occurring independently with the same average rate of repetition and measured in time or space (area).
Examples: sales forecasts, subject matter estimates, management assumptions. Approaches normal with high average rates.

CUSTOM
Empirically fitted discrete distribution when little data is available or when other theoretical distributions fail. Suitable for Delphi methods, can be multimodal or irregular. Examples: subject matter estimates, management assumptions, and qualitative estimates that are converted numerically.

LESS COMMONLY USED BUT IMPORTANT DISTRIBUTIONS

BERNOULLI
Single discrete trial version of Binomial (e.g., simulating success or failure of projects).

BETA 4
Highly flexible continuous distribution capable of taking on multiple shapes and scales.

DISCRETE UNIFORM
Range of discrete events with equal probability of occurrence (e.g., rolling a six-sided die).

EXPONENTIAL 2
High probably of low values, low probability of continuous high values (e.g., wait time).

GUMBEL
Tail-end extreme value simulations of continuous outcomes (e.g., market crashes).

LOGNORMAL
Variables with continuous non-negative and non-zero values (e.g., stock prices).

STUDENT'S T
Continuous-normal with fat tails or higher probability of extremes (e.g., risky returns).

WEIBULL 3
Continuous mean time before failure and reliability estimates (e.g., MTBF of an engine).

OTHER DISTRIBUTIONS: Arcsine, Beta, Beta 3, Cauchy, Chi-square, Cosine, Double Log, Erlang, Exponential, F, Fréchet, Gamma, Geometric, Gumbel Min, Gumbel Max, Hypergeometric, Laplace, Logistic, Lognormal 3, Negative Binomial, Parabolic, Generalized Pareto, Pareto, Pascal, Pearson V, Pearson VI, Pert, Power, Power 3, Rayleigh, Standard-Normal, Standard-T, Weibull

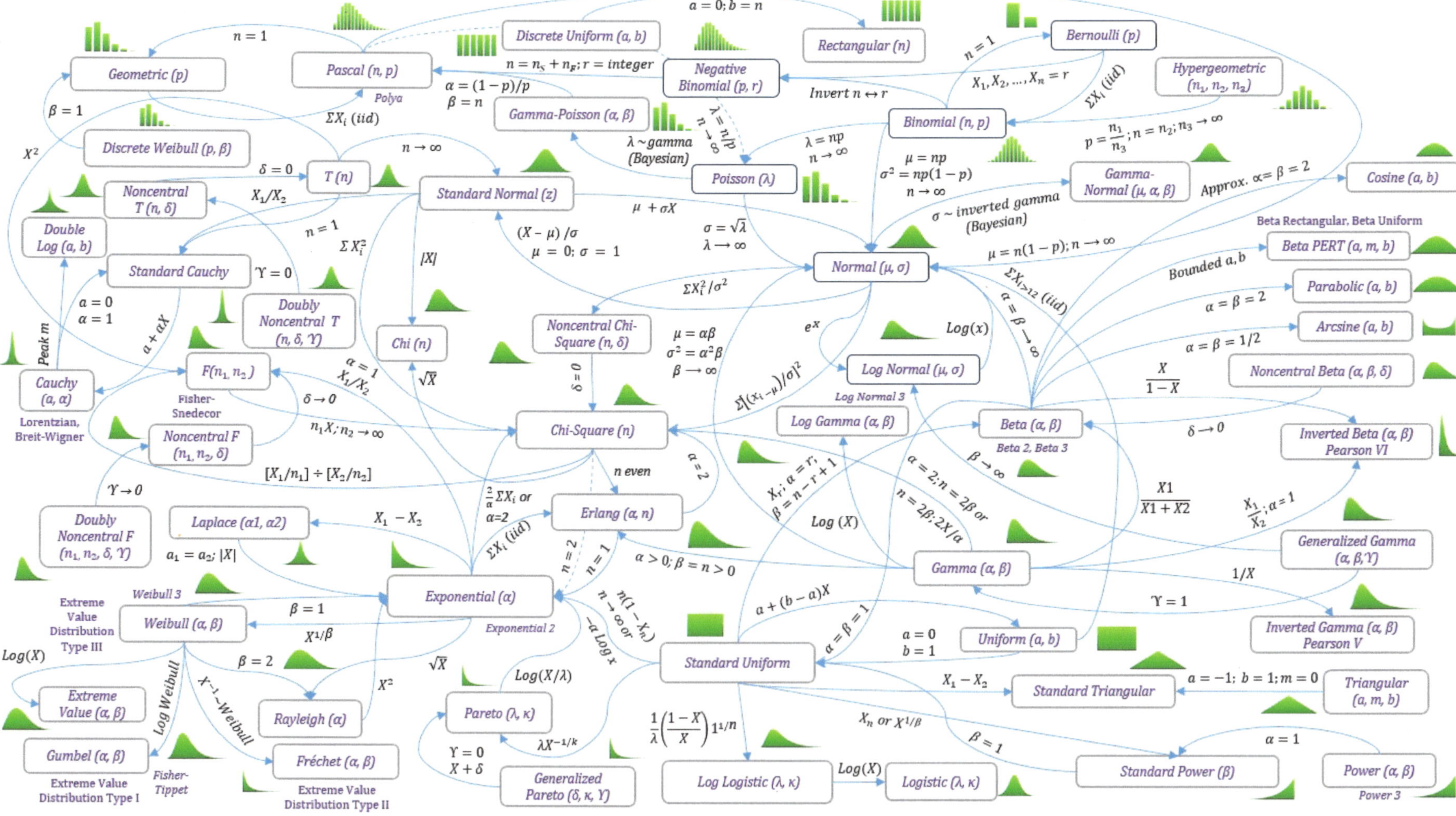
Geometric (p)
Pascal (n, p)
Polya
Discrete Uniform (a, b)
Negative Binomial (p, r)
Rectangular (n)
Bernoulli (p)
Hypergeometric (n_1, n_2, n_3)
Binomial (n, p)
Gamma-Poisson (α, β)
Discrete Weibull (p, β)
Poisson (λ)
Gamma-Normal (μ, α, β)
Cosine (a, b)
T (n)
Standard Normal (z)
Noncentral T (n, δ)
Double Log (a, b)
Standard Cauchy
Beta Rectangular, Beta Uniform
Beta PERT (a, m, b)
Normal (μ, σ)
Parabolic (a, b)
Doubly Noncentral T (n, δ, ϒ)
Chi (n)
Noncentral Chi-Square (n, δ)
Arcsine (a, b)
Log Normal (μ, σ)
Log Normal 3
Noncentral Beta (α, β, δ)
Cauchy (α, α)
Lorentzian, Breit-Wigner
F(n_1, n_2)
Fisher-Snedecor
Noncentral F (n_1, n_2, δ)
Chi-Square (n)
Log Gamma (α, β)
Beta (α, β)
Beta 2, Beta 3
Inverted Beta (α, β) Pearson VI
Doubly Noncentral F (n_1, n_2, δ, ϒ)
Laplace (α1, α2)
Erlang (α, n)
Generalized Gamma (α, β, ϒ)
Gamma (α, β)
Exponential (α)
Exponential 2
Weibull 3
Extreme Value Distribution Type III
Weibull (α, β)
Inverted Gamma (α, β) Pearson V
Uniform (a, b)
Standard Uniform
Extreme Value (α, β)
Rayleigh (α)
Pareto (λ, κ)
Standard Triangular
Triangular (a, m, b)
Gumbel (α, β)
Extreme Value Distribution Type I
Fisher-Tippet
Fréchet (α, β)
Extreme Value Distribution Type II
Generalized Pareto (δ, κ, ϒ)
Log Logistic (λ, κ)
Logistic (λ, κ)
Standard Power (β)
Power (α, β)
Power 3

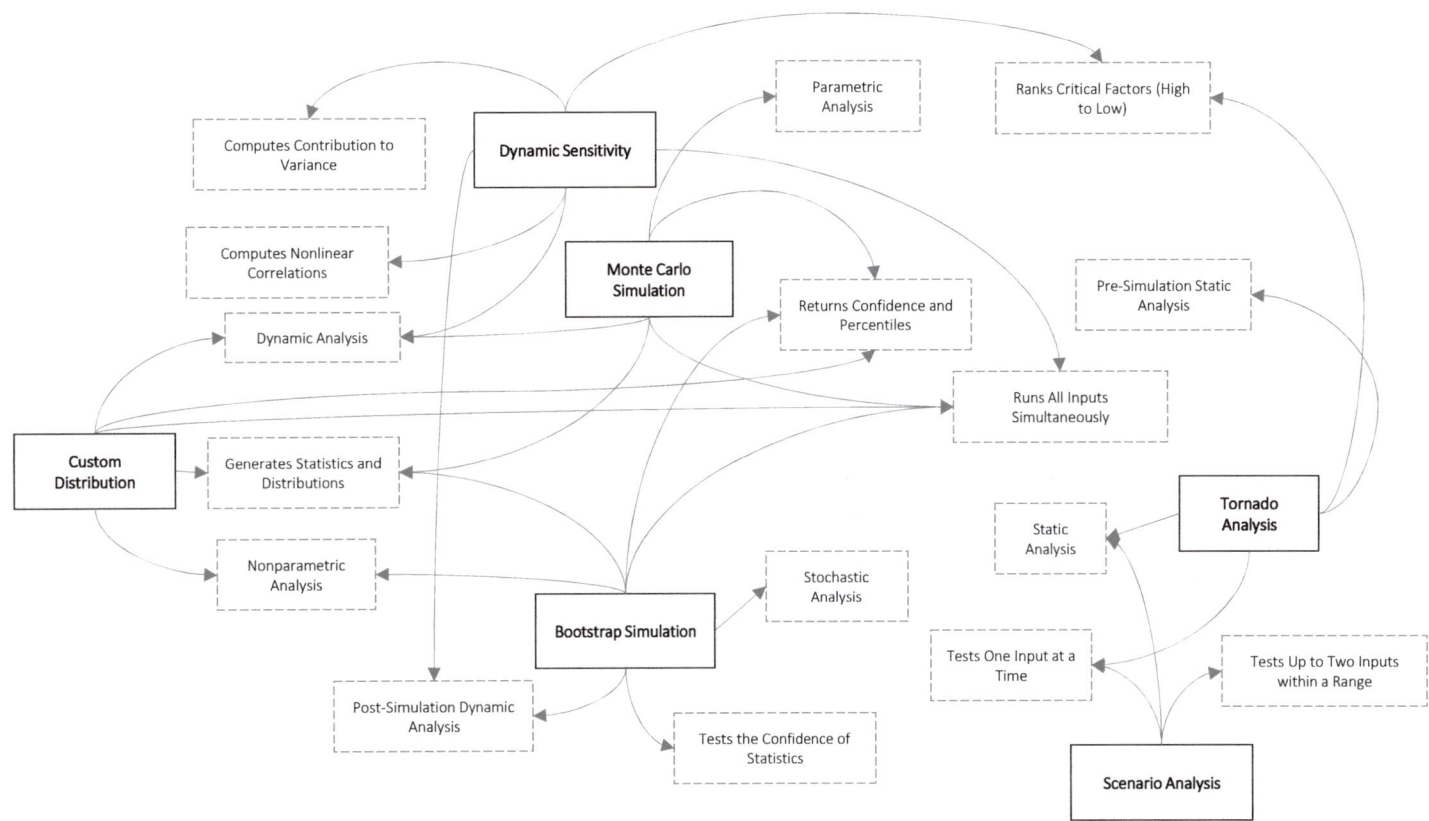

Dynamic Sensitivity
Computes Contribution to Variance
Computes Nonlinear Correlations
Dynamic Analysis
Parametric Analysis
Ranks Critical Factors (High to Low)
Monte Carlo Simulation
Returns Confidence and Percentiles
Pre-Simulation Static Analysis
Runs All Inputs Simultaneously
Custom Distribution
Generates Statistics and Distributions
Nonparametric Analysis
Bootstrap Simulation
Stochastic Analysis
Post-Simulation Dynamic Analysis
Tests the Confidence of Statistics
Tornado Analysis
Static Analysis
Tests One Input at a Time
Tests Up to Two Inputs within a Range
Scenario Analysis

ANALYTICAL TOOLS

DISTRIBUTIONAL FITTING
What distribution and distributional parameters do you use? This technique fits historical empirical data to probability distributions using Akaike Information Criterion (AIC), Anderson–Darling (AD), Chi-Square, Kolmogorov–Smirnov (KS), Kuiper's Statistic, and Schwarz/Bayes Information Criterion (SC/BIC).

DISTRIBUTIONAL ANALYSIS
Distributional Analysis (PDF, CDF, ICDF of 50 distributions). Distributional Charts and Tables (compares PDF & CDF shapes and characteristics). Overlay Charts (overlays empirically simulated output forecasts for a visual comparison of the moments).

CORRELATED SIMULATION
Runs correlated simulations by setting pairwise nonlinear correlations among multiple input assumptions. Normal, T, and Quasi-Normal Copulas are used in the convolution simulation. Correlations affect the second moment or risk of an output forecast distribution.

DATA DIAGNOSTICS
Executes multiple tests on existing dataset to determine its characteristics prior to running forecast models: autocorrelation, heteroskedasticity, lags, micronumerosity, multicollinearity, nonlinearity, and seasonality. Certain tests are relevant only for time-series, cross-sectional, or panel data types.

SCENARIO ANALYSIS
Runs multiple scenarios quickly and effortlessly by changing one or two input parameters a prespecified range for a heat map of the output variable.

TORNADO ANALYSIS
Static impacts of each variable on the outcome of the model by perturbing each input variable a preset amount, captures the final result, lists the pre-simulation perturbations ranked from most significant to least. Performed to identify critical factors to set as simulation assumptions to run.

DYNAMIC SENSITIVITY
Applies dynamic perturbations created after simulations and calculates contribution to variance.

HYPOTHESIS TESTS
Determines if two variables are statistically identical or different from one another.

BOOSTRAP SIMULATION
Estimates reliability or accuracy of forecast statistics, answers confidence/precision questions.

OVERLAY CHARTS
Overlays multiple assumptions and simulated forecast charts to compare their characteristics.

OTHER ANALYTICAL TOOLS: Check Model, Data Deseasonalization, Data Diagnostics, Data Open & Import, Distributional Fitting (Single, Multiple, Percentile), Principal Component Analysis, Seasonality Test, Segmentation Clustering, Statistical Tests, and Structural Break

WAYS OF SAVING A MODEL AND RESULTS: Generate live Excel charts after simulation runs, Tornado, and Sensitivity analyses, as well as:

COPY/PASTE CHARTS
Copy and paste the simulation and forecast charts into PowerPoint/Word.

CUSTOM DISTRIBUTION
Create and save nonparametric custom distributions based on actual empirical data.

DATA EXTRACTION
Simulated assumptions and forecasts' raw data can be extracted into Excel or text files.

EXCEL FILE
One file saves all assumptions, forecasts, decisions, constraints, objectives, and profiles.

REPORT GENERATION
Run simulation, forecasting, analytical methods, and optimization reports.

RISK SIMULATOR PROFILE
Create multiple profiles and scenarios of simulation and optimization variable settings.

RISK SIM FILE
Save live Risk Simulator charts for future retrieval without having to re-run simulations.

STATISTICS TABLE
Generate reports of statistical results as tables in Excel for archiving.

Akaike Information Criterion (AIC)
Rewards goodness-of-fit but also includes a penalty that is an increasing function of the number of estimated parameters (although AIC penalizes the number of parameters less strongly than other methods).

Anderson–Darling (AD)
When applied to testing if a normal distribution adequately describes a set of data, it is one of the most powerful statistical tools for detecting departures from normality and is powerful for testing normal tails. However, in non-normal distributions with skew and kurtosis, this test lacks power compared to other methods.

Chi-Square (CS)
Used to exclusively test discrete distributions where data are statistically categorized into various groups. The CS approach cannot be readily used to fit continuous distributions.

DISTRIBUTIONAL FITTING

Kolmogorov–Smirnov (KS)
A nonparametric test for the equality of continuous probability distributions that can be used to compare a sample with a reference probability distribution, making it useful for testing abnormally shaped distributions and non-normal distributions. Use the KS by default if the underlying distribution is unknown.

Kuiper's Statistic (K)
Related to the KS test making it as sensitive in the tails as at the median and also making it invariant under cyclic transformations of the independent variable, rendering it invaluable when testing for cyclic variations over time. In comparison, the AD test provides equal sensitivity at the tails as the median, but it does not provide the cyclic invariance.

Schwarz/Bayes Information Criterion (SC/BIC)
The SC/BIC test introduces a penalty term for the number of parameters in the model with a larger penalty than AIC.

HYPOTHESIS TEST
The null hypothesis being tested is such that the fitted distribution is the same distribution as the population from which the sample data to be fitted comes. Thus, if the computed p-value is lower than a critical alpha level (typically 0.10 or 0.05), then the distribution is the wrong distribution (reject the null hypothesis). Conversely, the higher the p-value, the better the distribution fits the data (do not reject the null hypothesis, which means the fitted distribution is the correct distribution, or null hypothesis of H_0: Error = 0, where error is defined as the difference between the empirical data and the theoretical distribution). Roughly, you can think of p-value as a percentage explained. The higher the p-value, the better the data fits the selected probability distribution.

Interpreting Simulation Statistics: First Moment

The First Moment – A Measure of Returns

- Central Tendency – Mean, Median, and Mode
- A measure of location or shift
- Tells of the *Expected Value* of an uncertain variable

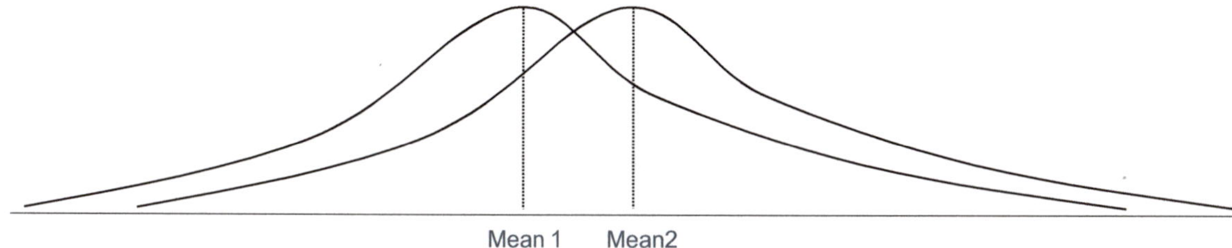

- May be deceiving... *Flaw of Averages* example
- Probability that the average will occur is very close to 0%

Interpreting Simulation Statistics: Second Moment

Second Moment – A Measure of Risk

- A measure of width, range, risk, and uncertainty
- Standard deviation, volatility, uncertainty, variance, width, percentiles, inter-quartile ranges, coefficient of variation...

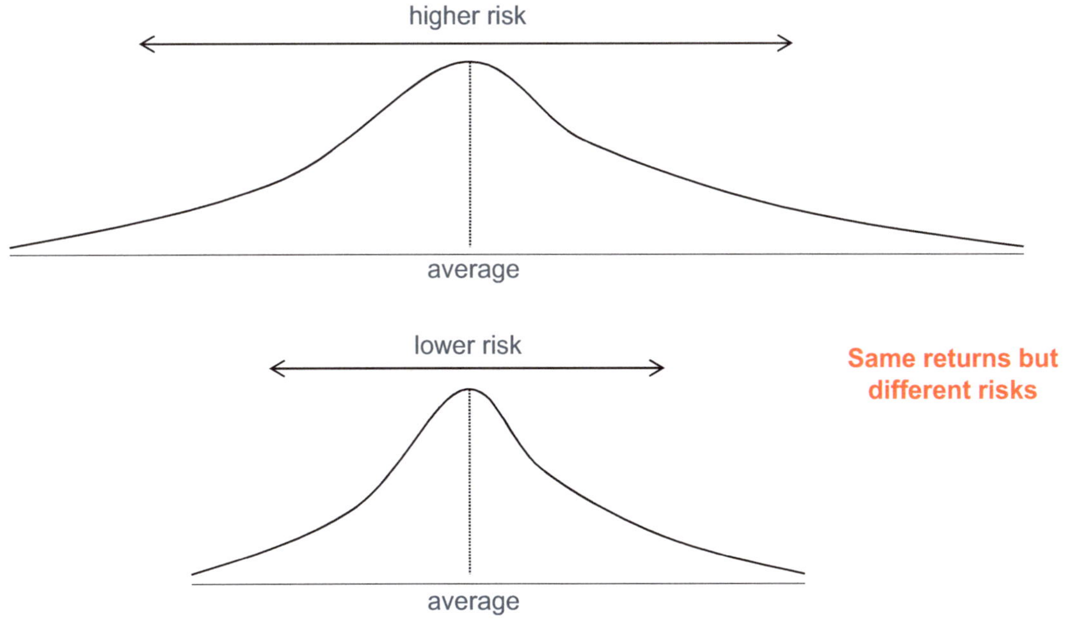

The Intuition of Risk

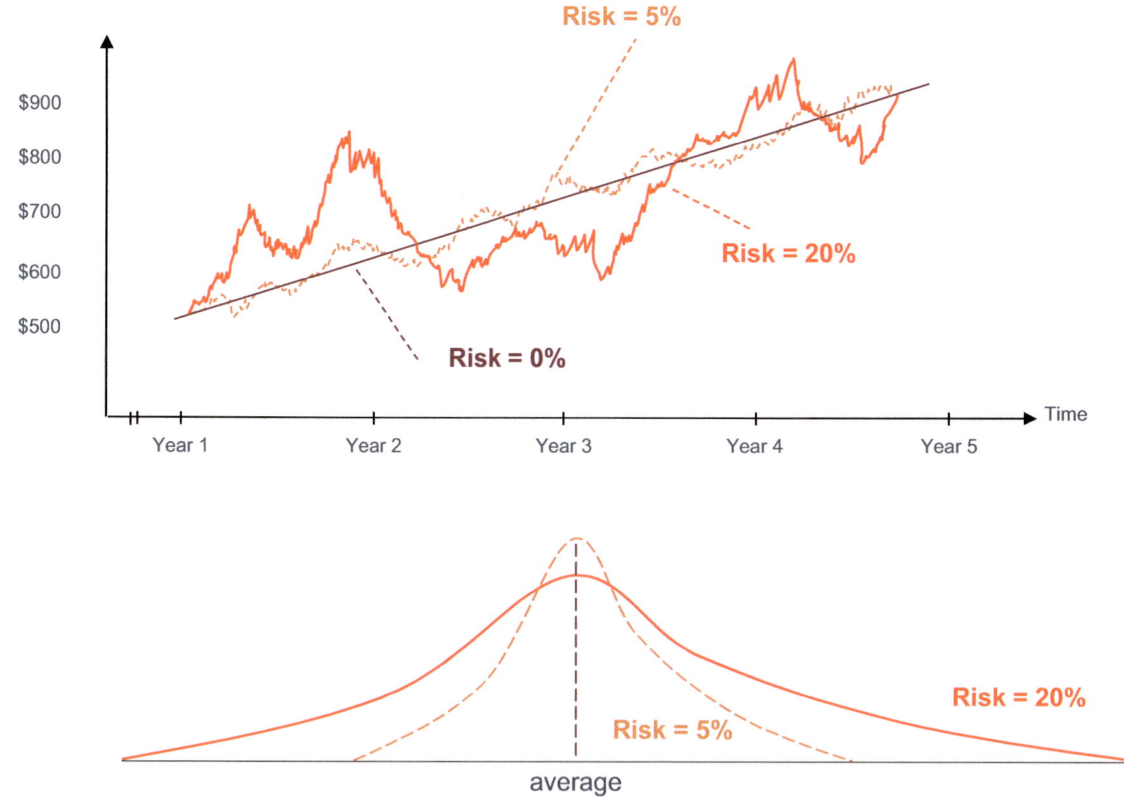

So, What Is Standard Deviation?

Simply defined as the average deviation of each point around the mean!

Sample Statistic for Standard Deviation:

$$s = \sqrt{\frac{\sum(x - \bar{x})^2}{n - 1}}$$

Population Parameter for Standard Deviation:

$$\sigma = \sqrt{\frac{\sum(x - \mu)^2}{N}}$$

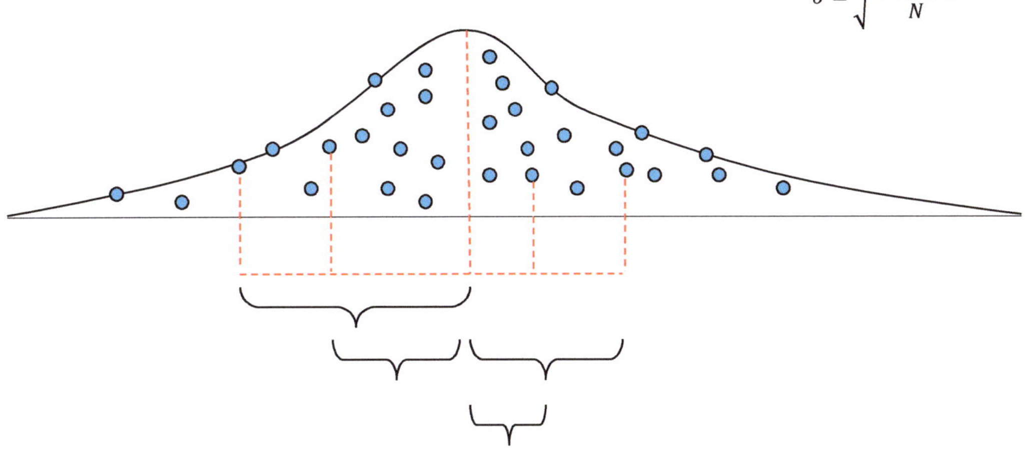

Take all the deviations or distances between the mean and average them up!

Interpreting Simulation Statistics: Third Moment

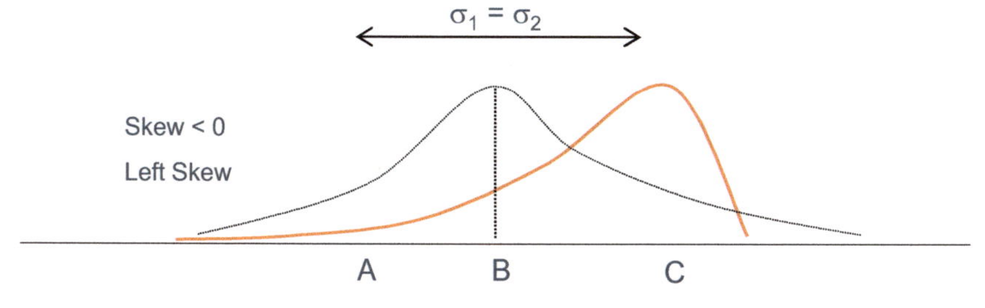

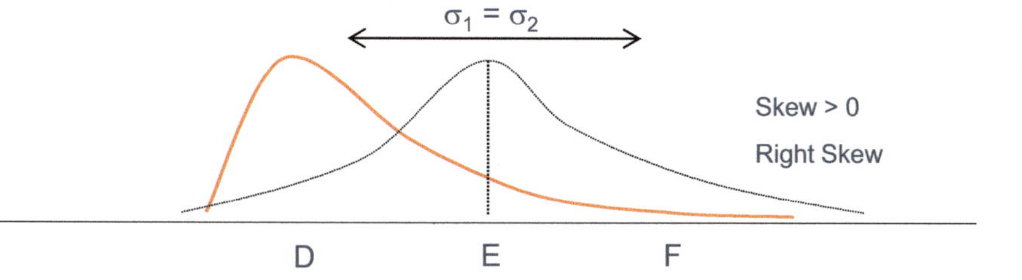

Sample Statistic and Population Paremeter for Skew Coefficient:

$$skew = \frac{n}{(n-1)(n-2)}\sum\left(\frac{x_i - \bar{x}}{s}\right)^3$$

Where are the Mean, Median, and Mode of the two distributions?

Real Options Valuation

Interpreting Simulation Statistics: Fourth Moment

Fourth Moment – A Measure of Kurtosis

Kurtosis measures the probabilities of extreme events… catastrophic losses (e.g., stock market crashes)

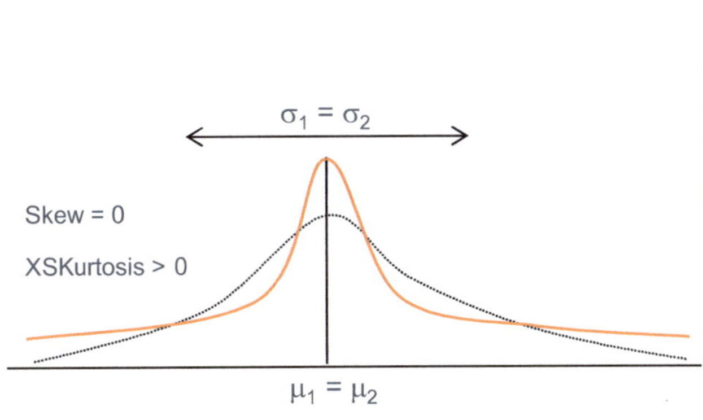

A higher kurtosis means a higher chance of extreme events occurring… the essence of risk management!

Note: Risk Simulator reports the Excess Kurtosis, which means we set 0 as the baseline.

Sample Statistic and Population Paremeter for Excess Kurtosis Coefficient:

$$\text{excess kurtosis} = \frac{n(n+1)}{(n-1)(n-2)(n-3)}\sum\left(\frac{x_i-\bar{x}}{s}\right)^4 - \frac{3(n-1)^2}{(n-2)(n-3)}$$

Discounted Cash Flow / ROI Model

Base Year	*2017*	*Sum PV Net Benefits*	***$4,762.09***	*Discount Type*	Discrete End-of-Year Discounting
Start Year	*2017*	*Sum PV Investments*	***$1,634.22***		
Market Risk-Adjusted Discount Rate	*15.00%*	*Net Present Value*	***$3,127.87***	*Model*	Include Terminal Valuation
Private-Risk Discount Rate	*5.00%*	*Internal Rate of Return*	***55.68%***		
Terminal Period Growth Rate	*2.00%*	*Return on Investment*	***191.40%***		
Effective Tax Rate	*40.00%*	*Profitability Index*	***2.91***		

	2017	2018	2019	2020	2021	2022	2023	2024	2025	2026
Product A Avg Price/Unit	$10.00	$10.50	$11.00	$11.50	$12.00	$12.50	$13.00	$13.50	$14.00	$14.50
Product B Avg Price/Unit	$12.25	$12.50	$12.75	$13.00	$13.25	$13.50	$13.75	$14.00	$14.25	$14.50
Product C Avg Price/Unit	$15.15	$15.30	$15.45	$15.60	$15.75	$15.90	$16.05	$16.20	$16.35	$16.50
Product A Sale Quantity ('000s)	50	50	50	50	50	50	50	50	50	50
Product B Sale Quantity ('000s)	35	35	35	35	35	35	35	35	35	35
Product C Sale Quantity ('000s)	20	20	20	20	20	20	20	20	20	20
Total Revenues	*$1,231.75*	*$1,268.50*	*$1,305.25*	*$1,342.00*	*$1,378.75*	*$1,415.50*	*$1,452.25*	*$1,489.00*	*$1,525.75*	*$1,562.50*
Direct Cost of Goods Sold	$184.76	$190.28	$195.79	$201.30	$206.81	$212.33	$217.84	$223.35	$228.86	$234.38
Gross Profit	*$1,046.99*	*$1,078.23*	*$1,109.46*	*$1,140.70*	*$1,171.94*	*$1,203.18*	*$1,234.41*	*$1,265.65*	*$1,296.89*	*$1,328.13*
Operating Expenses	$157.50	$157.50	$157.50	$157.50	$157.50	$157.50	$157.50	$157.50	$157.50	$157.50
Sales, General and Admin. Costs	$15.75	$15.75	$15.75	$15.75	$15.75	$15.75	$15.75	$15.75	$15.75	$15.75
Operating Income (EBITDA)	*$873.74*	*$904.98*	*$936.21*	*$967.45*	*$998.69*	*$1,029.93*	*$1,061.16*	*$1,092.40*	*$1,123.64*	*$1,154.88*
Depreciation	$10.00	$10.00	$10.00	$10.00	$10.00	$10.00	$10.00	$10.00	$10.00	$10.00
Amortization	$3.00	$3.00	$3.00							
EBIT	*$860.74*	*$891.98*	*$923.21*							
Interest Payments	$2.00	$2.00	$2.00							
EBT	*$858.74*	*$889.98*	*$921.21*							
Taxes	$343.50	$355.99	$368.49							
Net Income	*$515.24*	*$533.99*	*$552.73*							
Noncash: Depreciation Amortization	$13.00	$13.00	$13.00							
Noncash: Change in Net Working Capital	$0.00	$0.00	$0.00							
Noncash: Capital Expenditures	$0.00	$0.00	$0.00							
Free Cash Flow	*$528.24*	*$546.99*	*$565.73*							
Investment Outlay	*$500.00*		*$1,500.00*							
Net Free Cash Flow	*($1,105.97)*	*$546.99*	*$565.73*							
Financial Analysis										
Present Value of Free Cash Flow	*$528.24*	*$475.64*	*$427.77*							
Present Value of Investment Outlay	*$500.00*	*$0.00*	*$1,134.22*							
Discounted Payback Period	*3.47 Years*									

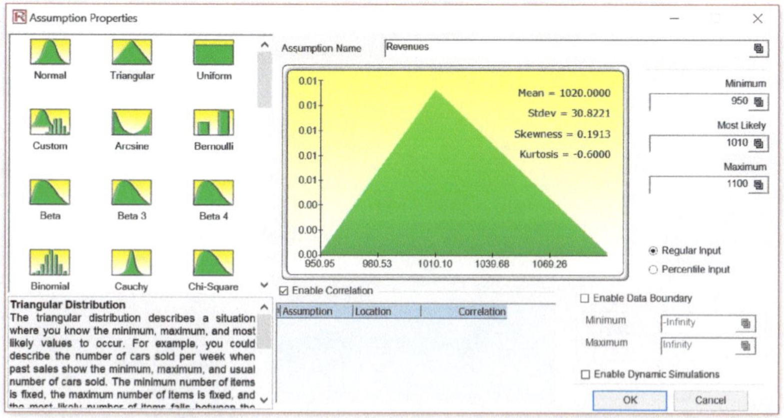

Tornado Analysis

- One of the powerful simulation tools is the tornado analysis—it captures the static impacts of each variable on the outcome of the model. That is, the tool automatically perturbs each variable in the model a preset amount, captures the fluctuation on the model's forecast or final result, and lists the resulting perturbations ranked from the most significant to the least. The question we try to answer here is, what are the critical success drivers that affect the model's output the most?
- The target cell's precedents in the model are used in creating the tornado chart. Precedents are all the input and intermediate variables that affect the outcome of the model. For instance, if the model consists of $A = B + C$, and where $C = D + E$, then B, D, and E are the precedents for A (C is not a precedent as it is only an intermediate calculated value). If the precedent variables are simple inputs, then the testing range will be a simple perturbation based on the range chosen (e.g., the default is ±10%). Each precedent variable can be perturbed at different percentages if required. A wider range is important as it is better able to test extreme values rather than smaller perturbations around the expected values. In certain circumstances, extreme values may have a larger, smaller, or unbalanced impact (e.g., nonlinearities may occur where increasing or decreasing economies of scale and scope creep in for larger or smaller values of a variable) and only a wider range will capture this nonlinear impact.
- It is important to note that Tornado and Spider Analysis is performed BEFORE running a simulation, in order to identify the critical factors to simulate, as compared to Sensitivity Analysis that is run after a simulation has been completed.
- Tornado and Spider charts are static analyses whereas a Sensitivity Analysis is a dynamic analysis.

- Tornado chart lists the precedent variable that has the most impact to the least.
- A red bar on the right indicates a negative correlation while a green bar on the right indicates a positive correlation between each input precedent and the result.
- A Tornado analysis report is also generated by the software, complete with an analysis table of the perturbations and results.

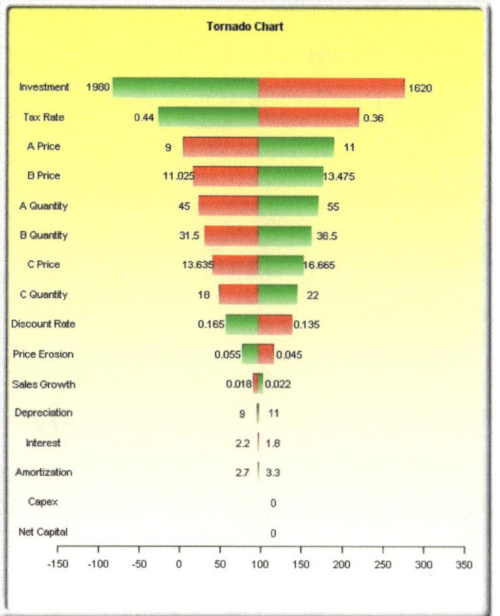

Tornado and Spider Charts

Statistical Summary

One of the powerful simulation tools is the tornado chart—it captures the static impacts of each variable on the outcome of the model. That is, the tool automatically perturbs each precedent variable in the model a user-specified preset amount, captures the fluctuation on the model's forecast or final result, and lists the resulting perturbations ranked from the most significant to the least. Precedents are all the input and intermediate variables that affect the outcome of the model. For instance, if the model consists of A = B + C, where C = D + E, then B, D, and E are the precedents for A (C is not a precedent as it is only an intermediate calculated value). The range and number of values perturbed is user-specified and can be set to test extreme values rather than smaller perturbations around the expected values. In certain circumstances, extreme values may have a larger, smaller, or unbalanced impact (e.g., nonlinearities may occur where increasing or decreasing economies of scale and scope creep occurs for larger or smaller values of a variable) and only a wider range will capture this nonlinear impact.

A tornado chart lists all the inputs that drive the model, starting from the input variable that has the most effect on the results. The chart is obtained by perturbing each precedent input at some consistent range (e.g., ±10% from the base case) one at a time, and comparing their results to the base case. A spider chart looks like a spider with a central body and its many legs protruding. The positively sloped lines indicate a positive relationship, while a negatively sloped line indicates a negative relationship. Further, spider charts can be used to visualize linear and nonlinear relationships. The tornado and spider charts help identify the critical success factors of an output cell in order to identify the inputs to simulate. The identified critical variables that are uncertain are the ones that should be simulated. Do not waste time simulating variables that are neither uncertain nor have little impact on the results.

Result

	Base Value: 96.6261638553219			Input Changes		
Precedent Cell	Output Downside	Output Upside	Effective Range	Input Downside	Input Upside	Base Case Value
Investment	$276.63	($83.37)	360.00	$1,620.00	$1,980.00	$1,800.00
Tax Rate	$219.73	($26.47)	246.20	36.00%	44.00%	40.00%
A Price	$3.43	$189.83	186.40	$9.00	$11.00	$10.00
B Price	$16.71	$176.55	159.84	$11.03	$13.48	$12.25
A Quantity	$23.18	$170.07	146.90	45.00	55.00	50.00
B Quantity	$30.53	$162.72	132.19	31.50	38.50	35.00
C Price	$40.15	$153.11	112.96	$13.64	$16.67	$15.15
C Quantity	$48.05	$145.20	97.16	18.00	22.00	20.00
Discount Rate	$138.24	$57.03	81.21	13.50%	16.50%	15.00%
Price Erosion	$116.80	$76.64	40.16	4.50%	5.50%	5.00%
Sales Growth	$90.59	$102.69	12.10	1.80%	2.20%	2.00%
Depreciation	$95.08	$98.17	3.08	$9.00	$11.00	$10.00
Interest	$97.09	$96.16	0.93	$1.80	$2.20	$2.00
Amortization	$96.16	$97.09	0.93	$2.70	$3.30	$3.00
Capex	$96.63	$96.63	0.00	$0.00	$0.00	$0.00
Net Capital	$96.63	$96.63	0.00	$0.00	$0.00	$0.00

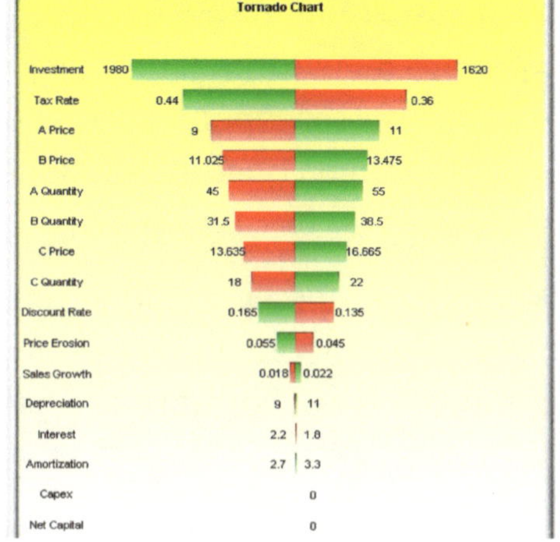

Simulation Forecast Results

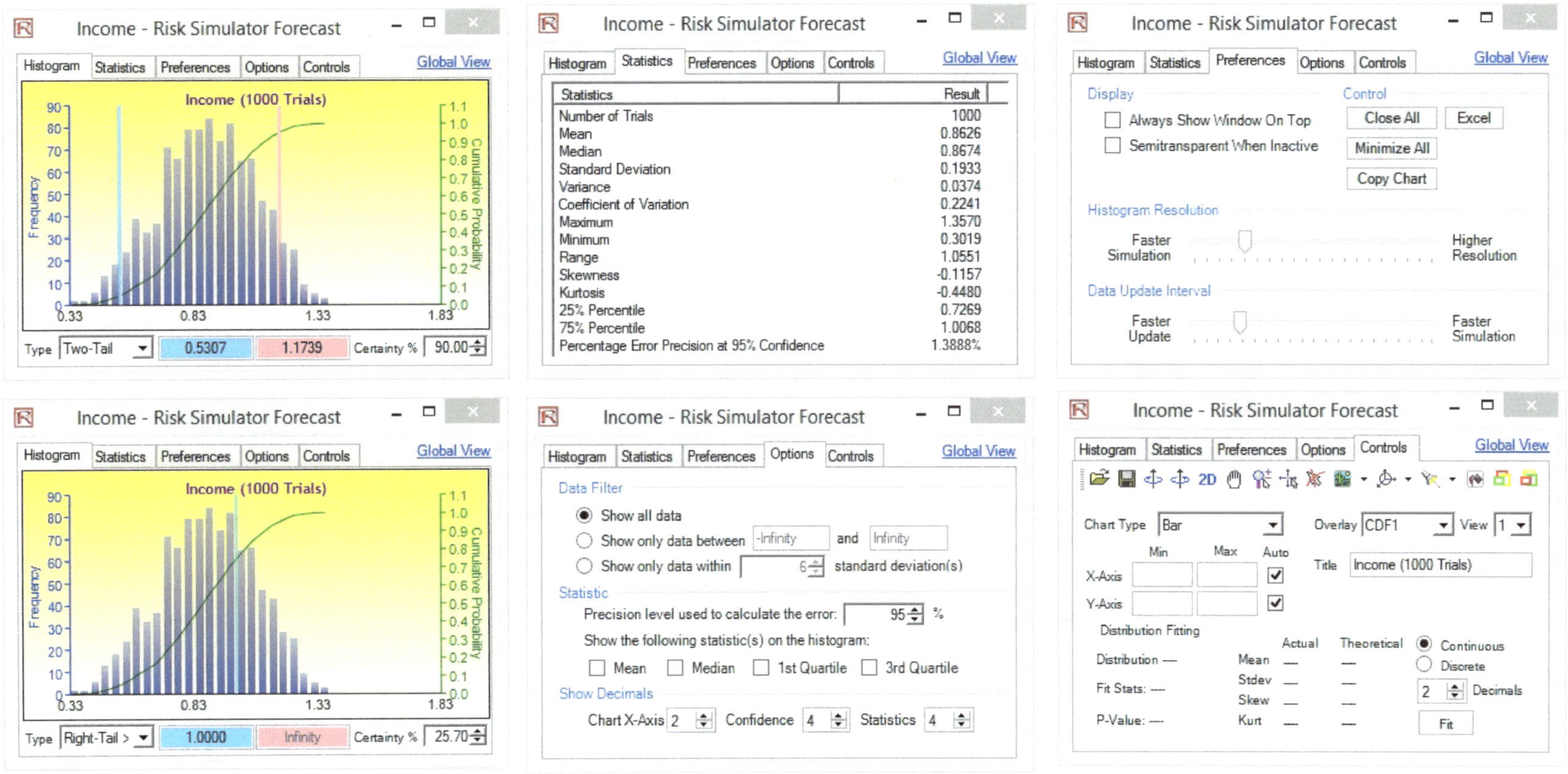

Income - Risk Simulator Forecast

Histogram | Statistics | Preferences | Options | Controls | Global View

Income (1000 Trials)

Frequency 0 10 20 30 40 50 60 70 80 90

0.33 0.83 1.33 1.83

Cumulative Probability 0.0 0.1 0.2 0.3 0.4 0.5 0.6 0.7 0.8 0.9 1.0 1.1

Type Two-Tail 0.5307 1.1739 Certainty % 90.00

Income - Risk Simulator Forecast

Histogram | Statistics | Preferences | Options | Controls | Global View

Statistics	Result
Number of Trials	1000
Mean	0.8626
Median	0.8674
Standard Deviation	0.1933
Variance	0.0374
Coefficient of Variation	0.2241
Maximum	1.3570
Minimum	0.3019
Range	1.0551
Skewness	-0.1157
Kurtosis	-0.4480
25% Percentile	0.7269
75% Percentile	1.0068
Percentage Error Precision at 95% Confidence	1.3888%

Income - Risk Simulator Forecast

Histogram | Statistics | Preferences | Options | Controls | Global View

Display

Always Show Window On Top

Semitransparent When Inactive

Control

Close All | Excel

Minimize All

Copy Chart

Histogram Resolution

Faster Simulation — Higher Resolution

Data Update Interval

Faster Update — Faster Simulation

Income - Risk Simulator Forecast

Histogram | Statistics | Preferences | Options | Controls | Global View

Income (1000 Trials)

Frequency 0 10 20 30 40 50 60 70 80 90

0.33 0.83 1.33 1.83

Cumulative Probability 0.0 0.1 0.2 0.3 0.4 0.5 0.6 0.7 0.8 0.9 1.0 1.1

Type Right-Tail > 1.0000 Infinity Certainty % 25.70

Income - Risk Simulator Forecast

Histogram | Statistics | Preferences | Options | Controls | Global View

Data Filter

Show all data

Show only data between -Infinity and Infinity

Show only data within 6 standard deviation(s)

Statistic

Precision level used to calculate the error: 95 %

Show the following statistic(s) on the histogram:

Mean | Median | 1st Quartile | 3rd Quartile

Show Decimals

Chart X-Axis 2 | Confidence 4 | Statistics 4

Income - Risk Simulator Forecast

Histogram | Statistics | Preferences | Options | Controls | Global View

Chart Type Bar | Overlay CDF1 | View 1

Min | Max | Auto

X-Axis

Y-Axis

Title Income (1000 Trials)

Distribution Fitting

Distribution: —

Fit Stats: —

P-Value: —

Actual | Theoretical

Mean — —

Stdev — —

Skew — —

Kurt — —

Continuous

Discrete

2 Decimals

Fit

The Forecasting Methodologies

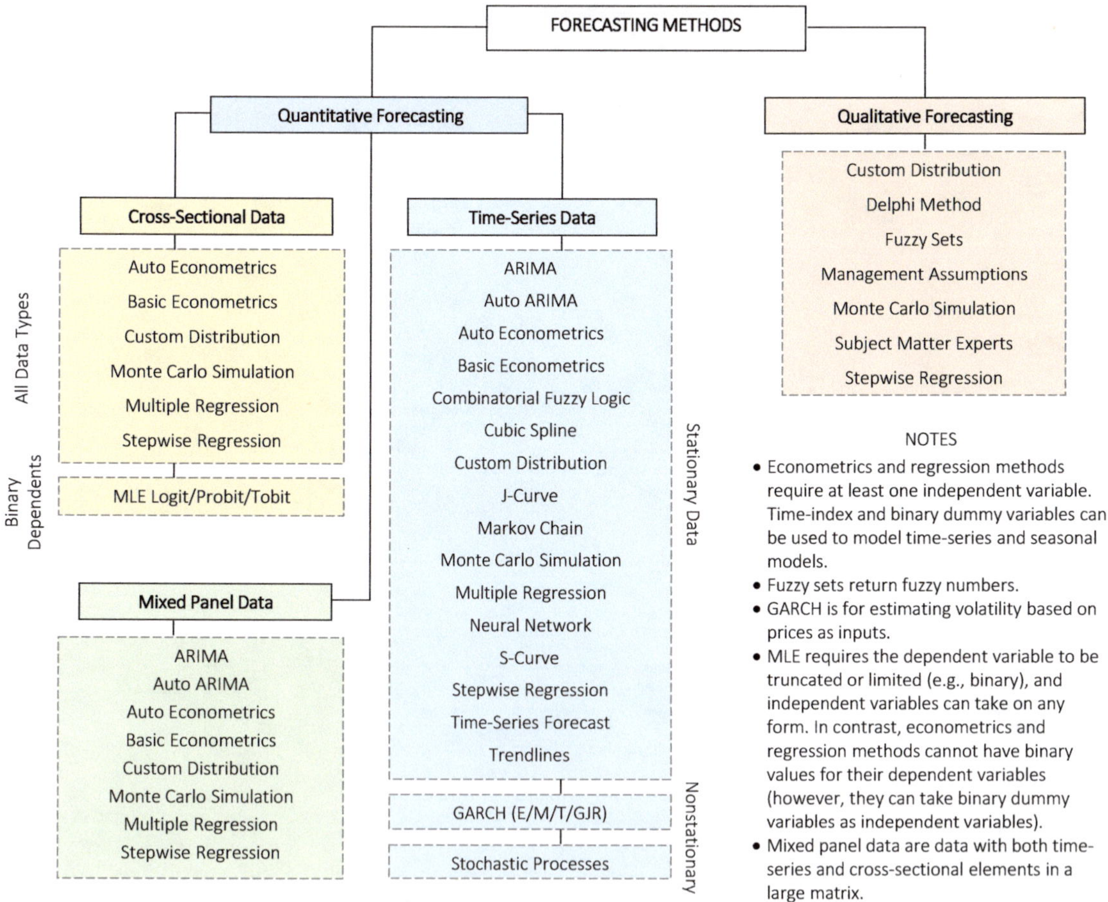

NOTES

- Econometrics and regression methods require at least one independent variable. Time-index and binary dummy variables can be used to model time-series and seasonal models.
- Fuzzy sets return fuzzy numbers.
- GARCH is for estimating volatility based on prices as inputs.
- MLE requires the dependent variable to be truncated or limited (e.g., binary), and independent variables can take on any form. In contrast, econometrics and regression methods cannot have binary values for their dependent variables (however, they can take binary dummy variables as independent variables).
- Mixed panel data are data with both time-series and cross-sectional elements in a large matrix.

Time-Series Forecasting

The eight most common time-series models, segregated by seasonality and trend, are listed below. For instance, if the data variable has no trend or seasonality, then a single moving-average model or a single exponential-smoothing model would suffice. However, if seasonality exists but no discernable trend is present, either a seasonal additive or seasonal multiplicative model would be better, and so forth.

	NO SEASONALITY	WITH SEASONALITY
WITHOUT TREND	Single Moving Average	Seasonal Additive
	Single Exponential Smoothing	Seasonal Multiplicative
WITH TREND	Double Moving Average	Holt–Winters Additive
	Double Exponential Smoothing	Holt–Winters Multiplicative

Year	Quarter	Period	Sales
2010	1	1	$684.20
2010	2	2	$584.10
2010	3	3	$765.40
2010	4	4	$892.30
2011	1	5	$885.40
2011	2	6	$677.00
2011	3	7	$1,006.60
2011	4	8	$1,122.10
2012	1	9	$1,163.40
2012	2	10	$993.20
2012	3	11	$1,312.50
2012	4	12	$1,545.30
2013	1	13	$1,596.20
2013	2	14	$1,260.40
2013	3	15	$1,735.20
2013	4	16	$2,029.70
2014	1	17	$2,107.80
2014	2	18	$1,650.30
2014	3	19	$2,304.40
2014	4	20	$2,639.40

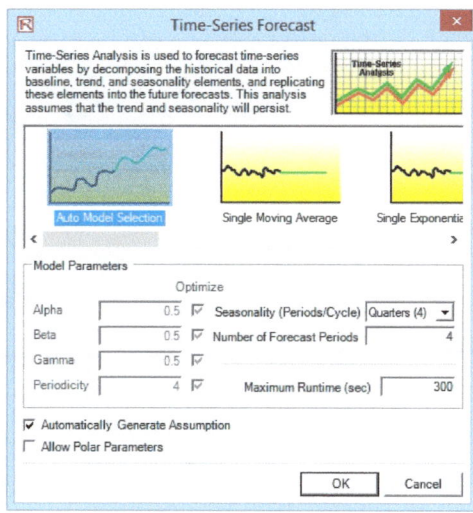

Time-Series Forecast

Time-Series Analysis is used to forecast time-series variables by decomposing the historical data into baseline, trend, and seasonality elements, and replicating these elements into the future forecasts. This analysis assumes that the trend and seasonality will persist.

Auto Model Selection | Single Moving Average | Single Exponentia

Model Parameters

Optimize

Alpha 0.5 ☑ Seasonality (Periods/Cycle) Quarters (4)

Beta 0.5 ☑ Number of Forecast Periods 4

Gamma 0.5 ☑

Periodicity 4 ☑ Maximum Runtime (sec) 300

☑ Automatically Generate Assumption

☐ Allow Polar Parameters

OK Cancel

Interpreting Time-Series Analysis Report

The figure here illustrates the sample results generated by using the *Forecasting* tool. The model selected by the software as the best-fitting model was a Holt–Winters' Multiplicative model. Notice that in the report, the model-fitting and forecast chart indicate that the trend and seasonality are picked up nicely by the Holt–Winters' Multiplicative model. The time-series analysis report provides the relevant optimized alpha, beta, and gamma parameters; the error measurements; fitted data; forecast values; and fitted-forecast graph. The parameters are simply for reference. Alpha captures the memory effect of the base level changes over time, beta is the trend parameter that measures the strength of the trend, while gamma measures the seasonality strength of the historical data. The analysis decomposes the historical data into these three elements and then recomposes them to forecast the future. The fitted data illustrates the historical data as well as the fitted data using the recomposed model and shows how close the forecasts are in the past (a technique called *backcasting*). The forecast values are either single-point estimates or assumptions (if the Automatically Generate Assumptions option is chosen and if a simulation profile exists). The graph illustrates these historical, fitted, and forecast values. The chart is a powerful communication and visual tool to see how good the forecast model is.

This time-series analysis module contains the eight time-series models. You can choose the specific model to run based on the trend and seasonality criteria or choose the Auto Model Selection, which will automatically iterate through all eight methods, optimize the parameters, and find the best-fitting model for your data. Alternatively, if you choose one of the eight models, you can also deselect the *optimize* checkboxes and enter your own alpha, beta, and gamma parameters. In addition, you would need to enter the relevant seasonality periods if you choose the automatic model selection or any of the seasonal models.

Holt-Winter's Multiplicative

Summary Statistics

Alpha, Beta, Gamma	RMSE	Alpha, Beta, Gamma	RMSE
0.00, 0.00, 0.00	914.824	0.00, 0.00, 0.00	914.824
0.10, 0.10, 0.10	415.322	0.10, 0.10, 0.10	415.322
0.20, 0.20, 0.20	187.202	0.20, 0.20, 0.20	187.202
0.30, 0.30, 0.30	118.795	0.30, 0.30, 0.30	118.795
0.40, 0.40, 0.40	101.794	0.40, 0.40, 0.40	101.794
0.50, 0.50, 0.50	102.143		

The analysis was run with alpha = 0.2429, beta = 1.0000, gamma = 0.7797, and seasonality = 4

Time-Series Analysis Summary

When both seasonality and trend exist, more advanced models are required to decompose the data into their base elements: a base-case level (L) weighted by the alpha parameter; a trend component (b) weighted by the beta parameter; and a seasonality component (S) weighted by the gamma parameter. Several methods exist but the two most common are the Holt-Winters' additive seasonality and Holt-Winters' multiplicative seasonality methods. In the Holt-Winter's additive model, the base case level, seasonality, and trend are added together to obtain the forecast fit.
The best-fitting test for the moving average forecast uses the root mean squared errors (RMSE). The RMSE calculates the square root of the average squared deviations of the fitted values versus the actual data points.

Mean Squared Error (MSE) is an absolute error measure that squares the errors (the difference between the actual historical data and the forecast-fitted data predicted by the model) to keep the positive and negative errors from canceling each other out. This measure also tends to exaggerate large errors by weighting the large errors more heavily than smaller errors by squaring them, which can help when comparing different time-series models. Root Mean Square Error (RMSE) is the square root of MSE and is the most popular error measure, also known as the quadratic loss function. RMSE can be defined as the average of the absolute values of the forecast errors and is highly appropriate when the cost of the forecast errors is proportional to the absolute size of the forecast error. The RMSE is used as the selection criteria for the best-fitting time-series model.

Mean Absolute Percentage Error (MAPE) is a relative error statistic measured as an average percent error of the historical data points and is most appropriate when the cost of the forecast error is more closely related to the percentage error than the numerical size of the error. Finally, an associated measure is the Theil's U statistic, which measures the naivety of the model's forecast. That is, if the Theil's U statistic is less than 1.0, then the forecast method used provides an estimate that is statistically better than guessing.

Period	Actual	Forecast Fit
1	684.20	
2	584.10	
3	765.40	
4	892.30	
5	885.40	684.20
6	677.00	667.55
7	1006.60	935.45
8	1122.10	1198.09
9	1163.40	1112.48
10	993.20	887.95
11	1312.50	1348.38
12	1545.30	1546.53
13	1596.20	1572.44
14	1260.40	1299.20
15	1735.20	1704.77
16	2029.70	1976.23
17	2107.80	2026.01
18	1650.30	1637.28
19	2304.40	2245.93
20	2639.40	2643.09
Forecast21		2713.69
Forecast22		2114.79
Forecast23		2900.42
Forecast24		3293.81
Forecast25		3346.55
Forecast26		2580.81
Forecast27		3506.19
Forecast28		3947.61
Forecast29		3979.41
Forecast30		3046.83

Error Measurements	
RMSE	71.8132
MSE	5157.1348
MAD	53.4071
MAPE	4.50%
Theil's U	0.3054

Actual vs. Forecast
Actual
Forecast

Linear, Nonlinear, Bivariate, and Multivariate Regression

Multiple Regression Analysis Data Set

Aggravated Assault	Bachelor's Degree	Police Expenditure Per Capita	Population in Millions	Population Density (Persons/Sq Mile)	Unemployment Rate
521	18308	185	4.041	79.6	7.2
367	1148	600	0.55	1	8.5
443	18068	372	3.665	32.3	5.7
365	7729	142	2.351	45.1	7.3
614	100484				
385	16728				
286	14630				
397	4008				
764	38927				
427	22322				
153	3711				
231	3136				
524	50508				
328	28886				
240	16996				
286	13035				
285	12973				
569	16309				
96	5227				
498	19235				
481	44487				
468	44213				
177	23619				
198	9106				
458	24917				
108	3872				
246	8945				
291	2373				
68	7128				
311	23624	349	7.73	1042	6.6

Multiple Regression Analysis

Multiple Regression Analysis can be used to run linear regressions with multiple independent variables. These variables can be applied through a series of lags or nonlinear transformations, or regressed in a stepwise fashion starting with the most correlated variable.

Multivariate Regression Y = F(X)

Dependent Variable: Aggravated Assault

Aggravated Assault	Bachelor's Degree	Police Expenditure Per Capita	Popu
521	18308	185	4.041
367	1148	600	0.55
443	18068	372	3.665
365	7729	142	2.351
614	100484	432	29.76
385	16728	290	3.294
286	14630	346	3.287

Options

Lag Regressors 1 Period(s) · Nonlinear Regression

Stepwise Correlation Method · Show All Steps · OK

p-Value: 0.1 · Cancel

Bootstrap Simulation

Linear, Nonlinear, Bivariate, and Multivariate Regression

Regression Analysis Report

Regression Statistics

R-Squared (Coefficient of Determination)	0.3272
Adjusted R-Squared	0.2508
Multiple R (Multiple Correlation Coefficient)	0.5720
Standard Error of the Estimates (SEy)	149.6720
Number of Observations	50

The R-Squared or Coefficient of Determination indicates that 0.33 of the variation in the dependent variable can be explained and accounted for by the independent variables in this regression analysis. However, in a multiple regression, the Adjusted R-Squared takes into account the existence of additional independent variables or regressors and adjusts this R-Squared value to a more accurate view of the regression's explanatory power. Hence, only 0.25 of the variation in the dependent variable can be explained by the regressors.

The Multiple Correlation Coefficient (Multiple R) measures the correlation between the actual dependent variable (Y) and the estimated or fitted (Y) based on the regression equation. This is also the square root of the Coefficient of Determination (R-Squared).

The Standard Error of the Estimates (SEy) describes the dispersion of data points above and below the regression line or plane. This value is used as part of the calculation to obtain the confidence interval of the estimates later.

Regression Results

	Intercept	Bachelor's Degree	Police Expenditure Per Capita	Population in Millions	Population Density (Persons/Sq Mile)	Unemployment Rate
Coefficients	57.9555	-0.0035	0.4644	25.2377	-0.0086	16.5579
Standard Error	108.7901	0.0035	0.2535	14.1172	0.1016	14.7996
t-Statistic	0.5327	-1.0066	1.8316	1.7877	-0.0843	1.1188
p-Value	0.5969	0.3197	0.0738	0.0807	0.9332	0.2693
Lower 5%	-161.2966	-0.0106	-0.0466	-3.2137	-0.2132	-13.2687
Upper 95%	277.2076	0.0036	0.9753	53.6891	0.1961	46.3845

Degrees of Freedom		Hypothesis Test	
Degrees of Freedom for Regression	5	Critical t-Statistic (99% confidence with df of 44)	2.6923
Degrees of Freedom for Residual	44	Critical t-Statistic (95% confidence with df of 44)	2.0154
Total Degrees of Freedom	49	Critical t-Statistic (90% confidence with df of 44)	1.6802

The Coefficients provide the estimated regression intercept and slopes. For instance, the coefficients are estimates of the true; population b values in the following regression equation $Y = b0 + b1X1 + b2X2 + ... + bnXn$. The Standard Error measures how accurate the predicted Coefficients are, and the t-Statistics are the ratios of each predicted Coefficient to its Standard Error.

The t-Statistic is used in hypothesis testing, where we set the null hypothesis (Ho) such that the real mean of the Coefficient = 0, and the alternate hypothesis (Ha) such that the real mean of the Coefficient is not equal to 0. A t-test is is performed and the calculated t-Statistic is compared to the critical values at the relevant Degrees of Freedom for Residual. The t-test is very important as it calculates if each of the coefficients is statistically significant in the presence of the other regressors. This means that the t-test statistically verifies whether a regressor or independent variable should remain in the regression or it should be dropped.

The Coefficient is statistically significant if its calculated t-Statistic exceeds the Critical t-Statistic at the relevant degrees of freedom (df). The three main confidence levels used to test for significance are 90%, 95% and 99%. If a Coefficient's t-Statistic exceeds the Critical level, it is considered statistically significant. Alternatively, the p-Value calculates each t-Statistic's probability of occurrence, which means that the smaller the p-Value, the more significant the Coefficient. The usual significant levels for the p-Value are 0.01, 0.05, and 0.10, corresponding to the 99%, 95%, and 90% confidence levels.

The Coefficients with their p-Values highlighted in blue indicate that they are statistically significant at the 90% confidence or 0.10 alpha level, while those highlighted in red indicate that they are not statistically significant at any other alpha levels.

Analysis of Variance

	Sums of Squares	Mean of Squares	F-Statistic	p-Value	Hypothesis Test	
Regression	479388.49	95877.70	4.28	0.0029	Critical F-statistic (99% confidence with df of 5 and 44)	3.4651
Residual	985675.19	22401.71			Critical F-statistic (95% confidence with df of 5 and 44)	2.4270
Total	1465063.68				Critical F-statistic (90% confidence with df of 5 and 44)	1.9828

The Analysis of Variance (ANOVA) table provides an F-test of the regression model's overall statistical significance. Instead of looking at individual regressors as in the t-test, the F-test looks at all the estimated Coefficients' statistical properties. The F-Statistic is calculated as the ratio of the Regression's Mean of Squares to the Residual's Mean of Squares. The numerator measures how much of the regression is explained, while the denominator measures how much is unexplained. Hence, the larger the F-Statistic, the more significant the model. The corresponding p-Value is calculated to test the null hypothesis (Ho) where all the Coefficients are simultaneously equal to zero, versus the alternate hypothesis (Ha) that they are all simultaneously different from zero, indicating a significant overall regression model. If the p-Value is smaller than the 0.01, 0.05, or 0.10 alpha significance, then the regression is significant. The same approach can be applied to the F-Statistic by comparing the calculated F-Statistic with the critical F values at various significance levels.

Forecasting

RMSE: 140.4048

Period	Actual (Y)	Forecast (F)	Error (E)
1	521.0000	299.5124	221.4876
2	367.0000	487.1243	(120.1243)
3	443.0000	353.2789	89.7211
4	365.0000	276.3296	88.6704
5	614.0000	776.1336	(162.1336)
6	385.0000	298.9993	86.0007
7	286.0000	354.8718	(68.8718)
8	397.0000	312.6155	84.3845
9	764.0000	529.7550	234.2450
10	427.0000	347.7034	79.2966
11	153.0000	266.2526	(113.2526)
12	231.0000	264.6375	(33.6375)
13	524.0000	406.8009	117.1991
14	328.0000	272.2226	55.7774
15	240.0000	231.7882	8.2118
16	286.0000	257.8862	28.1138
17	285.0000	314.9521	(29.9521)
18	569.0000	335.3140	233.6860
19	96.0000	282.0356	(186.0356)
20	498.0000	370.2062	127.7938
21	481.0000	340.8742	140.1258
22	468.0000	427.5118	40.4882
23	177.0000	274.5298	(97.5298)
24	198.0000	294.7795	(96.7795)
25	458.0000	295.2180	162.7820

Actual vs. Forecast

Diversifying Risk and Efficient Frontier

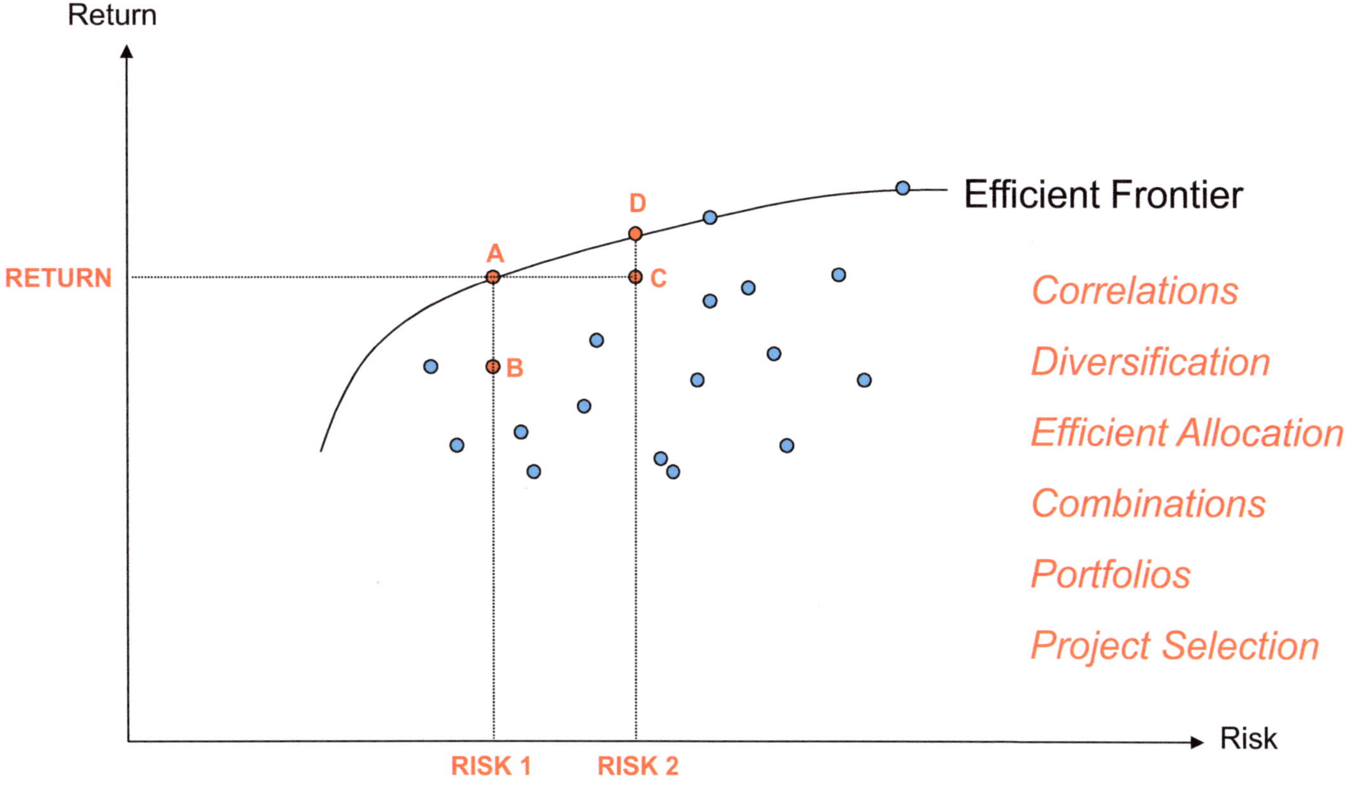

What does this picture tell you?

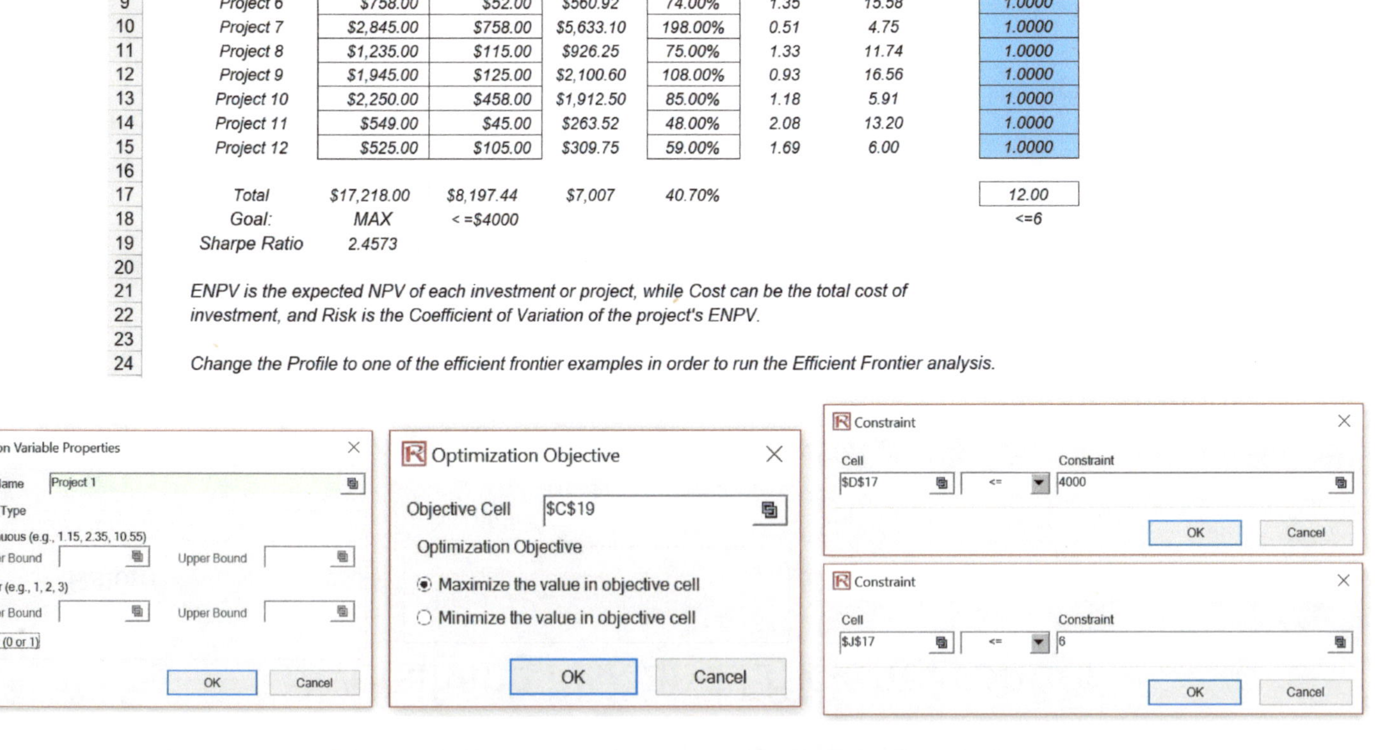

OPTIMAL PROJECT SELECTION FOR A PORTFOLIO WITH EFFICIENT FRONTIER SUBJECT TO CONSTRAINTS

Projects	ENPV	Cost	Risk $	Risk %	Return to Risk Ratio	Profitability Index	Selection
Project 1	$458.00	$1,732.44	$54.96	12.00%	8.33	1.26	1.0000
Project 2	$1,954.00	$859.00	$1,914.92	98.00%	1.02	3.27	1.0000
Project 3	$1,599.00	$1,845.00	$1,551.03	97.00%	1.03	1.87	1.0000
Project 4	$2,251.00	$1,645.00	$1,012.95	45.00%	2.22	2.37	1.0000
Project 5	$849.00	$458.00	$925.41	109.00%	0.92	2.85	1.0000
Project 6	$758.00	$52.00	$560.92	74.00%	1.35	15.58	1.0000
Project 7	$2,845.00	$758.00	$5,633.10	198.00%	0.51	4.75	1.0000
Project 8	$1,235.00	$115.00	$926.25	75.00%	1.33	11.74	1.0000
Project 9	$1,945.00	$125.00	$2,100.60	108.00%	0.93	16.56	1.0000
Project 10	$2,250.00	$458.00	$1,912.50	85.00%	1.18	5.91	1.0000
Project 11	$549.00	$45.00	$263.52	48.00%	2.08	13.20	1.0000
Project 12	$525.00	$105.00	$309.75	59.00%	1.69	6.00	1.0000
Total	$17,218.00	$8,197.44	$7,007	40.70%			12.00
Goal:	MAX	< =$4000					<=6
Sharpe Ratio	2.4573						

ENPV is the expected NPV of each investment or project, while Cost can be the total cost of investment, and Risk is the Coefficient of Variation of the project's ENPV.

Change the Profile to one of the efficient frontier examples in order to run the Efficient Frontier analysis.

ASSET ALLOCATION OPTIMIZATION MODEL

Asset Class Description	Annualized Returns	Volatility Risk	Allocation Weights	Required Minimum Allocation	Required Maximum Allocation	Return to Risk Ratio	Returns Ranking (Hi-Lo)	Risk Ranking (Lo-Hi)	Return to Risk Ranking (Hi-Lo)	Allocation Ranking (Hi-Lo)
Asset Class 1	10.54%	12.36%	10.00%	5.00%	35.00%	0.8524	9	2	7	1
Asset Class 2	11.25%	16.23%	10.00%	5.00%	35.00%	0.6929	7	8	10	1
Asset Class 3	11.84%	15.64%	10.00%	5.00%	35.00%	0.7570	6	7	9	1
Asset Class 4	10.64%	12.35%	10.00%	5.00%	35.00%	0.8615	8	1	5	1
Asset Class 5	13.25%	13.28%	10.00%	5.00%	35.00%	0.9977	5	4	2	1
Asset Class 6	14.21%	14.39%	10.00%	5.00%	35.00%	0.9875	3	6	3	1
Asset Class 7	15.53%	14.25%	10.00%	5.00%	35.00%	1.0898	1	5	1	1
Asset Class 8	14.95%	16.44%	10.00%	5.00%	35.00%	0.9094	2	9	4	1
Asset Class 9	14.16%	16.50%	10.00%	5.00%	35.00%	0.8584	4	10	6	1
Asset Class 10	10.06%	12.50%	10.00%	5.00%	35.00%	0.8045	10	3	8	1
Portfolio Total	***12.6419%***	***4.58%***	***100.00%***							
Return to Risk Ratio	***2.7596***									

Specifications of the optimization model:

Objective: *Maximize Return to Risk Ratio (C18)*
Decision Variables: *Allocation Weights (E6:E15)*
Restrictions on Decision Variables: *Minimum and Maximum Required (F6:G15)*
Constraints: *Portfolio Total Allocation Weights 100% (E17 is set to 100%)*

Additional specifications:

1. One can always maximize portfolio total returns or minimize the portfolio total risk.
2. Incorporate Monte Carlo simulation in the model by simulating the returns and volatility of each asset class and apply Simulation-Optimization techniques.
3. The portfolio can be optimized as is without simulation using Static Optimization techniques.

Portfolio Risk and Returns

- The previous slide shows a portfolio with 10 asset classes, where each asset class has its own set of annualized returns and annualized volatilities. These return and risk measures are annualized values such that they can be consistently compared across different asset classes. Returns are computed using the geometric average of the relative returns while the risks are computed using the logarithmic relative stock returns approach.
- The Allocation Weights in column E hold the decision variables, which are the variables that need to be tweaked and tested such that the total weight is constrained at 100% (cell E17). Typically, to start the optimization, we will set these cells to a uniform value, where in this case, cells E6 to E15 are set at 10% each. In addition, each decision variable may have specific restrictions in its allowed range. In this example, the lower and upper allocations allowed are 5% and 35%, as seen in columns F and G. This means that each asset class may have its own allocation boundaries. Next, column H shows the return to risk ratio, which is simply the return percentage divided by the risk percentage, where the higher this value, the higher the *bang for the buck*. The remainder of the model shows the individual asset class rankings by returns, risk, return to risk ratio, and allocation. In other words, these rankings show at a glance which asset class has the lowest risk, or the highest return, and so forth.
- The portfolio's total return in cell C17 is *SUMPRODUCT(C6:C15, E6:E15)*, that is, the sum of the allocation weights multiplied by the annualized returns for each asset class. In other words, we have $R_P = \omega_A R_A + \omega_B R_B + \omega_C R_C + \omega_D R_D$ where R_P is the return on the portfolio, $R_{A,B,C,D}$ are the individual returns on the projects, and $\omega_{A,B,C,D}$ are the respective weights or capital allocation across each project.
- In addition, the portfolio's diversified risk in cell D17 is computed by taking $\sigma_P = \sqrt{\sum_{i=1}^{n} \omega_i^2 \sigma_i^2 + \sum_{i=1}^{n} \sum_{j=1}^{m} 2\omega_i \omega_j \rho_{i,j} \sigma_i \sigma_j}$
- Here, $\rho_{i,j}$ are the respective cross-correlations between the asset classes. Hence, if the cross-correlations are negative, there are risk diversification effects, and the portfolio risk decreases. However, to simplify the computations here, we assume zero correlations among the asset classes through this portfolio risk computation but assume the correlations when applying simulation on the returns as will be seen later. Therefore, instead of applying static correlations among these different asset returns, we apply the correlations in the simulation assumptions themselves, creating a more dynamic relationship among the simulated return values.

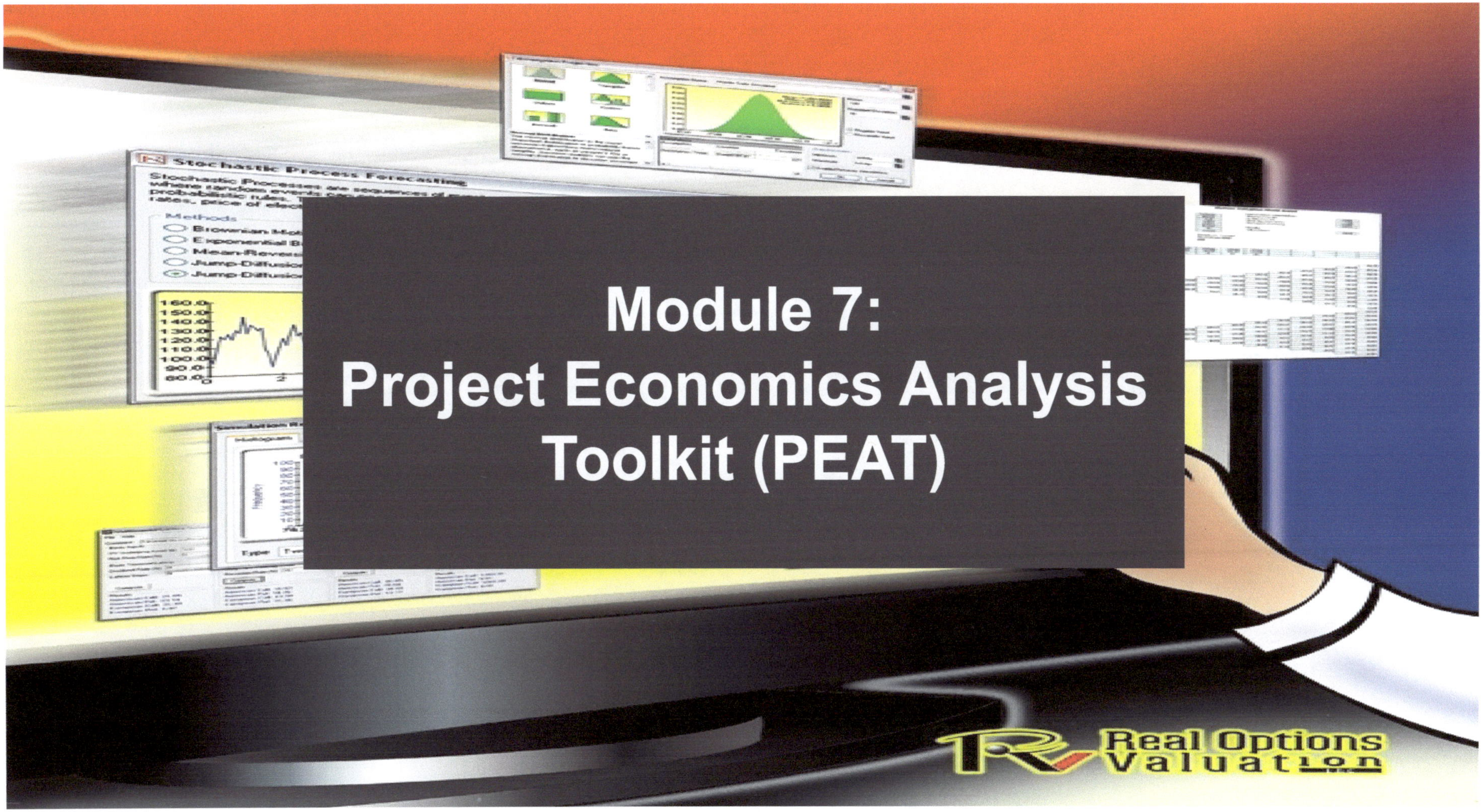

Module 7: Project Economics Analysis Toolkit (PEAT)

Financial and Economic Portfolios

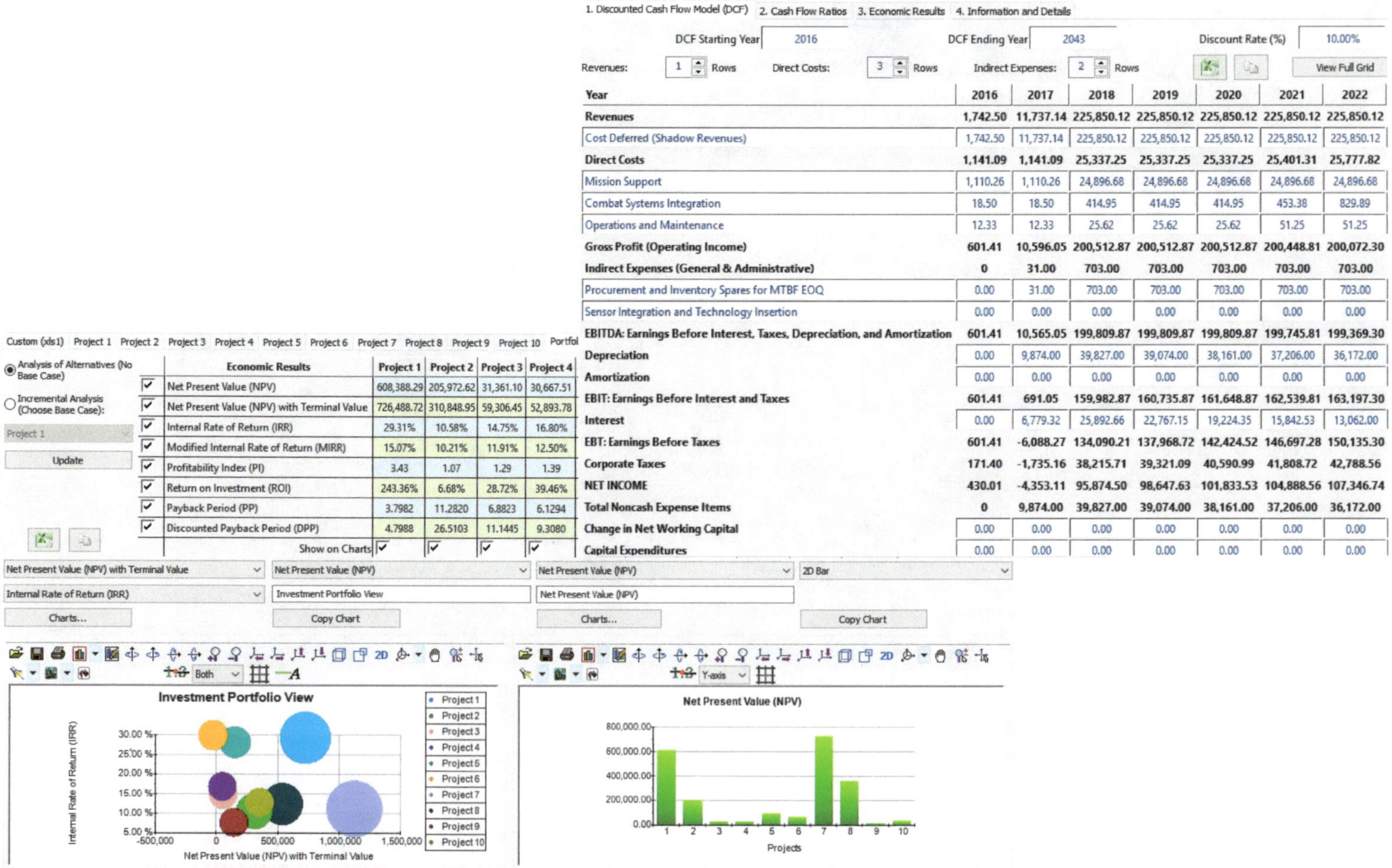

1. Discounted Cash Flow Model (DCF) | 2. Cash Flow Ratios | 3. Economic Results | 4. Information and Details

DCF Starting Year: 2016 | DCF Ending Year: 2043 | Discount Rate (%): 10.00%

Revenues: 1 Rows | Direct Costs: 3 Rows | Indirect Expenses: 2 Rows | View Full Grid

Year	2016	2017	2018	2019	2020	2021	2022
Revenues	1,742.50	11,737.14	225,850.12	225,850.12	225,850.12	225,850.12	225,850.12
Cost Deferred (Shadow Revenues)	1,742.50	11,737.14	225,850.12	225,850.12	225,850.12	225,850.12	225,850.12
Direct Costs	1,141.09	1,141.09	25,337.25	25,337.25	25,337.25	25,401.31	25,777.82
Mission Support	1,110.26	1,110.26	24,896.68	24,896.68	24,896.68	24,896.68	24,896.68
Combat Systems Integration	18.50	18.50	414.95	414.95	414.95	453.38	829.89
Operations and Maintenance	12.33	12.33	25.62	25.62	25.62	51.25	51.25
Gross Profit (Operating Income)	601.41	10,596.05	200,512.87	200,512.87	200,512.87	200,448.81	200,072.30
Indirect Expenses (General & Administrative)	0	31.00	703.00	703.00	703.00	703.00	703.00
Procurement and Inventory Spares for MTBF EOQ	0.00	31.00	703.00	703.00	703.00	703.00	703.00
Sensor Integration and Technology Insertion	0.00	0.00	0.00	0.00	0.00	0.00	0.00
EBITDA: Earnings Before Interest, Taxes, Depreciation, and Amortization	601.41	10,565.05	199,809.87	199,809.87	199,809.87	199,745.81	199,369.30
Depreciation	0.00	9,874.00	39,827.00	39,074.00	38,161.00	37,206.00	36,172.00
Amortization	0.00	0.00	0.00	0.00	0.00	0.00	0.00
EBIT: Earnings Before Interest and Taxes	601.41	691.05	159,982.87	160,735.87	161,648.87	162,539.81	163,197.30
Interest	0.00	6,779.32	25,892.66	22,767.15	19,224.35	15,842.53	13,062.00
EBT: Earnings Before Taxes	601.41	-6,088.27	134,090.21	137,968.72	142,424.52	146,697.28	150,135.30
Corporate Taxes	171.40	-1,735.16	38,215.71	39,321.09	40,590.99	41,808.72	42,788.56
NET INCOME	430.01	-4,353.11	95,874.50	98,647.63	101,833.53	104,888.56	107,346.74
Total Noncash Expense Items	0	9,874.00	39,827.00	39,074.00	38,161.00	37,206.00	36,172.00
Change in Net Working Capital	0.00	0.00	0.00	0.00	0.00	0.00	0.00
Capital Expenditures	0.00	0.00	0.00	0.00	0.00	0.00	0.00

Custom (xls1) | Project 1 | Project 2 | Project 3 | Project 4 | Project 5 | Project 6 | Project 7 | Project 8 | Project 9 | Project 10 | Portfol

◉ Analysis of Alternatives (No Base Case)
○ Incremental Analysis (Choose Base Case): Project 1

Update

Economic Results	Project 1	Project 2	Project 3	Project 4
Net Present Value (NPV)	608,388.29	205,972.62	31,361.10	30,667.51
Net Present Value (NPV) with Terminal Value	726,488.72	310,848.95	59,306.45	52,893.78
Internal Rate of Return (IRR)	29.31%	10.58%	14.75%	16.80%
Modified Internal Rate of Return (MIRR)	15.07%	10.21%	11.91%	12.50%
Profitability Index (PI)	3.43	1.07	1.29	1.39
Return on Investment (ROI)	243.36%	6.68%	28.72%	39.46%
Payback Period (PP)	3.7982	11.2820	6.8823	6.1294
Discounted Payback Period (DPP)	4.7988	26.5103	11.1445	9.3080
Show on Charts	✓	✓	✓	✓

Net Present Value (NPV) with Terminal Value | Net Present Value (NPV) | Net Present Value (NPV) | 2D Bar

Internal Rate of Return (IRR) | Investment Portfolio View | Net Present Value (NPV)

Charts... | Copy Chart | Charts... | Copy Chart

Investment Portfolio View

Internal Rate of Return (IRR): 30.00 %, 25.00 %, 20.00 %, 15.00 %, 10.00 %, 5.00 %

Net Present Value (NPV) with Terminal Value: -500,000, 0, 500,000, 1,000,000, 1,500,000

Project 1, Project 2, Project 3, Project 4, Project 5, Project 6, Project 7, Project 8, Project 9, Project 10

Net Present Value (NPV)

800,000.00, 600,000.00, 400,000.00, 200,000.00, 0.00

Projects: 1, 2, 3, 4, 5, 6, 7, 8, 9, 10

Economic and Non-economic Portfolios

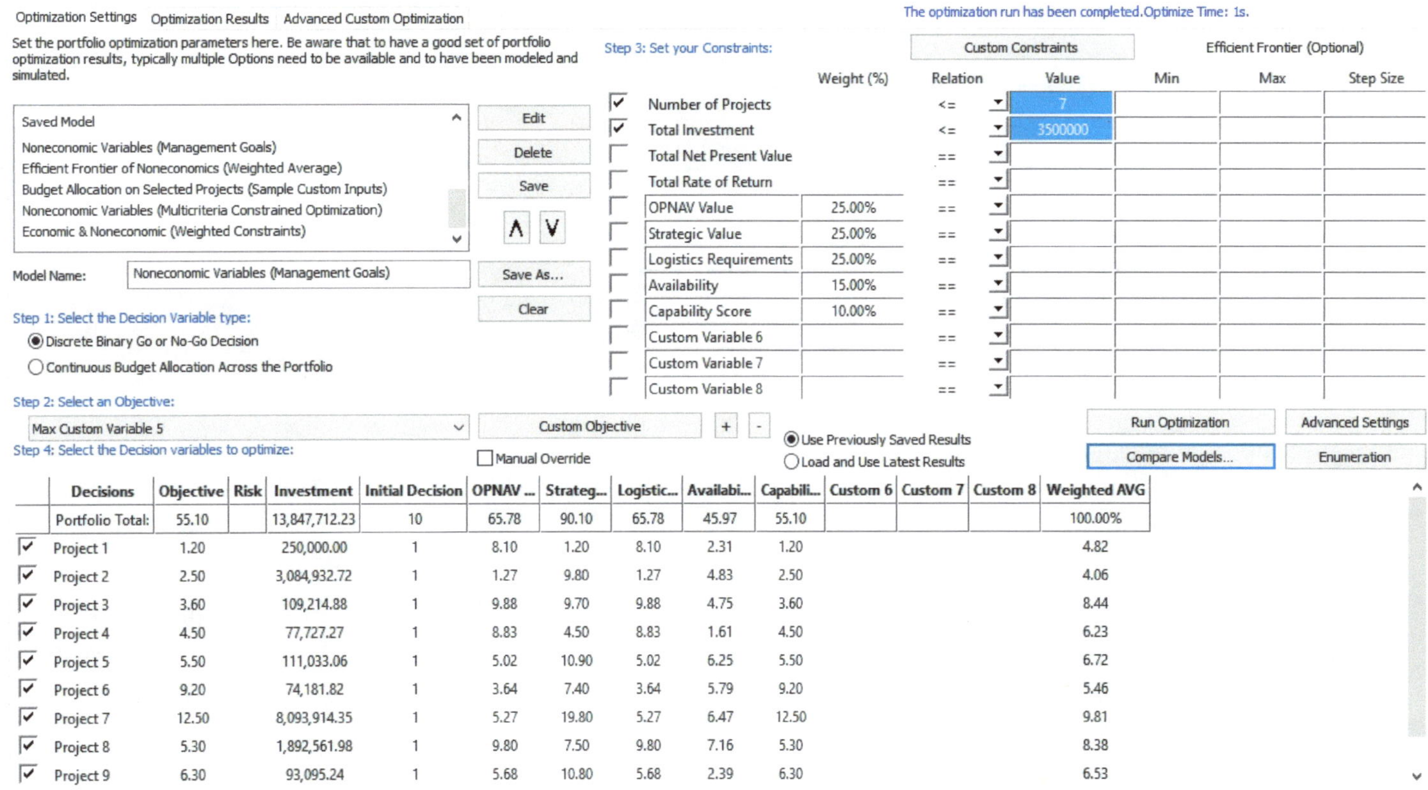

Decisions	Objective	Risk	Investment	Initial Decision	OPNAV ...	Strateg...	Logistic...	Availabi...	Capabili...	Custom 6	Custom 7	Custom 8	Weighted AVG
Portfolio Total:	55.10		13,847,712.23	10	65.78	90.10	65.78	45.97	55.10				100.00%
Project 1	1.20		250,000.00	1	8.10	1.20	8.10	2.31	1.20				4.82
Project 2	2.50		3,084,932.72	1	1.27	9.80	1.27	4.83	2.50				4.06
Project 3	3.60		109,214.88	1	9.88	9.70	9.88	4.75	3.60				8.44
Project 4	4.50		77,727.27	1	8.83	4.50	8.83	1.61	4.50				6.23
Project 5	5.50		111,033.06	1	5.02	10.90	5.02	6.25	5.50				6.72
Project 6	9.20		74,181.82	1	3.64	7.40	3.64	5.79	9.20				5.46
Project 7	12.50		8,093,914.35	1	5.27	19.80	5.27	6.47	12.50				9.81
Project 8	5.30		1,892,561.98	1	9.80	7.50	9.80	7.16	5.30				8.38
Project 9	6.30		93,095.24	1	5.68	10.80	5.68	2.39	6.30				6.53

Slice and Dice – Multicriteria Portfolios

- We have multiple value metrics (e.g., economic, noneconomic, strategic, operational, logistic).
- Portfolio selection and optimization can be run to maximize each of these value metrics to create a cross-tabulation matrix (below). Each "model" below is an optimal portfolio under each value metric.
- We then prioritize the program/capability by the Count (a high count indicates that regardless of what value metric we use, that specific capability is still dominant). The portfolios are also constrained portfolios (subject to cost, schedule, risk, budget, and other constraints).

Compare Model Results

Index	1	2	3	4	5	Count
Model	Model 1	Model 2	Model 3	Model 4	Model 5	
Objective Function	55.6000	59.3000	55.6000	33.0600	38.9000	
Optimized Constraint 1	7.0000	7.0000	7.0000	7.0000	7.0000	
Optimized Constraint 2	2,588,872.3394	2,413,054.1576	2,588,872.3394	2,585,326.8849	2,413,054.1576	
Option 1	1	0	1	1	0	3
Option 2	0	0	0	0	0	0
Option 3	1	1	1	1	1	5
Option 4	1	1	1	0	1	4
Option 5	1	1	1	1	1	5
Option 6	0	1	0	1	1	3
Option 7	0	0	0	0	0	0
Option 8	1	1	1	1	1	5
Option 9	1	1	1	1	1	5
Option 10	1	1	1	1	1	5

1 = Selected Program/Capability
0 = Rejected Program/Capability

Models 1 to 5 are run based on five different value metrics, where each portfolio is still subject to multiple constraints and limitations (budget and risk).

Count shows the number of times a specific Program/Capability Option is selected under various value objectives.

Budgetary Constraints

- Portfolios are optimized based on constraints and limitations; for example, budgetary levels can be applied (below).
- The Investment Efficient Frontier analysis based on the budget will show different programs/options that should be added or replaced based on various budgetary levels.
- The analysis can be done on any economic and non-economic values.

Objective Function	6.1286	6.7465	6.9478	6.9478	6.9478
Frontier Variable	2,000,000	2,500,000	3,000,000	3,500,000	4,000,000
Optimized Constraint	1,978,818	2,487,042	2,718,646	2,718,646	2,718,646
Option1	1	1	1	1	1
Option2	0	1	1	1	1
Option3	1	1	1	1	1
Option4	1	1	1	1	1
Option5	1	0	1	1	1
Option6	0	0	1	1	1
Option7	0	0	0	0	0
Option8	1	1	1	1	1
Option9	0	0	1	1	1
Option10	0	1	1	1	1

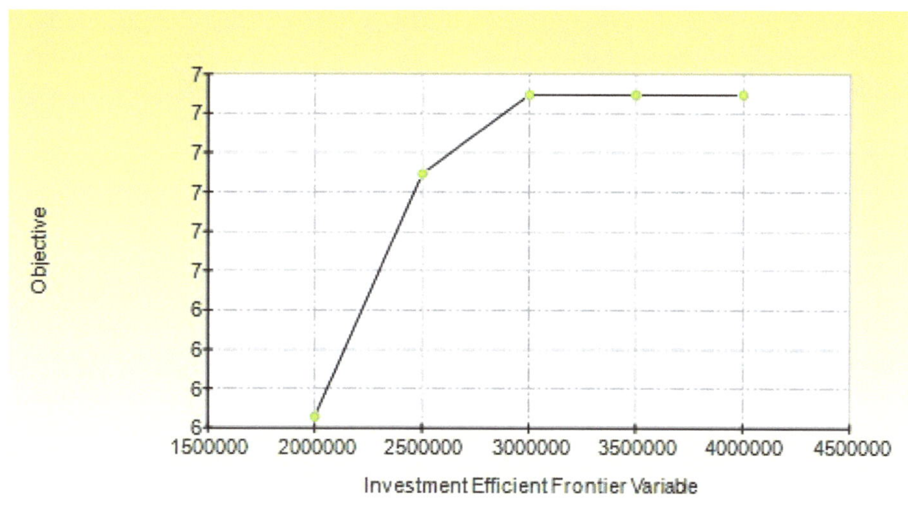

Investment Efficient Frontier

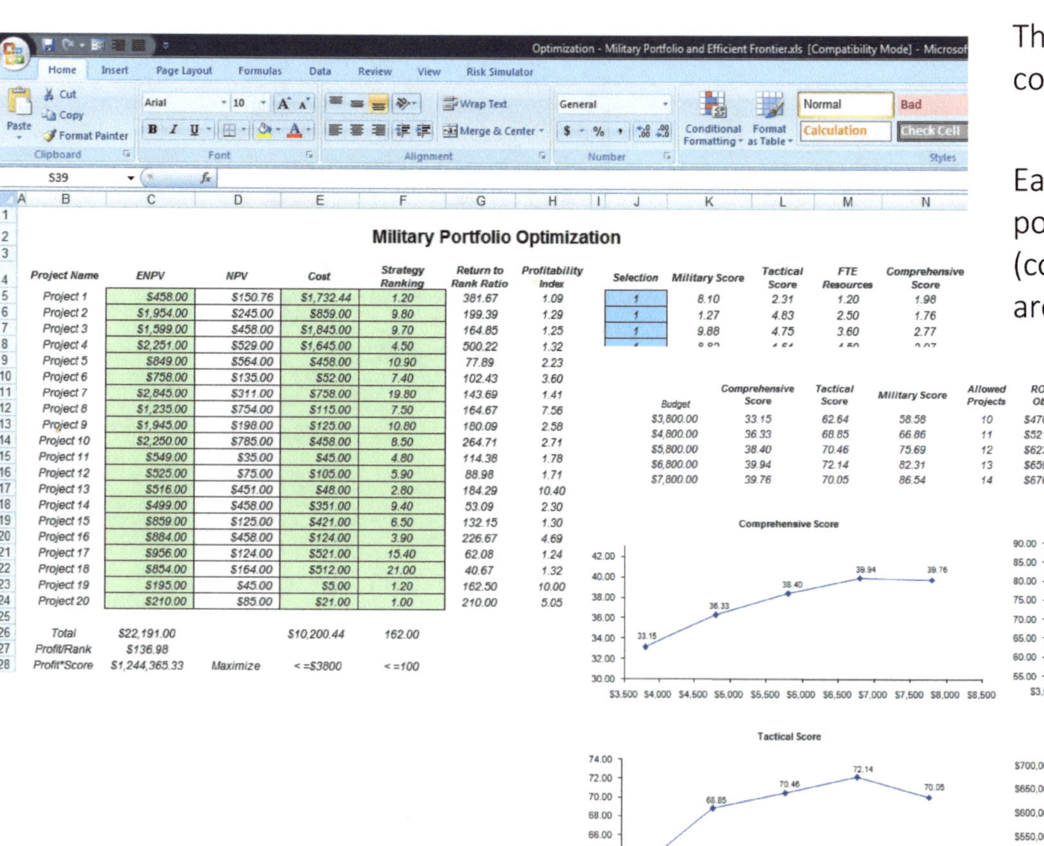

Military Portfolio Optimization

Project Name	ENPV	NPV	Cost	Strategy Ranking	Return to Rank Ratio	Profitability Index
Project 1	$458.00	$150.76	$1,732.44	1.20	381.67	1.09
Project 2	$1,954.00	$245.00	$859.00	9.80	199.39	1.29
Project 3	$1,599.00	$458.00	$1,845.00	9.70	164.85	1.25
Project 4	$2,251.00	$529.00	$1,645.00	4.50	500.22	1.32
Project 5	$849.00	$564.00	$458.00	10.90	77.89	2.23
Project 6	$758.00	$135.00	$52.00	7.40	102.43	3.60
Project 7	$2,845.00	$311.00	$758.00	19.80	143.69	1.41
Project 8	$1,235.00	$754.00	$115.00	7.50	164.67	7.56
Project 9	$1,945.00	$198.00	$125.00	10.80	180.09	2.58
Project 10	$2,250.00	$785.00	$458.00	8.50	264.71	2.71
Project 11	$549.00	$35.00	$45.00	4.80	114.38	1.78
Project 12	$525.00	$75.00	$105.00	5.90	88.98	1.71
Project 13	$516.00	$451.00	$48.00	2.80	184.29	10.40
Project 14	$499.00	$458.00	$351.00	9.40	53.09	2.30
Project 15	$859.00	$125.00	$421.00	6.50	132.15	1.30
Project 16	$884.00	$458.00	$124.00	3.90	226.67	4.69
Project 17	$956.00	$124.00	$521.00	15.40	62.08	1.24
Project 18	$854.00	$164.00	$512.00	21.00	40.67	1.32
Project 19	$195.00	$45.00	$5.00	1.20	162.50	10.00
Project 20	$210.00	$85.00	$21.00	1.00	210.00	5.05
Total	$22,191.00		$10,200.44	162.00		
Profit/Rank	$136.98					
Profit*Score	$1,244,365.33	Maximize	<=$3800	<=100		

Selection	Military Score	Tactical Score	FTE Resources	Comprehensive Score
1	8.10	2.31	1.20	1.98
1	1.27	4.83	2.50	1.76
1	9.88	4.75	3.60	2.77

Budget	Comprehensive Score	Tactical Score	Military Score	Allowed Projects	ROI-RANK Objective
$3,800.00	33.15	62.64	58.58	10	$470,235.60
$4,800.00	36.33	68.85	66.86	11	$521,645.92
$5,800.00	38.40	70.46	75.69	12	$623,557.79
$6,800.00	39.94	72.14	82.31	13	$659,947.99
$7,800.00	39.76	70.05	86.54	14	$676,279.81

The x-axis shows budgetary levels and constraints.

Each point along the frontier is an optimal portfolio for that budgetary level (combinations of programs and capabilities are chosen at that budget level).

Time-Sequenced Optimized Portfolios

In some instances, a list of capabilities or programs/options can be considered for execution in the future. In fact, some programs and systems may require sequencing (platform or base systems need to be up and running before add-on systems can be implemented) or initial proofs of concept (Milestone A before additional funding is authorized for Milestones B and C).

Actual Capabilities Redacted

Capability	Optimal on Budget	Optimal Cost-Risk	BMD Must-Have	BMD Cost-Risk
Capability 1	ACB16	ACB16	ACB16	ACB18
Capability 2	ACB18	Later	ACB14	ACB14
Capability 3	Later	Later	Later	Later
Capability 4	ACB14	ACB14	ACB16	ACB16
Capability 5	ACB16	ACB14	ACB16	ACB16
Capability 6	ACB14	ACB16	ACB18	ACB18
Capability 7	ACB14	ACB14	ACB16	ACB16
Capability 8	Later	ACB18	ACB18	Later
Capability 9	ACB16	ACB14	ACB18	ACB16
Capability 10	ACB14	ACB14	ACB16	ACB16
Capability 11	ACB14	ACB14	ACB14	ACB14
Capability 12	ACB16	ACB16	ACB18	ACB18
Capability 13	ACB14	ACB14	ACB16	ACB16
Capability 14	ACB14	ACB14	ACB16	ACB16
Capability 15	ACB14	ACB16	ACB16	ACB18
Capability 16	ACB14	ACB14	ACB14	ACB16
Capability 17	ACB14	ACB14	ACB14	ACB16
Capability 18	ACB14	ACB14	ACB14	ACB16
Capability 19	ACB16	ACB18	Later	Later
Capability 20	ACB16	ACB16	Later	ACB18
Capability 21	ACB16	ACB16	Later	ACB18
Capability 22	Later	Later	Later	Later
Capability 23	ACB16	ACB16	ACB16	ACB18

ACB 14 + ACB 16 + ACB 18
*rounded to the nearest 0.1

	Optimal on Budget	Optimal Cost-Risk	BMD Must-Have	BMD Cost-Risk
Total Capabilities ACB14	11	11	5	2
Total Capabilities ACB16	8	7	9	10
Total Capabilities ACB18	1	2	4	7
EMV ACB14	310.98	299.74	115.56	61.02
EMV ACB16	149.87	151.58	268.03	280.96
EMV ACB18	42.24	57.94	127.93	151.58
Total Cost ACB14	$146.00	$139.00	$149.00	$129.00
Total Cost ACB16	$141.00	$129.00	$150.00	$137.00
Total Cost ACB18	$126.00	$95.00	$141.00	$129.00
Total Spent on ACB14-18	$413.00	$363.00	$440.00	$395.00
Probability of Under Budget ACB14	29.70%	97.90%	41.50%	90.80%
Probability of Under Budget ACB16	72.23%	90.90%	16.25%	99.90%
Probability of Under Budget ACB18	94.80%	99.90%	72.90%	90.90%
ACB14 Median 50th Percentile on Budget	$153.20	$142.90	$152.60	$132.30
ACB14 Median 85th Percentile on Budget	$160.22	$146.60	$166.60	$146.30
ACB14 Median 95th Percentile on Budget	$164.30	$148.70	$173.90	$153.50
ACB16 Median 50th Percentile on Budget	$145.40	$137.90	$156.50	$139.50
ACB16 Median 85th Percentile on Budget	$153.50	$147.30	$164.80	$143.30
ACB16 Median 95th Percentile on Budget	$157.80	$152.70	$169.20	$145.30
ACB18 Median 50th Percentile on Budget	$128.90	$95.30	$145.10	$137.90
ACB18 Median 85th Percentile on Budget	$142.90	$101.30	$153.50	$147.30
ACB18 Median 95th Percentile on Budget	$150.20	$104.30	$158.40	$152.70

Risk and Uncertainty in Input Assumptions and Projected Outcomes

In many instances, SME judgment and input assumptions are fraught with uncertainties and risks. Before running optimization and capital budgeting analytics, we will be applying sensitivity analysis (see Tornado chart below) to identify which input assumptions and data points have the highest impact on the results. More detailed analysis and additional data refinement will be performed on these inputs.

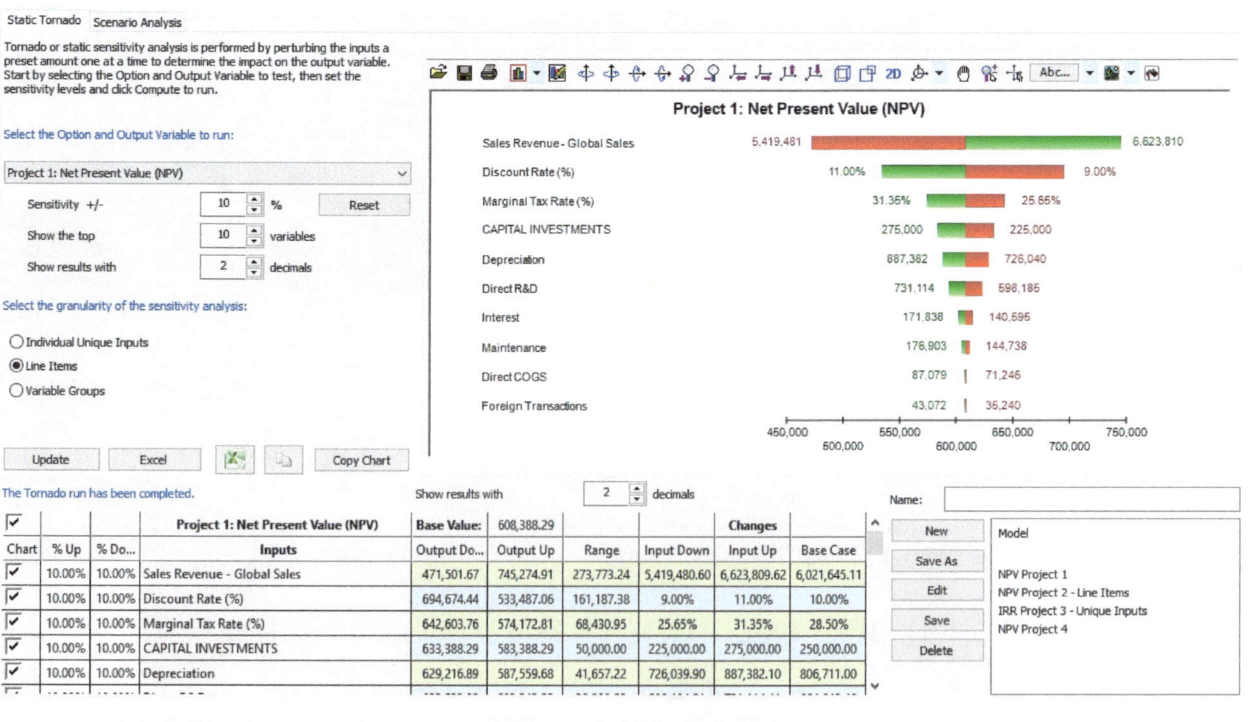

Chart	% Up	% Do...	Project 1: Net Present Value (NPV) Inputs	Base Value: Output Do...	608,388.29 Output Up	Range	Input Down	Changes Input Up	Base Case
✓	10.00%	10.00%	Sales Revenue - Global Sales	471,501.67	745,274.91	273,773.24	5,419,480.60	6,623,809.62	6,021,645.11
✓	10.00%	10.00%	Discount Rate (%)	694,674.44	533,487.06	161,187.38	9.00%	11.00%	10.00%
✓	10.00%	10.00%	Marginal Tax Rate (%)	642,603.76	574,172.81	68,430.95	25.65%	31.35%	28.50%
✓	10.00%	10.00%	CAPITAL INVESTMENTS	633,388.29	583,388.29	50,000.00	225,000.00	275,000.00	250,000.00
✓	10.00%	10.00%	Depreciation	629,216.89	587,559.68	41,657.22	726,039.90	887,382.10	806,711.00

Risk Simulation

Monte Carlo risk simulation of millions of trials will be performed on uncertain inputs to obtain probability distributions instead of single-point estimates. These distributions are then used in the portfolio optimization process. We can then determine the probability that a portfolio will be under or over budget, the chances of a schedule overrun and by how much, and the levels of uncertainty and risk of each portfolio.

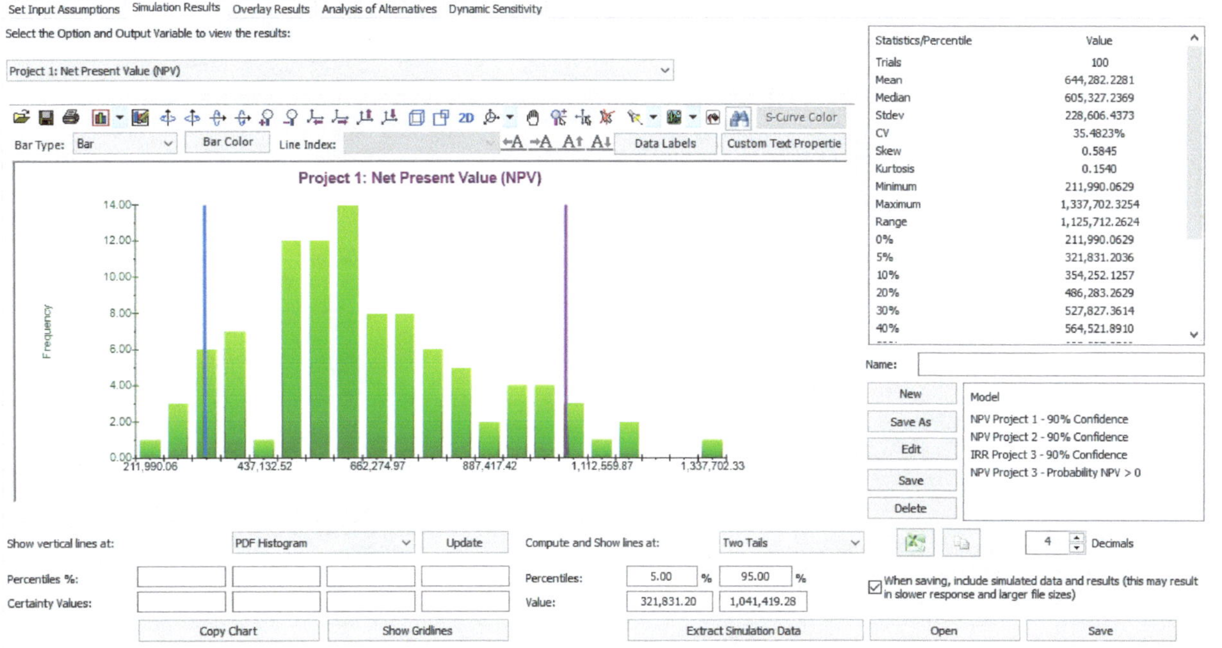

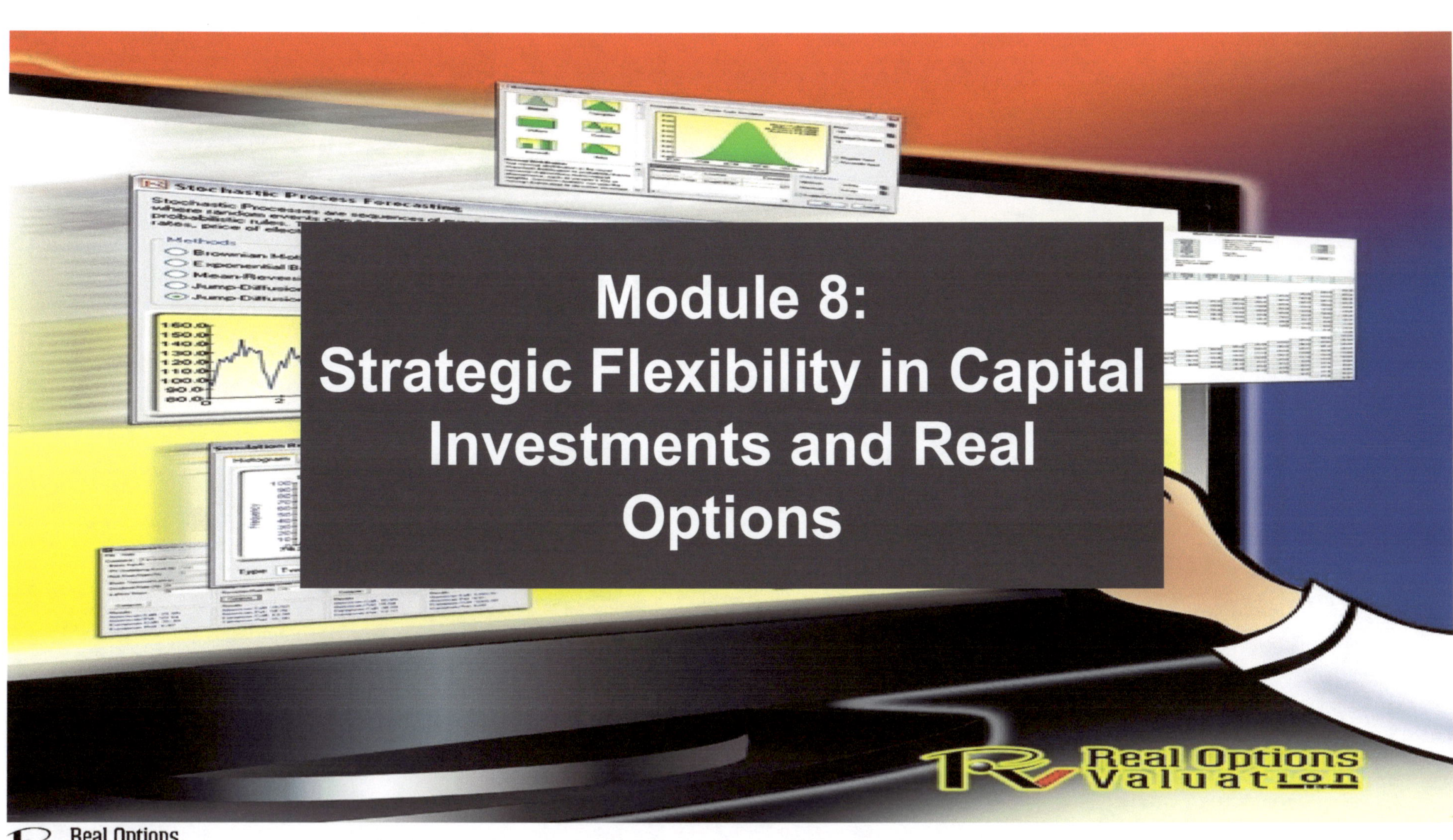
Module 8:
Strategic Flexibility in Capital Investments and Real Options
Real Options Valuation

What the Business Journals are saying...

Harvard Business Review (September/October 1998)

"Unfortunately, the financial tool most widely relied on to estimate the value of a strategy is the discounted cash flow which assumes that we will follow a predetermined plan regardless of how events unfold. A better approach to valuation would incorporate both the uncertainty inherent in business and the active decision making required for a strategy to succeed. It would help executives to think strategically on their feet by capturing the value of doing just that – of managing actively rather than passively and real options can deliver that extra insight."

Business Week (June 1999)

"The real options revolution in decision making is the next big thing to sell to clients and has the potential to be the next major business breakthrough."

"Doing this analysis has provided a lot of intuition you didn't have in the past... and that as it takes hold, it's clear that a new generation of business analysts will be schooled in options thinking. Silicon Valley is fast embracing the concepts of real options analytics, in its tradition of fail fast so that other options may be sought after."

Industry Week (December 6, 1999)

"With the degree of change going on in industry, the old models just don't work anymore... one promising tool for determining the strategic worth of an acquisition is Real Options Valuation."

"In contrast, the beauty of Real Options theory – an approach that ties the value of small initial investments to later opportunities for big payoffs – is that it works well with uncertainty and encourages management flexibility."

Overview of Real Options (RO)

- WHAT: What is RO?
- WHY: Why is RO superior (or is it?) compared to most traditional valuation methodologies? Differences and similarities?
- WHO: What companies are using RO?
- WHEN: When and under what circumstances is RO most amenable and applicable?
- WHERE: Industries and characteristics of firms using RO?
- HOW: How is RO used?

What Is Real Options?

- A systematic and integrated decision analysis approach
- Incorporates financial theory, economic analysis, applied decision sciences, investment finance, options theory, and statistical modeling in valuing real assets as opposed to financial assets
- Useful in a risky and uncertain business environment where business decisions are flexible and dynamic
- Applicable within the context of strategic decision making, valuing, and justifying investment opportunities and capital expenditures in e-commerce, e-business, IT, research and development, biotechnology, and high-tech industries

Why Real Options?

Traditional Net Present Value approach:

- Provides single decision pathway
- Allows only one future outcome
- Locks in a single risk rate
- Requires all assumptions to be determined at the outset

Real Options approach:

- Allows multiple decision pathways
- Maximizes financial flexibility
- Recognizes managerial decision making
- Incorporates new assumptions over time
- Allows variable risk

The Intuition: Straight DCF Analysis

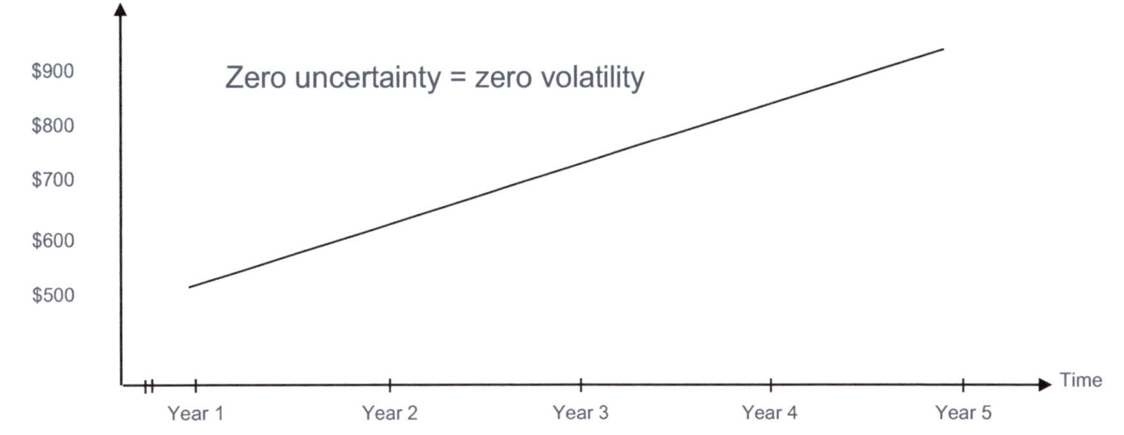

This straight-line cash-flow projection is the basis of DCF analysis. It assumes a static and known set of future cash flows.

The Intuition: DCF with Simulation

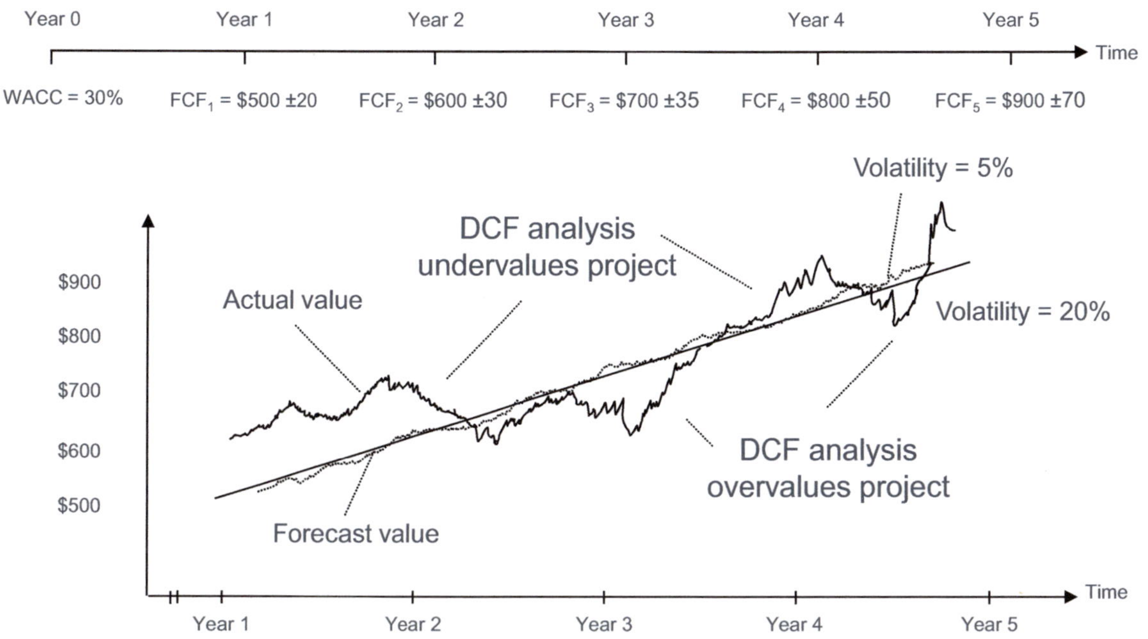

This graph shows that, in reality, at different times, actual cash flows may be above, below, or at the forecast value line due to uncertainty and risk. The higher the risk, the higher the volatility and the higher the fluctuation of actual cash flows around the forecast value. When volatility is zero, the values collapse to the forecast straight-line static value.

The Intuition: Real Options Analysis

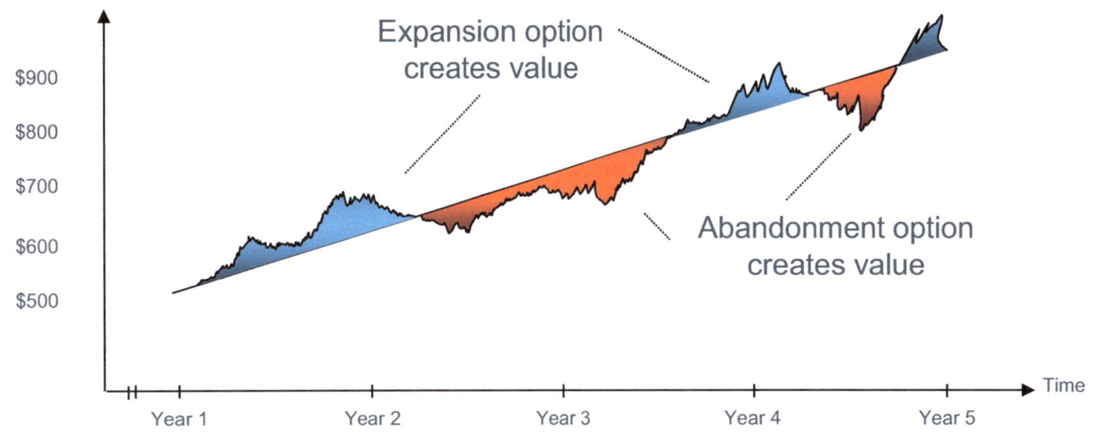

If a firm is strategically positioned to take advantage of these fluctuations, there is value in uncertainty. Options analysis also provides trigger points and optimal timing (i.e., when it is optimal to execute).

Integrated Risk Management

1 QUALITATIVE MANAGEMENT SCREENING

RISK IDENTIFICATION

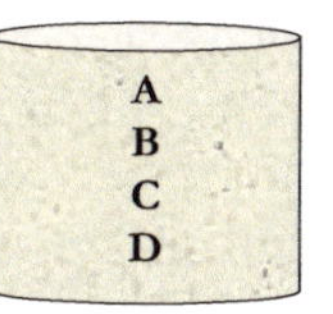

Start with a list of projects or strategies to be evaluated that have already been through qualitative screening…

2 FORECAST PREDICTION MODELING

RISK PREDICTION

Back-fitting, Forecasting and Scenario Analysis

ARIMA, GARCH, Fuzzy Logic, Markov Chains, Time Series Models…

…with the assistance of forecasting algorithms, future outcomes can be predicted...

3 BASE CASE STATIC MODELS

RISK MODELING

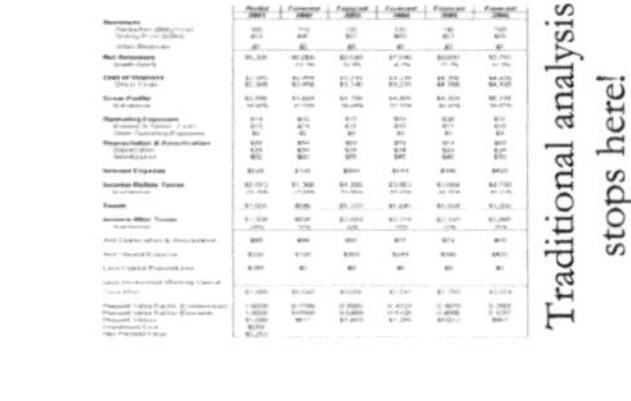

Traditional analysis stops here!

…create traditional static base case financial or economic models for each project…

4 DYNAMIC MONTE CARLO RISK SIMULATION

RISK ANALYSIS

Simulate thousands of scenario outcomes

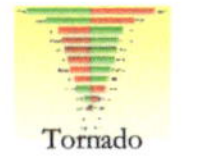

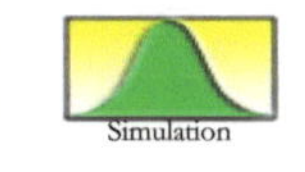

…Tornado analysis identifies critical success factors, then dynamic sensitivities and Monte Carlo risk simulations are run…

5 REAL OPTIONS PROBLEM FRAMING

RISK MITIGATION

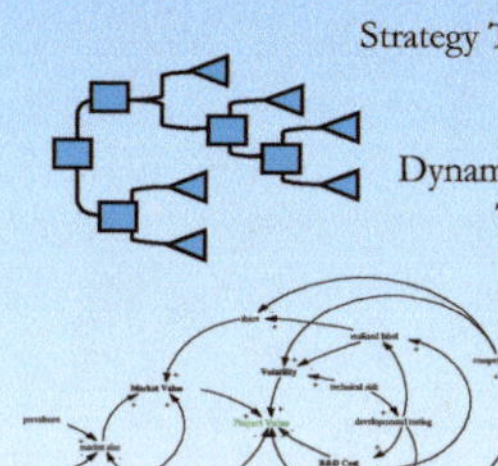

…strategic real options are framed to hedge and mitigate downside risks and take advantage of upside potential…

6 REAL OPTIONS VALUATION AND MODELING

RISK HEDGING

Simulation

$$\frac{\delta S}{S} = \mu \delta t + \sigma \varepsilon \sqrt{\delta t}$$

Differential Equations

Binomial Lattices

…the real options are valued using binomial lattices and closed-form partial-differential models with simulation…

7 PORTFOLIO AND RESOURCE OPTIMIZATION

RISK DIVERSIFICATION

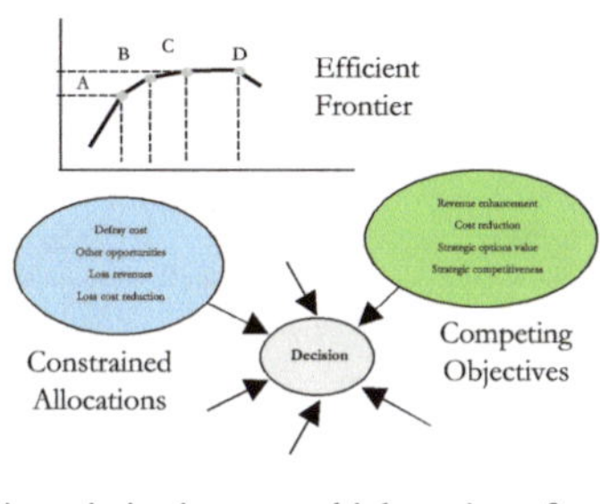

…stochastic optimization on multiple projects for efficient asset allocation subject to resource constraints…

8 REPORTS, PRESENTATION, AND UPDATES

RISK MANAGEMENT

…create reports, make decisions, and update analysis iteratively when uncertainty is resolved over time…

Real Options Valuation

Who Uses Real Options?
Sample Quick Cases

Aeronautics
Boeing, Airbus

Oil and Gas
BP, Shell

High Tech
Intel, Seagate

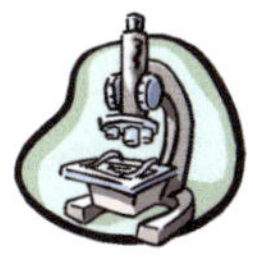

Pharmacology
Merck, Pfizer

Research & Development
Portfolios, Motorola, Unilever, 3M

IT Infrastructure
Credit Suisse, Halliburton

Electric/Utility
Peaker Plants, Coal-Coke Fired

Military & Government
Navy, Marines, Air Force, Army

Real Estate
Development, Management

Banking
Basel II/III, Credit/Market Risk

Truncating the Downside Risk and Taking Advantage of the Upside Opportunity

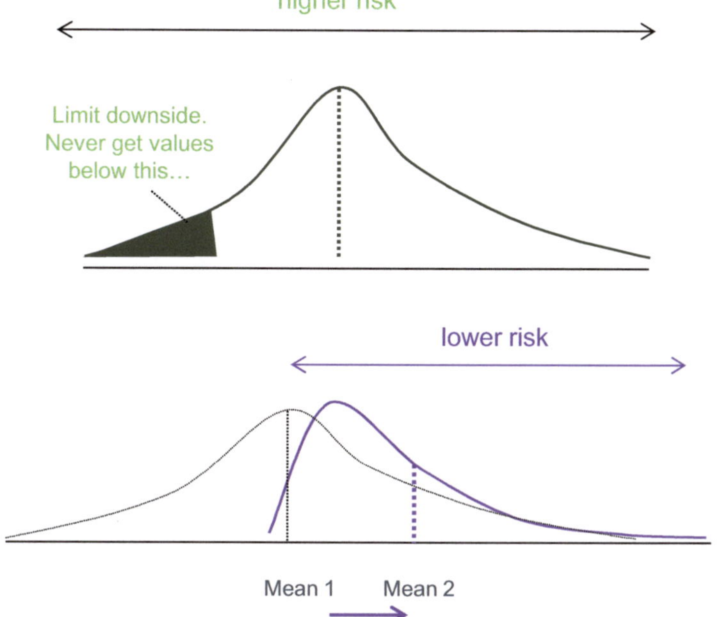

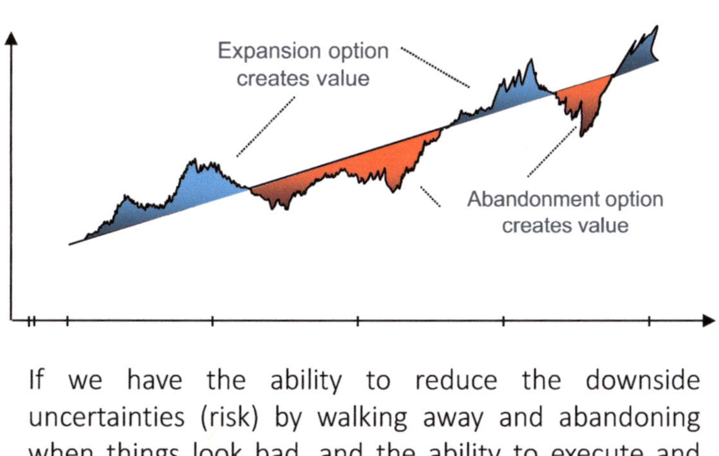

If we have the ability to reduce the downside uncertainties (risk) by walking away and abandoning when things look bad, and the ability to execute and continue with a path only when things are looking up (in real life, we make midcourse corrections along the way when uncertainties become resolved over the passage of time, actions, and events), we can truncate the downside and shift expectations to the right.

Real options will reduce risk (chop off the left tail downside, thereby reducing the distributional width and variability) and shift the distribution to the right and increase the expected value (mean returns).

When Are Real Options Applicable?

Do not randomly apply it everywhere!

Only when options exist

Only if the cost-benefit of the project fits

Know the 5 requirements for applying real options

- A financial model must exist or can be built.
- Uncertainty exists and is resolved through time, events and actions.
- Uncertainty unfolding changes decisions and actions.
- Flexibility or options must exist.
- Management must be credible enough to execute options optimally.

Understand the caveats and criticisms of real options

Financial Options versus Real Options

FINANCIAL OPTIONS

- Short maturity, usually in months
- Underlying variable driving its value is equity price or price of a financial asset (usually a stock price)
- Cannot control option value by manipulating stock prices
- Values are usually small
- Competitive or market effects are irrelevant to its value and pricing
- Have been around and traded for over four decades
- Usually solved using closed-form partial differential equations and simulation/variance reduction techniques for exotic options
- Marketable and traded security with comparables and pricing info
- Management assumptions and actions have no bearing on valuation although used for hedging/speculation
- Strategies of creating new vehicles by buying/selling combinations (butterflies, straddles, strangles)

REAL OPTIONS

- Longer maturity, usually in years
- Underlying variables are free cash flows, which in turn are driven by competition, demand, and management
- Can increase strategic option value by management decisions and flexibility
- Major million- and billion-dollar decisions
- Competition and market drive the value of a strategic option
- A recent development in corporate finance within the last two decades
- Usually solved using closed form equations and binomial lattices with simulation of the underlying variables, not on the option analysis
- Not traded and proprietary in nature, with no market comparables
- Management assumptions and actions drive the value of a real option—institute options to reduce risk and take advantage of upsides
- Strategies exist only for real options (abandon, barrier, contraction, defer and wait, expansion, switching, sequential compound)

Option Cost $5
Stock and Strike $100

Basic Option Payoff

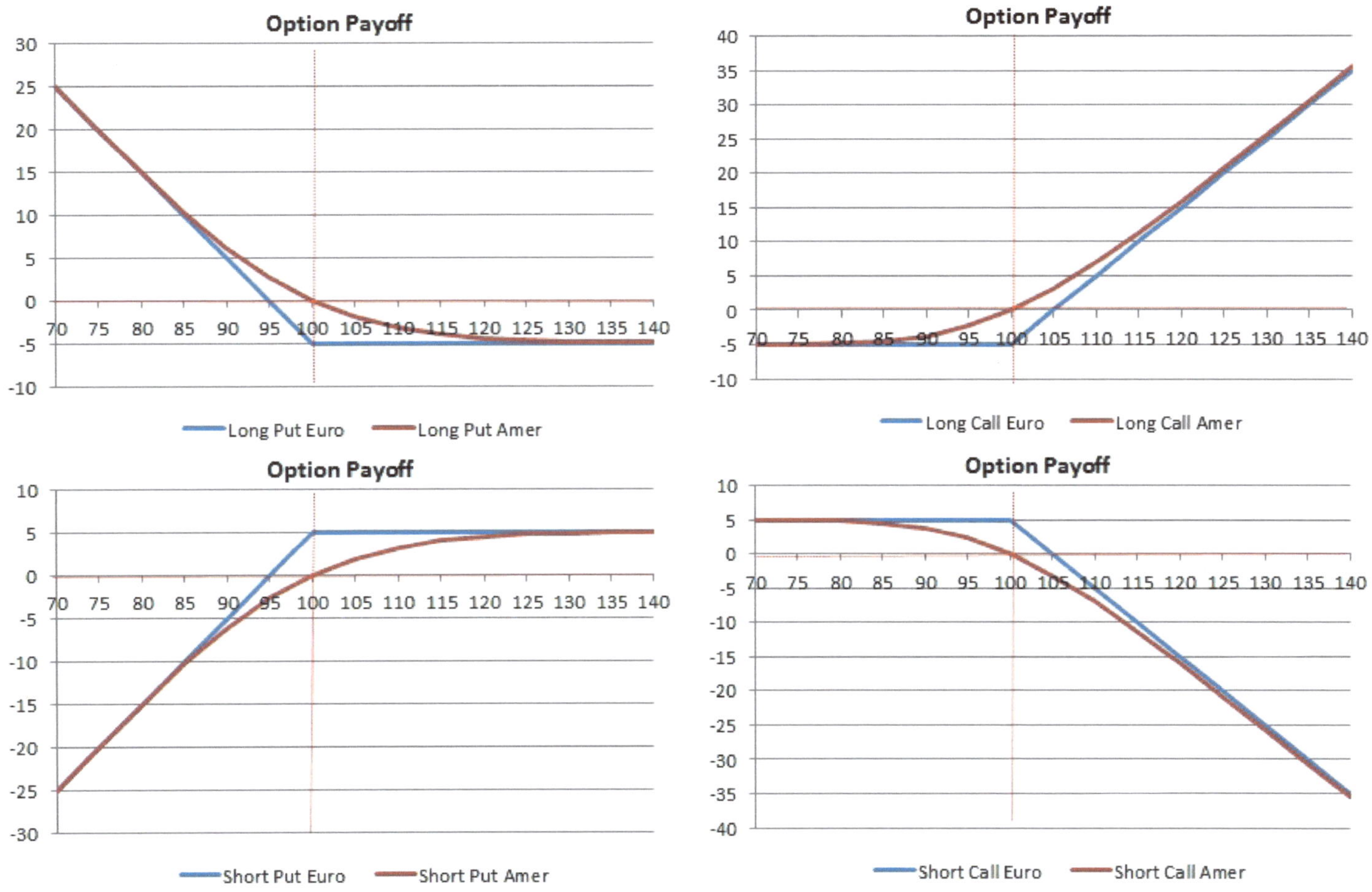

Option Payoff

30 25 20 15 10 5 0 -5 -10

70 75 80 85 90 95 100 105 110 115 120 125 130 135 140

Long Put Euro — Long Put Amer

Option Payoff

40 35 30 25 20 15 10 5 0 -5 -10

70 75 80 85 90 95 100 105 110 115 120 125 130 135 140

Long Call Euro — Long Call Amer

Option Payoff

10 5 0 -5 -10 -15 -20 -25 -30

70 75 80 85 90 95 100 105 110 115 120 125 130 135 140

Short Put Euro — Short Put Amer

Option Payoff

10 5 0 -5 -10 -15 -20 -25 -30 -35 -40

70 75 80 85 90 95 100 105 110 115 120 125 130 135 140

Short Call Euro — Short Call Amer

Real Options Math Can Be Painful!

$$C = \alpha S^{\psi} - \alpha\phi(S,T,\beta,I,I) + \phi(S,T,1,I,I) - \phi(S,T,1,X,I) - X(S,T,0,I,I) + X\phi(S,T,0,X,I)$$

$$\phi(S,T,\gamma,H,I) = e^{\lambda}S^{\gamma}\left[N(d) - \left(\frac{I}{S}\right)^{\kappa} N\left(d - \frac{s\ln(I/S)}{\sigma\sqrt{T}}\right)\right]$$

$$\alpha = (I-X)I^{-\beta} \text{ and } \beta = \left(\frac{1}{2} - \frac{b}{\sigma^2}\right) + \sqrt{\left(\frac{b}{\sigma^2} - \frac{1}{2}\right)^2 + 2\frac{r}{\sigma^2}}$$

$$Put = C(X,S,T,r-b,-b,\sigma)$$

$$C(S,X,T) = Sup(C + \psi(S/S')^q, S-X)^+$$

$$\psi = (1 - e^{(b-r)T}\Phi\left[\frac{\ln(S/X) + (b+\sigma^2/2)T}{\sigma\sqrt{T}}\right](S'))(S'/q)$$

$$q = \frac{N + 1 + \sqrt{(N^2 + N + 8r/(1-e^{-rT})\sigma^2 + 1}}{2}$$

Solving S' with the Newton - Raphson algorithm

Framing Options: Strategy Tree
Two-Stage Sequential Phased Options

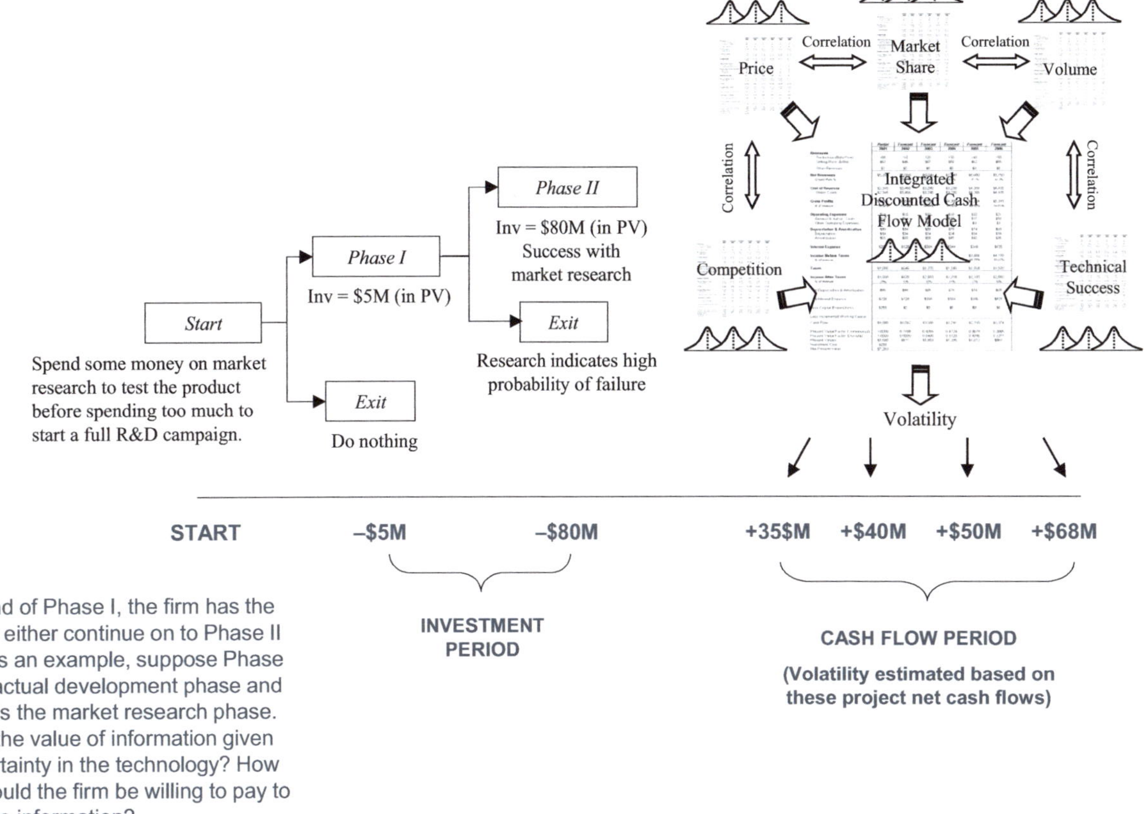

At the end of Phase I, the firm has the option to either continue on to Phase II or not. As an example, suppose Phase II is the actual development phase and Phase I is the market research phase. What is the value of information given an uncertainty in the technology? How much would the firm be willing to pay to obtain the information?

Framing Options: Strategy Tree
Complex Multi-Stage Phased Options

In reality, an R&D project will yield intellectual property and patent rights that the firm can easily license off (Abandon). In addition, at any phase, the project's development can be slowed down (Contract) or accelerated (Expand) depending on the outcome of each phase.

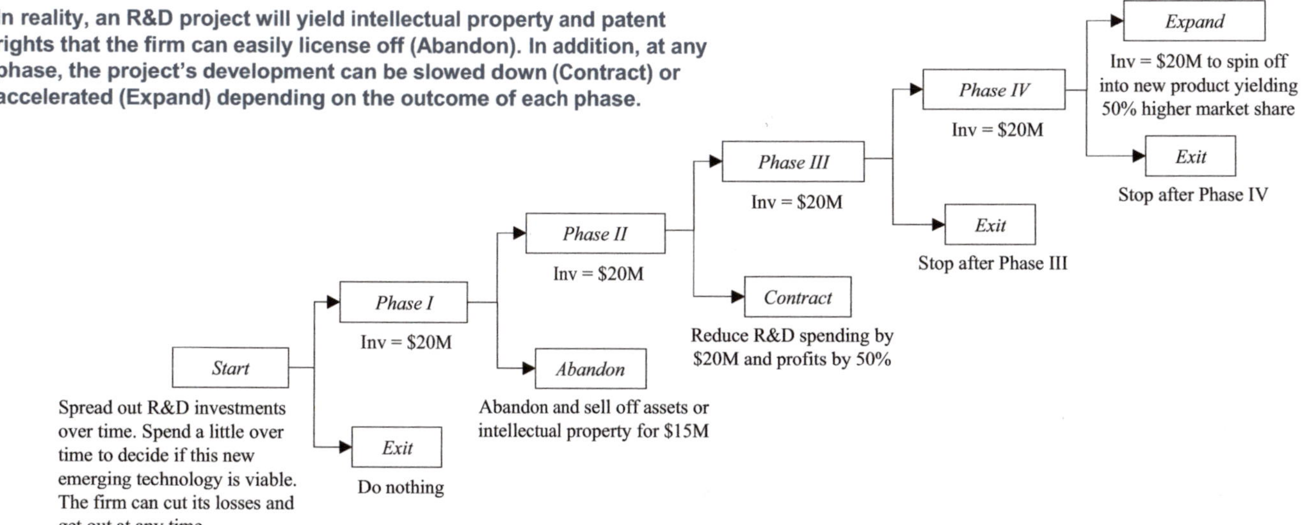
Start
Spread out R&D investments over time. Spend a little over time to decide if this new emerging technology is viable. The firm can cut its losses and get out at any time.
Phase I
Inv = $20M
Exit
Do nothing
Phase II
Inv = $20M
Abandon
Abandon and sell off assets or intellectual property for $15M
Phase III
Inv = $20M
Contract
Reduce R&D spending by $20M and profits by 50%
Phase IV
Inv = $20M
Exit
Stop after Phase III
Expand
Inv = $20M to spin off into new product yielding 50% higher market share
Exit
Stop after Phase IV

Another potential issue is synergy. Even if the development of the current technology is unsuccessful, the knowledge and insights gained may be applicable to some other product (Technology B).

The new technology will yield a potential 50% increase in projected revenues if implemented. However, Technology B can be applied only after the success of Phase IV's R&D efforts.

An NPV analysis cannot account for these options to make midcourse corrections over time, when uncertainty becomes resolved.

Framing Options: Strategy Tree Complex Multi-Stage Phased Options

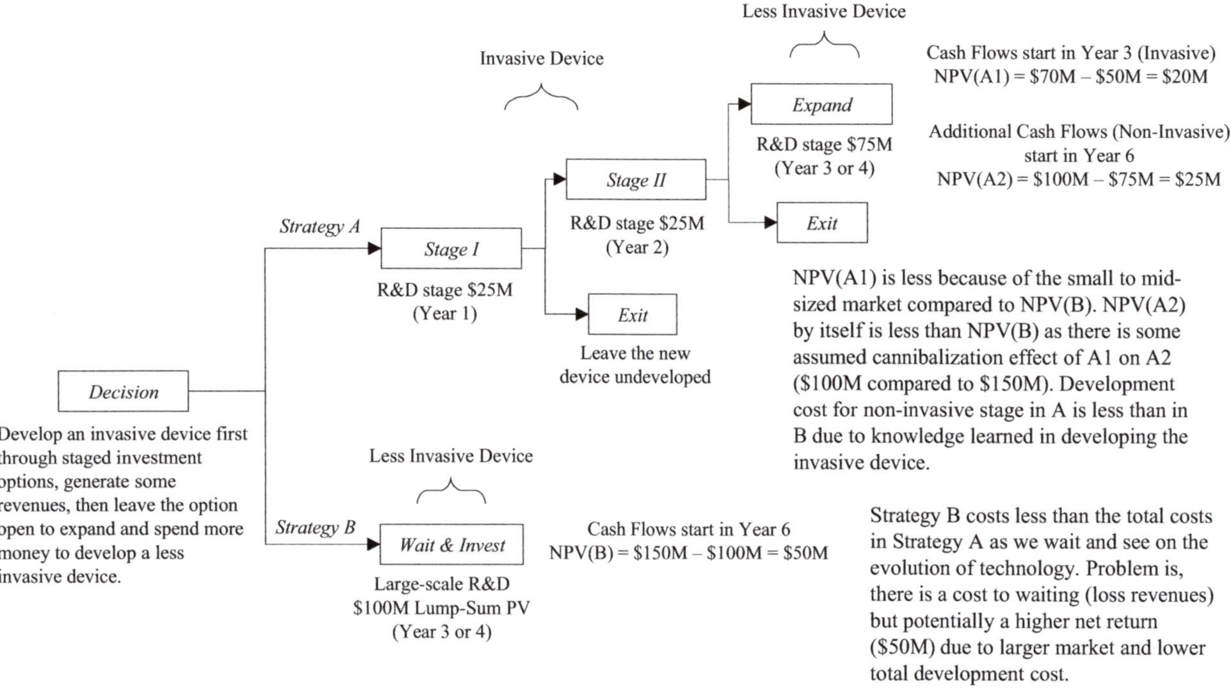
Less Invasive Device
Invasive Device
Cash Flows start in Year 3 (Invasive)
NPV(A1) = $70M – $50M = $20M
Expand
R&D stage $75M
(Year 3 or 4)
Additional Cash Flows (Non-Invasive)
start in Year 6
NPV(A2) = $100M – $75M = $25M
Stage II
R&D stage $25M
(Year 2)
Exit
Strategy A
Stage I
R&D stage $25M
(Year 1)
Exit
Leave the new
device undeveloped
NPV(A1) is less because of the small to mid-sized market compared to NPV(B). NPV(A2) by itself is less than NPV(B) as there is some assumed cannibalization effect of A1 on A2 ($100M compared to $150M). Development cost for non-invasive stage in A is less than in B due to knowledge learned in developing the invasive device.
Decision
Develop an invasive device first through staged investment options, generate some revenues, then leave the option open to expand and spend more money to develop a less invasive device.
Less Invasive Device
Strategy B
Wait & Invest
Large-scale R&D
$100M Lump-Sum PV
(Year 3 or 4)
Cash Flows start in Year 6
NPV(B) = $150M – $100M = $50M
Strategy B costs less than the total costs in Strategy A as we wait and see on the evolution of technology. Problem is, there is a cost to waiting (loss revenues) but potentially a higher net return ($50M) due to larger market and lower total development cost.

The decision whether to choose Strategy A or B depends on several considerations: How long is the delay before the revenues are obtained in B as compared to A? What is the cost of waiting if executing B versus A (net revenue and annualized cash flow losses in B as compared to A)? How much uncertainty and risks are involved in the device?

Real Options Valuation

Framing Options: Strategy Tree Analysis of Alternatives

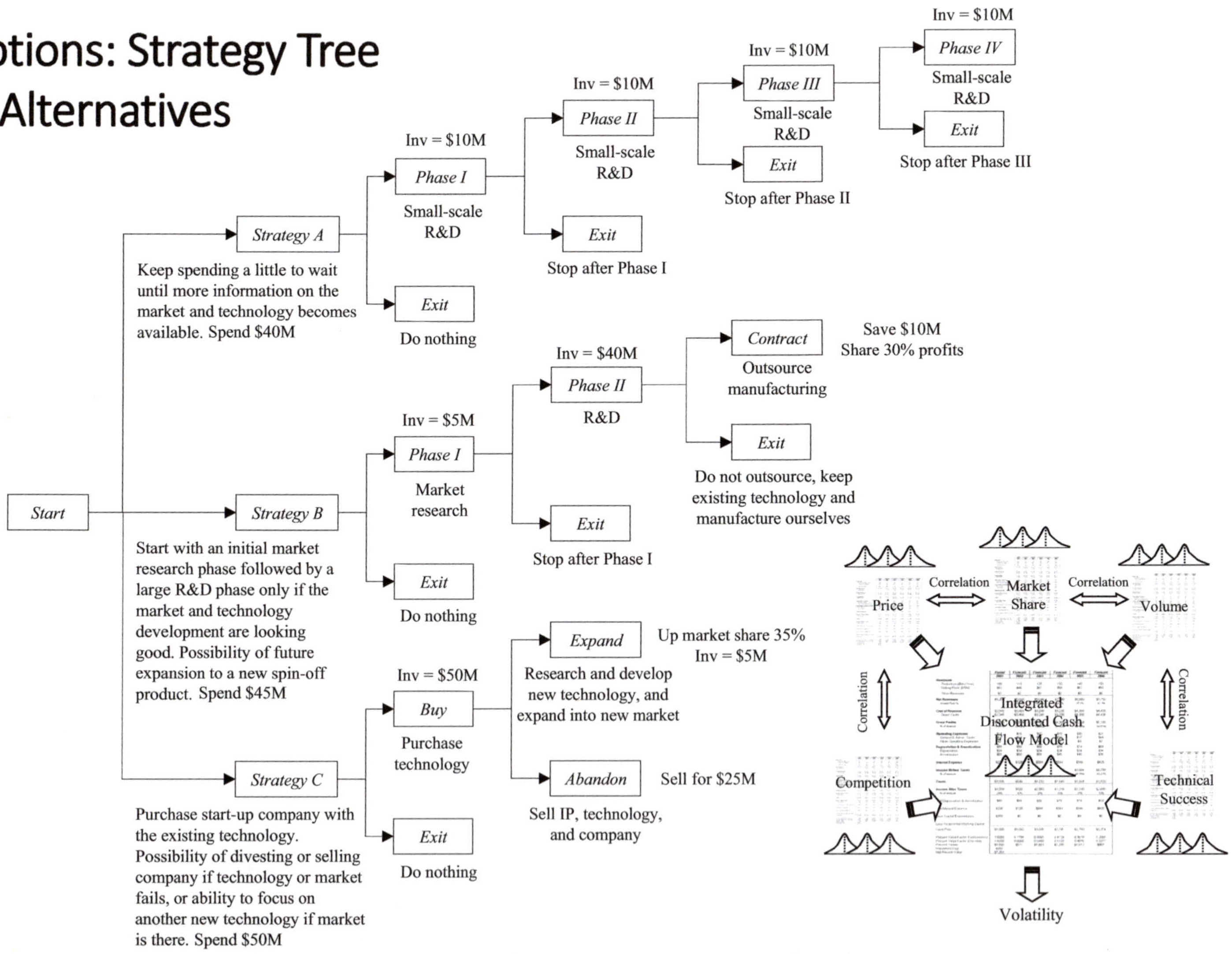

Framing Options: Strategy Tree Analysis of Alternatives

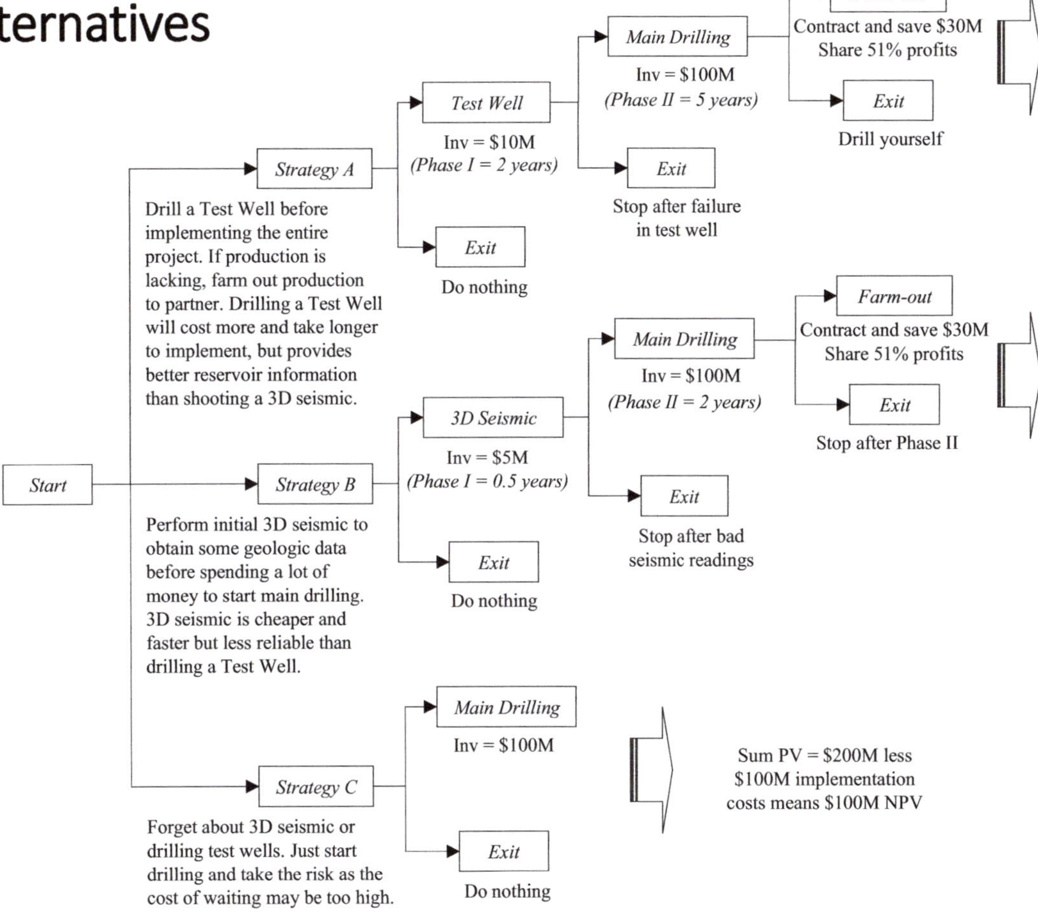
Start
Strategy A
Drill a Test Well before implementing the entire project. If production is lacking, farm out production to partner. Drilling a Test Well will cost more and take longer to implement, but provides better reservoir information than shooting a 3D seismic.
Test Well
Inv = $10M
(Phase I = 2 years)
Exit
Do nothing
Main Drilling
Inv = $100M
(Phase II = 5 years)
Exit
Stop after failure in test well
Farm-out
Contract and save $30M
Share 51% profits
Exit
Drill yourself
Sum PV = $200M but we are delaying full drilling, thus creating an annualized dividend rate of 4% ($8M losses in net cash flow per year)
Strategy B
Perform initial 3D seismic to obtain some geologic data before spending a lot of money to start main drilling. 3D seismic is cheaper and faster but less reliable than drilling a Test Well.
3D Seismic
Inv = $5M
(Phase I = 0.5 years)
Exit
Do nothing
Main Drilling
Inv = $100M
(Phase II = 2 years)
Exit
Stop after bad seismic readings
Farm-out
Contract and save $30M
Share 51% profits
Exit
Stop after Phase II
Sum PV = $200M
Strategy C
Forget about 3D seismic or drilling test wells. Just start drilling and take the risk as the cost of waiting may be too high.
Main Drilling
Inv = $100M
Exit
Do nothing
Sum PV = $200M less $100M implementation costs means $100M NPV

Real Options Valuation

STRATEGIC REAL OPTIONS

ABANDONMENT
Exit and salvage or sell the assets to cut losses, stop before executing the next phase after completing the current phase, contractual Termination for Convenience. To have an abandonment option, the holder must first own the asset.

BARRIER
The option comes in-the-money or out-of-the-money if the underlying asset value exceeds or does not exceed some pre-specified fixed or fluctuating contractual barrier. This option typically has lower value to the holder than a similarly specified option without the barriers. Combinations of single, double, upper, lower, knock-in, and knock-out barriers can be constructed.

CONTRACTION
Outsourcing, alliances, co-marketing, subcontractors, joint ventures, foreign partnerships, and other strategic relationships whereby cost is reduced and part of the asset's profits is shared with the partner. To have a contraction option, the holder must first own the asset.

EXPANSION
Platform technologies, mergers and acquisitions (new technologies, market, clients, or vertical solution), reusability and scalability, pre-investments, and pre-building facilities (faster and cheaper to pre-invest now then restart development in the future). To have an expansion option, the holder must first own the asset.

SEQUENTIAL
Stage-gate implementation of high-risk project development, prototyping, drug development phases, technology demonstration, contracts with multiple stages with the option to exit at any time, built-in flexibility to execute different courses of action at specific stages of development, milestones, R&D, and phased investments over different time periods.

SIMULTANEOUS
Multiple assets or investments are executed simultaneously to reduce risks that one of these assets or projects fails. This is the same computation as a combination into a single asset for an option to wait and defer or execute. The result for Simultaneous options is typically less than Sequential options given the same parameters and asset valuation.

SWITCHING
Switching among multiple vendors, modular designs, multiple inputs, or raw materials. This option allows production risk mitigation through multiple vendors and a strong industrial base, and takes advantage of market-based cost fluctuations. Negatively correlated assets tend to generate greater option values (portfolio diversification effects).

EXECUTION TYPES
American Options: Any time up to and including maturity date.
Asian Options: Backward-looking, time-specific.
Bermudan Options: Any time except during blackouts and vesting.
European Options: One time at maturity only.
American ≥ Bermudan ≥ European except for plain-vanilla call options with zero dividends, where all values are identical.

WAIT & DEFER/EXECUTE
Proof of concept to better determine the costs, profitability, and schedule risks of a project. Holding on to the opportunity with contract in place while reducing large-scale implementation risks, low-rate initial production, R&D, prototyping, and right of first refusal. Ability to wait and see for valuable information to arrive before deciding to execute the option if optimal.

Abandonment, Contraction, Expansion, and Switching options imply that the option holder currently owns the asset and, therefore, can sell it (abandon), reduce output and save on expenses (contract), expand upon it (expand), or change it out to an alternative (switch). Further, Switching options imply that the option holder can sequentially switch back and forth the underlying assets with some predetermined switching cost. Abandonment, Barrier, Contraction, Expansion, and Wait & Defer options typically have a single underlying asset, and can be executed in a single phase or multiple-phased Sequential option. Sequential options usually imply multiple phases (more than one) and a single underlying asset, and can be combined with the other types of real options. Finally, Switching and Simultaneous options imply more than one underlying asset exists and can be executed in a single phase at once or executed over time in a multiple-phased Sequential option.

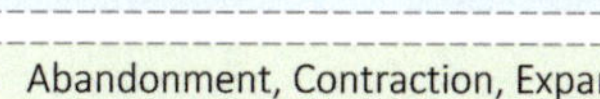

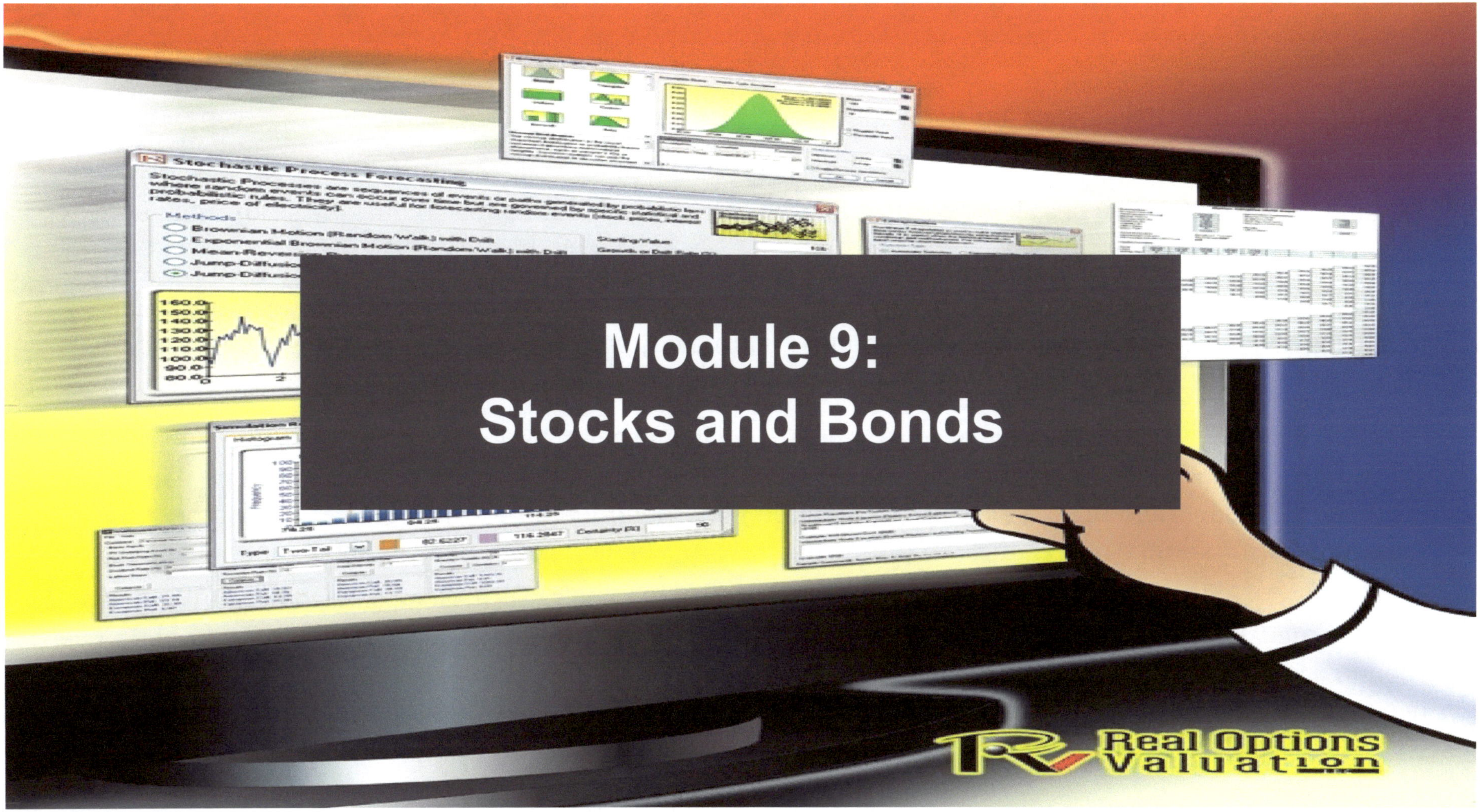

Module 9: Stocks and Bonds

Stocks and Bonds

The two main financing vehicles in a company are stocks (equity) and bonds. When these vehicles are traded in the market, sometimes they are repackaged and other derivative products are created, such as stock options and bond options. Other types of derivatives, such as forwards, futures, swaps, and swaptions, are typically created by the company to hedge its risks and to take advantage of upside opportunities.

- Risk and Return Trade-offs (arranged from low risk and low return to high risk and high return): US Treasury Bills–Notes–Bonds, Foreign Government Bonds, US Corporate Bonds, Foreign Corporate Bonds, Private Real Estate, US Common Stocks, Foreign Common Stocks, Commercial Real Estate, Junk Bonds, Derivatives (Options, Forwards, Futures, Swaps), Coins/Stamps/Art/Antiques/Collectibles.
- Bonds are considered debt and have specific payment covenants such as periodic coupon payments (typically annually and semiannually). Due to constant required payments, highly leveraged positions with significant debt imply a higher default probability and bankruptcy. Bond holders do not have voting rights, but they have seniority in payments in the event of bankruptcy.
- Common Stocks or common equity shareholders are owners of the company and have voting rights, but they take higher risk as residual claimants (last to be paid in a bankruptcy).
- Preferred Stocks are the hybrid of common stocks and bonds, with no voting rights but predetermined periodic dividend payments.

Stocks

- Considerations and Issues in Common Equity
  - IPO in the Primary Market and Public Stock Trades in Secondary Markets
  - High Flotation Costs
  - Proxy and Proxy Fight
  - Friendly vs. Hostile Takeovers, Poison Pills, and Golden Parachutes
  - Classification of Stocks (A, B, C)
  - Founders' Stocks (sole voting rights initially)
  - Corporations that are closely held versus publicly traded stocks
  - OTC unlisted trades (smaller stocks) versus Exchange listed trades NYSE/AMEX

Stocks II

- Stock price (P) is the sum of all present values of dividends (D). It is similar to the value of a bond (V), which is the sum of all present values of the coupon interest payments (INT) and the final payment at maturity (M):

$$\hat{P}_0 = \frac{D_1}{(1+k_S)^1} + \frac{D_1}{(1+k_S)^2} + \ldots + \frac{D_1}{(1+k_S)^\infty} = \sum_{t=1}^{\infty} \frac{D_t}{(1+k_S)^t} \qquad V_B = \sum_{i=1}^{N} \frac{INT}{(1+k_d)^N} + \frac{M}{(1+k_d)^N}$$

- Stock price valuation can be modeled depending on zero growth or constant growth (g). We can assume g = RR(ROE):

$$\hat{P}_0 = \frac{D}{k_S} \qquad k_S = \frac{D}{P_0}$$

Note: The expected rate of return = dividend yield when growth rate = 0.

$$\hat{P}_0 = \frac{D_0(1+g)}{k_S - g} = \frac{D_1}{k_S - g} \qquad k_S = \frac{D_1}{P_0} + g$$

Note: Constant growth rate can be computed using the Gordon Growth Model.

- Preferred stocks have fixed dividends; hence, the theoretical price of a preferred stock is:

$$V_{PS} = \frac{D_{PS}}{k_{PS}} \qquad k_{PS} = \frac{D_{PS}}{P_{PS}}$$

- What if there are no dividends? Use fundamental analysis. For example, P/E x Estimated Earnings = Intrinsic Price, where at market equilibrium, expected rate of return = required rate of return.

Stocks III

- Stock price is assumed to be stochastic because of all the exogenous factors that can impact its value over time... We can apply stochastic processes to attempt to model the distribution of stock prices such as using Brownian motion random walk Weiner processes.
- The stock market is assumed to be somewhat efficient. The Efficient Market Hypothesis (EMH) states:
  - Informationally efficient capital markets – security prices adjust rapidly to new information. This implies that if markets are efficient, the current price of a security fully reflects all the information currently available.
  - Weak Form Efficiency – current prices fully reflect all currently available historical market information. This implies that you cannot achieve excess returns using Technical Analysis. Tested using econometric autocorrelation tests, filters, trading rules, and differencing methods.
  - Semi-Strong Form Efficiency – current prices fully reflect all currently available historical and public market information. This implies that you cannot achieve excess returns using Fundamental Analysis. Tested with event studies (January effect, weekday effect) and fundamental ratios (P/E, B/M).
  - Strong Form Efficiency – current prices fully reflect all currently available historical, public, and private market information. This implies that private groups of investors cannot achieve excess returns. Tested by looking at insider trading and professional money managers' returns.
- Implications of EMH: Technical analysis has little to no value. Fundamental analysis is better where you should use a top-down approach (market, industry, firm). There is no superior performance by professional money managers as a group. Therefore, if the market is efficient, the best recommendation is to determine and quantify an investor's risk preferences, then perform a portfolio allocation among risky and riskless assets, and apply global diversification, with a focus on minimizing transaction costs and taxes.

Stock: Technical Analysis

- Suppose a stock pays a constant dividend of $1.82 and your required rate of return on the stock is 16%. What is the stock's implicit price?

$$\hat{P}_0 = \frac{1.82}{(1+0.16)^1} + \frac{1.82}{(1+0.16)^2} + \ldots + \frac{1.82}{(1+0.16)^{50}} + .. + \frac{1.82}{(1+0.16)^{100}} + \ldots + \frac{1.82}{(1+0.16)^{\infty}} \quad \text{or} \quad P = \frac{D}{k_S} = 1.82 \div 0.16 = \$11.38$$

Alternatively, if the stock is priced at $11.38 and its dividend is $1.82, the expected return on the stock is $k_S = \frac{D}{P} = 1.82 \div 11.38 = 16\%$.

- Assume the same stock as above but its dividends are expected to grow at 10% a year. What is its new implicit price? What is its expected required rate of return?

$$\hat{P}_0 = \frac{D_0(1+g)}{k_S - g} = \frac{D_1}{k_S - g} = \frac{1.82(1+0.1)}{0.16-0.10} = \$33.33 \qquad k_S = \frac{D_1}{P_0} + g = \frac{1.82(1+0.1)}{33.33} + 0.1 = 16\%$$

- Suppose the growth rate is 30% for the first 3 years and drops down to 10% after that. Assume that the dividend paid at time zero is $1.82 and a shareholder required rate of return at 16%. Calculate the value of this stock.

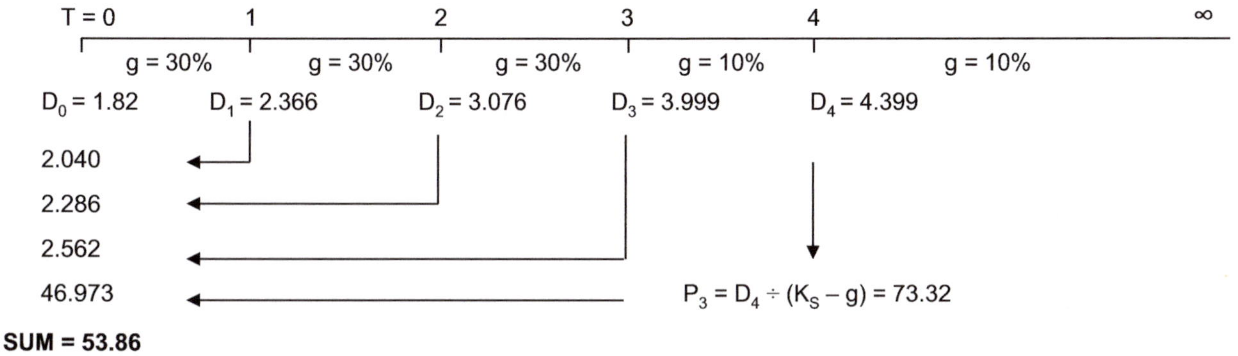

Technical vs. Fundamental Analysis

- Fundamental analysis – securities' prices are determined by the supply and demand for the underlying security based on economic fundamentals such as expected return and risk as well as company- or industry-specific variables.
- Efficient market hypothesis (EMH) – all information has already been absorbed into prices.
- Technical analysis – evidence of changes in supply and demand, and, hence, security price changes, through market signals and indicators.
- The major difference between these three views is the speed with which news and information are embedded into security prices.
- Fundamentalists look for reasons why the valuation band shifts upward. Price changes occur over a period of days or even weeks.
- Technicians look for signs that the valuation band has moved. Price changes will occur over long periods of time.
- Efficient market followers say when events happen, the price will shift instantaneously.

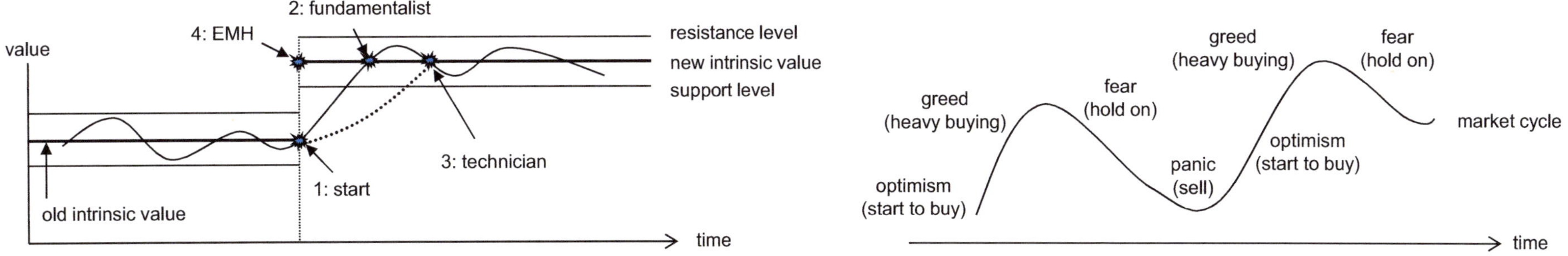

Technical vs. Fundamental Analysis II

- Advantages of technical analysis
  - Quick and easy
  - No messing with data or adjusting for accounting problems
  - Incorporates psychological as well as economic reasons behind price changes
  - Tells when to buy, but not why investors are buying
- Disadvantages of technical analysis
  - Efficient market followers say it doesn't work
  - If it worked, it would self-destruct – self-fulfilling prophesy
  - Interpretation of rules are too subjective and decision variables change over time
  - Technical analysis falls into two categories
  - General market movement indicators
  - Individual stock selection indicators
- Technicians take one of the following two views
  - Contrarian View – the majority of the investors are wrong, so wait and do the opposite. This view comes from the greed or panic view in the investment process. As the market advances, investors are afraid that they will be left behind and their greed tells them to buy. As the market plunges, they panic and sell. In the end, investors tend to do the wrong thing at the right time.
  - Momentum View (Follow-the-smart-money) – smart investors know what they are doing, so, you had better jump on the bandwagon.
  - Market Indicators View – there are multiple market metrics and indicators that can help predict the movement of stock prices in the near future

Technical vs. Fundamental Analysis III: Contrarian View

- Mutual fund cash position – a good indicator of institutional investors' expectations
  - Mutual fund ratio (MFR) = mutual fund cash ÷ total fund assets
  - MFR > 13% funds bearish, contrarians bullish (buying)
  - MFR < 7% funds bullish, contrarians bearish (selling)
- Investor credit balances in brokerage accounts
  - Falling balances mean investors bullish, contrarians bearish (sell)
  - Rising balances mean investors bearish, contrarians bullish (buy)
- Investment advisory opinions – opinions by analysts
  - Investment advisory opinion ratio (IAOR) = bearish opinions ÷ total opinions
  - IAOR ≥ 60%, bearish market, contrarians bullish (buy)
  - IAOR ≤ 20%, bullish market, contrarians bearish (sell)
- OTC versus NYSE Volume
  - Volume Ratio (VR) = OTC Volume ÷ NYSE Volume
  - VR ≥ 112%, high bullish speculation, contrarians bearish (sell)
  - VR ≤ 87%, bearish, contrarians bullish (buy)
- CBOE Put-Call Ratio
  - Put Call Ratio (PCR) = Puts ÷ Calls
  - PCR ≥ 0.9, market bearish, contrarians bullish (buy)
  - PCR ≤ 0.7, bullish, contrarians bearish (sell)
- Futures traders bullish on stock index futures
  - 70% or more speculators are bullish, contrarians bearish (sell)
  - 30% or less speculators are bullish, contrarians bullish (buy)

Technical vs. Fundamental Analysis IV: Momentum View

- Confidence Index
  - Confidence Index = Barron's Average Yield on Top 10 Grade Corporate Bonds ÷ Dow Jones Average 40 Bonds
  - Confidence Index = Quality Bonds Yield ÷ Average Bonds Yields
  - In periods of confidence, investors sell quality bonds and buy lower quality bonds, quality bond prices fall and yield rises, CI rises in confidence periods, and yield spread narrows
- T-Bill and Eurodollar yield spread
  - Yield spread widens in times of international crisis as money flows into safer US Treasuries
- Short sales by specialists
  - Specialist Short Sales = Specialists' Short Sales ÷ NYSE Total Short Sales
  - Below 30% implies bullish and specialists are buying
  - Above 50% implies bearish and specialists are selling
- Debit balances in brokerage accounts (Margin Debt)
  - Increase in debit balances implies purchasing by astute buyers (bullish)
  - Decrease in debit balances implies selling by astute traders (bearish)
- Miscellaneous stock price and volume techniques
  - Support and resistance levels
  - Moving average lines
  - Relative strength ratios (RS = Stock Price ÷ Market Price)

Technical vs. Fundamental Analysis V: Market Indicators View

- Market Breadth – using the advance decline (AD) line
  - If the AD line moves with the index, the movement is broadly based across the entire market and not tied to a specific sector
- Short Interest
  - Short Interest Ratio (SIR) = Outstanding Short Interest ÷ Average Daily Volume
  - SIR above 4.0 implies potential demand and is a bullish sign
  - SIR below 3.0 implies potential for short selling and is a bearish sign
- Stocks above their 200-day moving average
  - If greater than 80%, the market is overbought and is bearish
  - If less than 20%, the market is oversold and is bullish

Bonds

- Types of bonds: Treasury bonds (bills, notes, and bonds), zero coupon bonds, corporate bonds, agency bonds, municipal bonds, and foreign bonds.
- Terminology: Par face value, coupon payments, coupon interest rates and maturity, call provision (higher coupons or sold at a discount), sinking fund provision, convertibles (lower coupons), warrants (lower coupons), income bond, indexed bond, discount bond, premium bond.
- Yield to Maturity: YTM is the cost (K_d) of a bond if the bond is held to maturity. This is the Interest Rate on the standard time value of money inputs (N, I, PV, FV, PMT).
- Types of bond risks
  - Interest rate risk: prices decrease when general interest rates increase
  - Reinvestment rate risk: risk of subsequent decreases in interest rates leading to a lower income bond in the portfolio or that revenues received at maturity cannot be reinvested at a similarly high paying interest bond
  - Default and credit risk: corporate bonds defaulting, especially junk bonds
  - Sovereign and country risk: foreign bonds, especially in developing countries or emerging markets
- Bond price behavior
  - Bond prices move inversely to interest rates
  - Bond price volatility is directly related to its maturity
  - Price volatility increases at a decreasing rate as term to maturity increases
  - Price volatility is inversely related to the bond's coupon rate
  - Price changes are asymmetrical as bond prices go up faster when interest rates fall

Bonds II

- Bond Ratings
  - S&P (AAA, AA, A, BBB – BB, B, CCC, D)
  - Moody's (Aaa, Aa, A, Baa – Ba, B, Caa, C)
  - Bonds rated BBB or Baa or higher are considered investment-grade bonds
  - Junk bonds if rated lower than BBB or Baa are high-risk and high-yield speculative bonds
- Asset-backed securities – credit card receivables, certificate for auto receivables, mortgage bonds, indentures/debentures
- Municipals – general obligation (using taxing power to repay) versus revenue bonds (paying from the earning power of a specific project, e.g., tolls)
- Foreign bonds – by foreign borrower issuing in another country in local currency, Yankee bonds, Samurai bonds and Bulldog bonds; e.g., a French multinational selling foreign Yankee bonds denominated in US dollars to US or other investors
- Eurobond – sold in a foreign country but denominated in a local currency – Eurodollar, Euroyen, and Eurosterling bonds; e.g., a US multinational selling US dollar denominated Eurobonds in the Virgin Islands

Bond Valuation

Value of a Bond:

$$V_B = \sum_{t=1}^{N} \frac{INT_t}{(1+k_d)^t} + \frac{M}{(1+k_d)^N} = INT[PVIFA_{Kd,N}] + M[PVIF_{Kd,N}]$$

Value of a Bond:
(semiannual coupons)

$$V_B = \sum_{t=1}^{2N} \frac{INT_t/2}{(1+\frac{k_d}{2})^t} + \frac{M}{(1+\frac{k_d}{2})^{2N}} = \frac{INT}{2}[PVIFA_{\frac{Kd}{2},2N}] + M[PVIF_{\frac{Kd}{2},2N}]$$

Value of a Bond:
(perpetuity consol)

$$V_B = \frac{INT}{k_d}$$

Yield to Maturity:

$$YTM \approx \frac{C + \frac{Par - Price}{Years}}{\frac{Par + Price}{2}}$$

Yield to Call:

$$V_B = \sum_{t=1}^{N} \frac{INT_t}{(1+k_d)^t} + \frac{Call\,Price}{(1+k_d)^N}$$

where Current Yield = Interest / Value

Macaulay Duration:

$$\sum_{i=1}^{n} \frac{PVCF_i}{V_B} time$$

Modified Duration:

$$\frac{Macaulay}{\left(1 + \frac{YTM}{\#coupons}\right)}$$

Convexity:

$$\frac{d^2P}{di^2} = \frac{\sum_{t=1}^{n} \frac{CF}{(1+i)^t}(t^2+t)}{(1+i)^2}$$

where DP/P = –MD[Di] + ½C[Di]^2

Real Options Valuation

Bond Valuation II

- Consider a $1000 par bond with a 12% coupon rate (CR) and a 25-year maturity. If the bond has a 12% required rate of return (RRR) and interest is paid annually, calculate its value.

$$V_B = \frac{120}{(1+0.12)^1} + \frac{120}{(1+0.12)^2} + \ldots + \frac{120}{(1+0.12)^{25}} + \frac{1000}{(1+0.12)^{25}} = 1000$$

Excel: NPER = 25, FV = 1000, PMT = 120, RATE =12%, calculate PV = –1000.

Note: If CR = RRR, the bond sells at par! In this example, the value of the bond is $1000.

- For a 25-year bond paying 12% coupons, with a required rate of return at 16% and semiannual interest payments, what is its value?

Excel: FV = 1000, PMT = 120, N = 25 x 2 = 50, RATE = 0.16/2 = 0.08, calculate PV = –754.98

Note: if the coupon rate is lower than the prevailing interest rate (RRR), the bond value $754.98 is less than par.

Bond Valuation III

- What are the approximate YTM and actual YTM for a $900 bond price, offering $100 annual coupons maturing in 20 years where the par face value is $1000?

$$YTM \approx \frac{C + \frac{Par - Price}{Years}}{\frac{Par + Price}{2}} \qquad YTM \approx \frac{100 + \frac{1000 - 900}{20}}{\frac{1000 + 900}{2}} = 11.05\%$$

Actual YTM, use Excel: PV = –900, FV = 1000, NPER = 20, PMT = 100, calculate RATE = 11.28%.

- Calculate both the YTM and YTC of a 20-year semiannual 10% coupon bond that is callable in 5 years for $1100 and is currently selling for $1150.

YTM: NPER = 2 x 20, PMT = 100/2 = 50, PV = –1150, FV = 1000, calculate RATE = 4.22% x 2 = 8.44%.

Note: Remember to multiply by 2 for the interest as it should be annualized for this semiannual coupon bond.

YTC: NPER = 2 x 5, PMT = 100/2 = 50, PV = –1150, FV = 1100, calculate RATE = 3.99% x 2 = 7.98%.

Note: Remember that FV is the call price of $1100.

Bond Valuation IV

- Graph the relationship between the market value of a bond, the general market rate of interest, and the length of maturity.

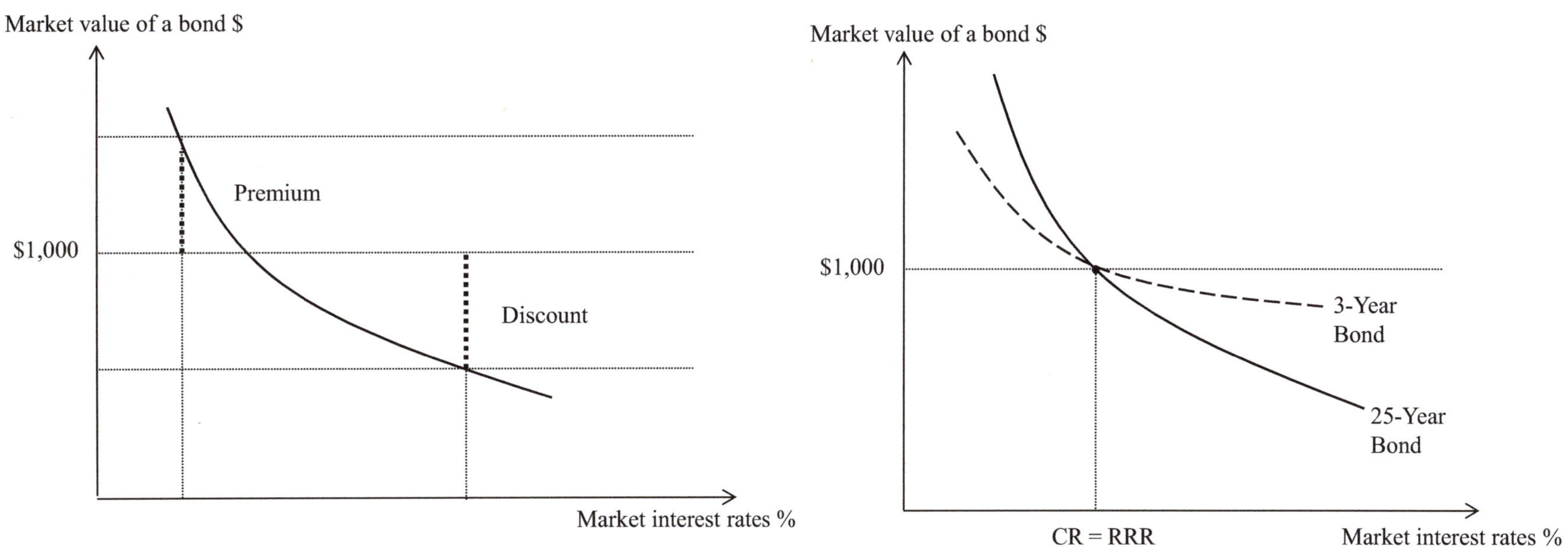

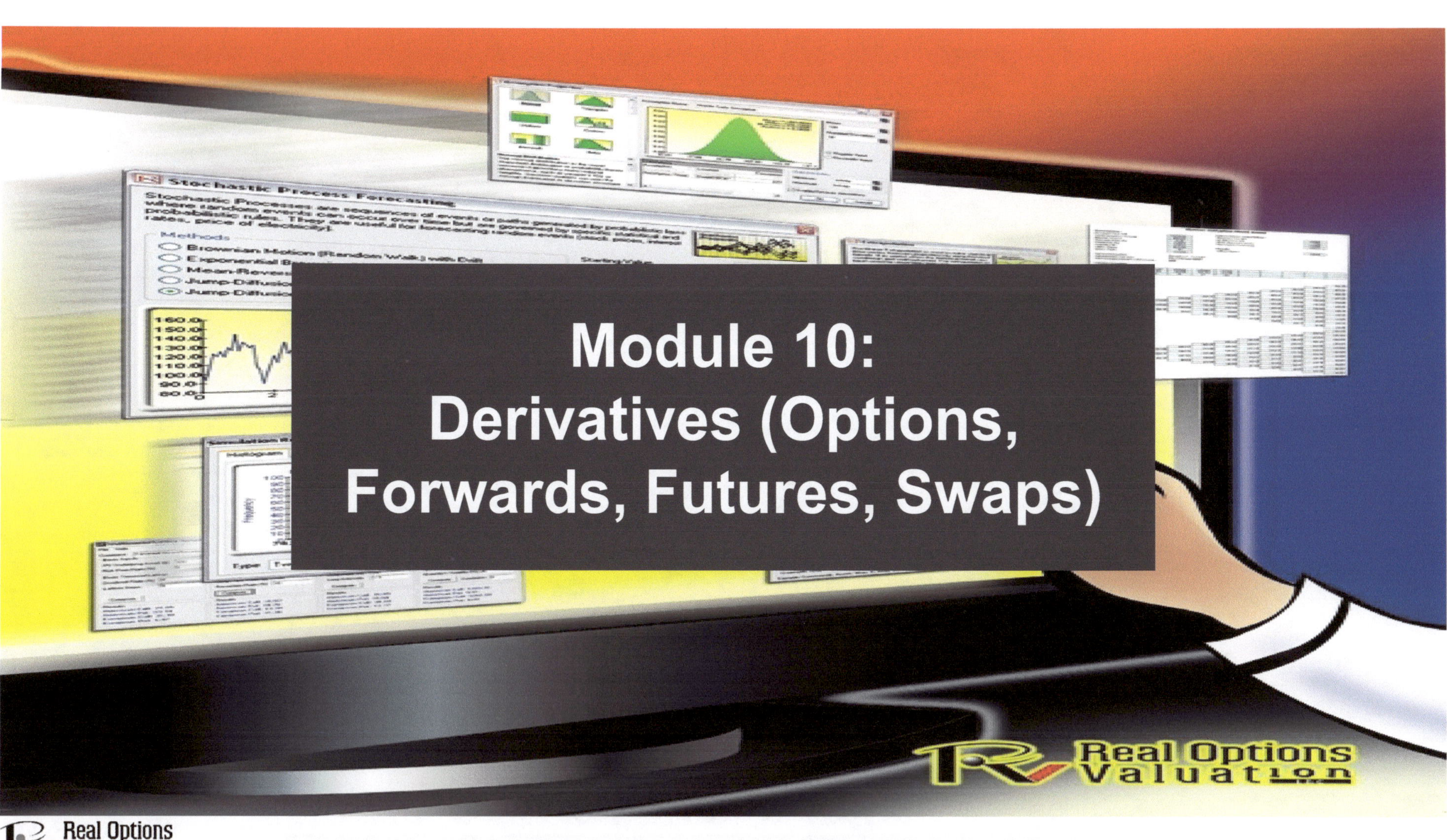
Module 10:
Derivatives (Options,
Forwards, Futures, Swaps)
Stochastic Process Forecasting
Methods
Real Options
Valuation

Financial Derivatives

- Financial derivatives: These are financial instruments whose payoffs depend on an underlying financial instrument or asset. The most common derivatives are forwards, futures, options, and swaps.
- Forwards: A forward contract is a contract negotiated in the present that provides the contract holder both the right and the full legal obligation to conduct a transaction at a specific time in the future involving a specific quantity and type of asset at a predetermined price., e.g., agree today to exchange a certain amount of dollars for marks with another party on a specific future date at a specific exchange rate. Forward contracts are a useful way of resolving uncertainty.
- Futures: A futures contract is a forward contract that has been highly standardized and closely specified. The futures contract, like the forward contract, calls for the exchange of some good at a future date for cash, with the payment for the good to occur at the future delivery date. The payment price is determined at the initial time of the contract. The buyer of the contract receives the good and pays for it.
- Differences between forwards and futures
    - Forwards are private contracts and are not traded on exchanges.
    - Futures are traded on organized exchanges.
    - Forwards are unique contracts satisfying the needs of the parties involved.
    - Futures are highly standardized since a futures contract specifies the quantity, quality, delivery date, and delivery mechanism and is standardized.
    - Forwards have default risk as the seller may not deliver and the buyer does not accept.
    - Futures are guaranteed by the exchange's clearinghouse.
    - Forwards require no cash transactions until delivery date.
    - Futures require traders to post margin money in order to trade.
    - Forwards are not regulated and are considered private arrangements.
    - Futures market and trading are regulated by the authorities.
    - Regardless of the institutional differences, forwards and futures are highly similar contracts and are priced according to identical economic concepts.

Financial Derivatives II

- Options: An options contract gives the owner the right but not the legal obligation to conduct a transaction involving an underlying asset at a predetermined future date and at a predetermined price (the exercise or strike price), but the option only provides the long position the right to decide whether or not to trade and the seller the obligation to perform.
  - The owner of a call option has the right to purchase the underlying good at a specified price for a specified time period, while the owner of a put option has the right to sell the underlying good at a specified time period. To acquire these rights, owners of options must buy them by paying a price called the premium to the seller of the option.
  - For every owner of an option, there must be a seller, called the option writer.
  - There are four possible positions: the buyer of the call option, the seller or writer of the call option, the buyer of a put option, and the seller or writer of a put option.
- Swaps: A swap is an agreement between two or more parties to exchange sets of cash flows over a specified period of time in the future. The parties agreeing to swap are called counterparties, and the cash flows are generally tied to the value of debt instruments or foreign exchange rates. The two major types of swaps are interest rate swaps and exchange rate swaps.
- Other types of derivatives include Options on Futures, Swaptions, and Exotics (combinations of different derivatives). These securities are created based on market demand and a need for such devices as well as due to the advances in financial engineering concepts, but pricing these vehicles is very difficult.
- Applications of financial derivatives: Derivatives have grown rapidly in the recent past because they add many important features to the markets including
  - Market completeness – allows for any and all identifiable payoffs to be obtained by trading securities available in the market to fulfill investors' trading needs.
  - Speculation – lets traders take high-level risk positions adding completeness.
  - Risk management – provides for risk hedging and risk management to shift risk to market speculators.
  - Arbitrage –makes the market more efficient because it is easier to arbitrage away any mispricing,.
  - Trading efficiency – allows for ease and more efficiency as trading market index futures or interest rate futures is easier than having large, diversified securities or Treasury portfolios.

Options

- An option is a contract that gives its holder the right to buy or sell an asset at some predetermined price within a specified period of time.
- An option does not obligate its owner to take any action.
- Call option is an option to buy a specified number of shares of a security within some future period.
- Put option is an option to sell a specified number of shares of a security within some future period.
- Exercise price is the strike price or the price stated in the option contract at which the security can be bought or sold.
- Option price is market price of the option contract.
- Expiration date is the date the option expires or matures.
- Formula value is the intrinsic value of an option, the value of a call option if it were exercised today, and is equal to the current stock price minus the strike price.
- Covered option is a call option written against a stock held in a portfolio.
- Naked option is an option sold without the stock to back it up.
- In-the-money call is a call option whose exercise price exceeds the current stock price.
- LEAP is Long-term Equity Anticipation security similar to conventional options except that it is a long-term option with maturities of up to 2½ years.

Options II

- American Options allow the owner to exercise the option at any time before or at expiration. European Options can only be exercised at expiration. If both options have the same characteristics, an American Option is worth more than, or at least the same as, a European Option.
- When the stock price S is above the strike price X, a call option has value and is said to be in-the-money, i.e., when $S - X > 0$, a call option is in-the-money.
- When the stock price S is at the strike price X, a call option has no value and is said to be at-the-money, i.e., when $S - X = 0$, a call option is at-the-money.
- When the stock price S is below the strike price X, a call option has no value and is said to be out-of-the-money, i.e., when $S - X < 0$, a call option is out-of-the-money.
- When the stock price S is above the strike price X, a put option has no value and is said to be out-of-the-money, i.e., when $S - X > 0$, a put option is out-of-the-money.
- When the stock price S is at the strike price X, a put option has no value and is said to be at-the-money, i.e., when $S - X = 0$, a put option is at-the-money.
- When the stock price S is below the strike price X, a put option has value and is said to be in-the-money, i.e., when $S - X < 0$, a put option is in-the-money.
- Why trade options?
  - Speculation (calls and puts are cheaper than stocks and more volatile)
  - Risk reduction (adjust risk-return of portfolio, eliminate risk, combine with other assets)
  - Transaction cost reduction
  - Tax reduction
  - Market restriction avoidance (avoid restriction on short selling by buying puts)
- Options are standardized to promote liquidity.
  - Chicago Board of Options Exchange – stocks, indexes, and Treasuries
  - Philadelphia Stock Exchange – stocks, futures, currencies, and indexes
  - American Stock Exchange – stocks and indexes
  - New York Stock Exchange – stocks and indexes
  - Chicago Mercantile Exchange – agricultural, stocks, and currencies

Option Payoff

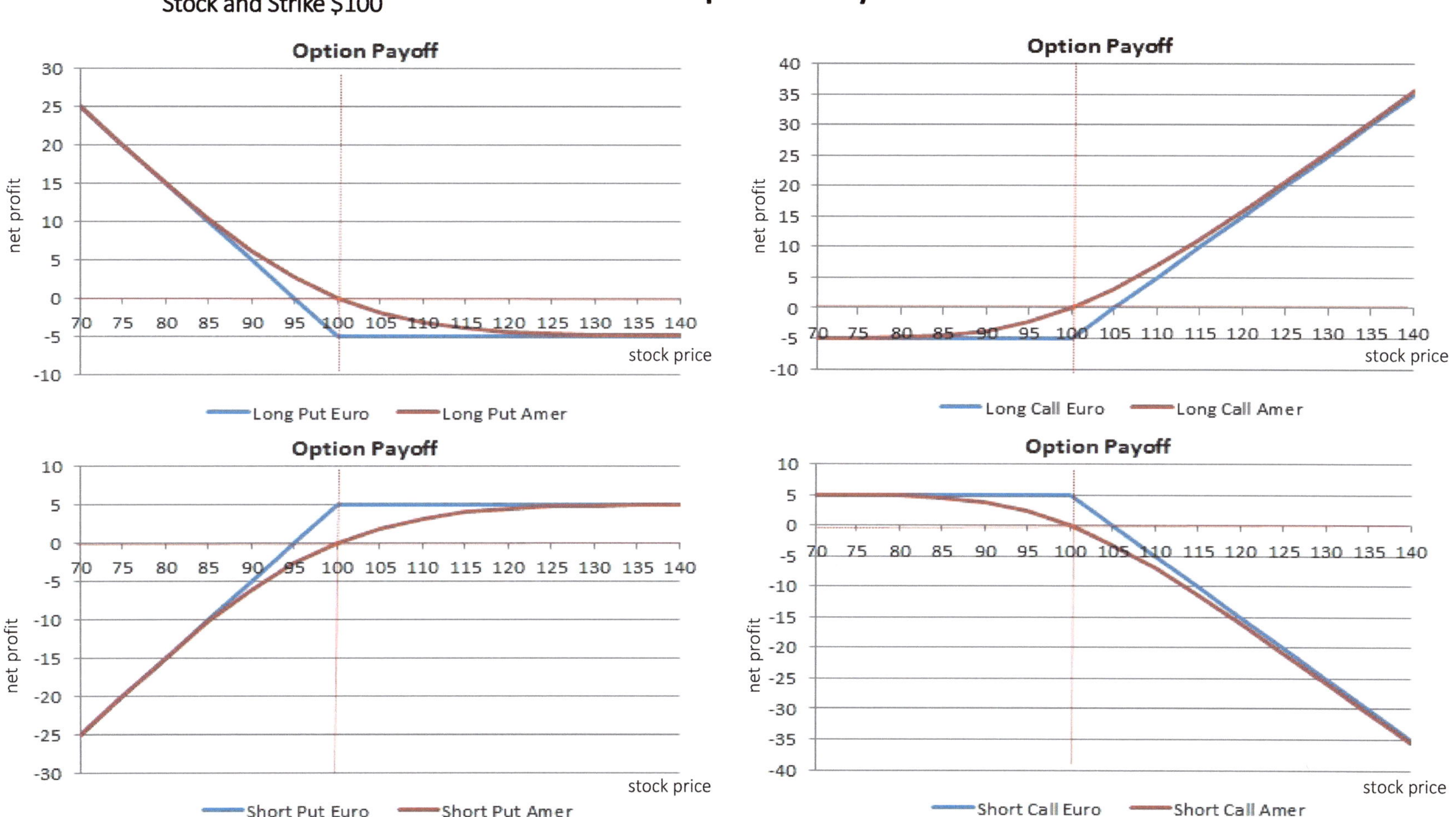

Real Options Valuation

Option Valuation: Closed-Form Models

- European options (calls and puts) can be solved easily with a Black–Scholes–Merton model. The Generalized Black–Scholes model shown below is an example of a closed-form mathematical solution. For example, using the required inputs below on the left, we can get the value of a European call option by substituting the input parameters into the closed-form equation. The value of the option is $12.3360.
- Using the same input parameters, we can also solve the option value using open-form simulation and binomial lattice approaches. The results of these approaches are shown in the next two slides.

$$Call = Se^{-qT}\Phi\left[\frac{\ln(S/X)+(rf-q+\sigma^2/2)T}{\sigma\sqrt{T}}\right]-Xe^{-rf(T)}\Phi\left[\frac{\ln(S/X)+(rf-q-\sigma^2/2)T}{\sigma\sqrt{T}}\right]$$

$$Call - Put = Stock - Xe^{-r(T-t)}$$

Closed Form

Stock Price	S	100.0000
Strike Price	X	100.0000
Maturity	T	1.0000
Risk-Free	rf	5.00%
Volatility	σ	25.00%
Dividend	q	0.00%
BS	**Call**	**12.3360**

Options Pricing Model assumptions:

1. The stocks underlying the call options provides no dividends during the life of the option.
2. No transaction costs are involved with the sale or purchase of either the stock or the option.
3. The short-term risk-free interest rate is known and is constant during the life of the option.
4. Security buyers may borrow any fraction of the purchase price at the short-term risk-free rate.
5. Short-term selling is permitted without penalty and sellers immediately receive the full cash proceeds at today's price for securities sold short.
6. A call option can be exercised only on its expiration date.
7. Security trading takes place in continuous time and stock prices move in continuous time.

Option Valuation: Simulation Models

- Monte Carlo Simulation Approach using an exponential Brownian Motion, simulates all possible paths over time T with subinterval δt.
- Epsilon is simulated seeds from the standard normal N(0,1) distribution.
- Many simulations are required for increased accuracy.
- Variance-reduction techniques are required for increased efficiency.

$$S_{t+1} = S_t e^{(rf - q - \sigma^2/2)\delta t + \sigma \varepsilon \sqrt{\delta t}}$$

To quantify the uncertainty and forecast the actual cash flows, multiple simulations are run.

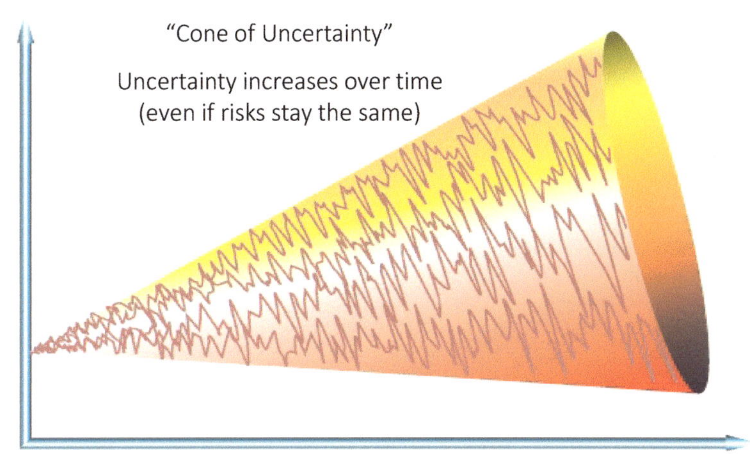
"Cone of Uncertainty"
Uncertainty increases over time
(even if risks stay the same)

Option Valuation: Lattices

- Comparison of approaches
- Black–Scholes: $12.3360
- Binomial:

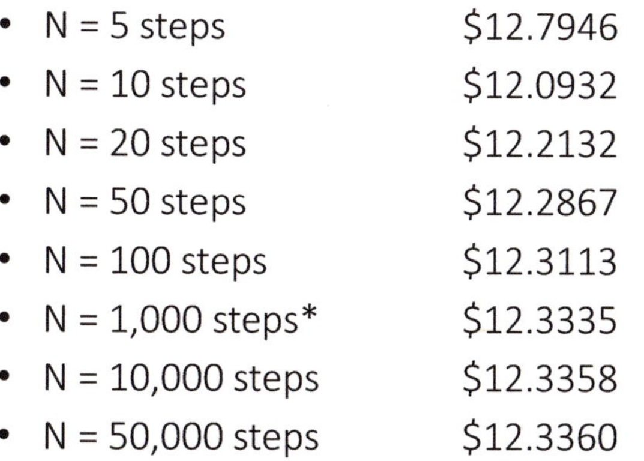

  - N = 5 steps $12.7946
  - N = 10 steps $12.0932
  - N = 20 steps $12.2132
  - N = 50 steps $12.2867
  - N = 100 steps $12.3113
  - N = 1,000 steps* $12.3335
  - N = 10,000 steps $12.3358
  - N = 50,000 steps $12.3360

  *Convergence typically happens around 500–1000 steps.

- Simulation: (10,000 simulations: $12.3360)

Maximum between executing the option or letting it expire
Letting it expire = $0 (expires out-of-the-money worthless)
Executing the option = $S_0u^5 - X$ = $174.9 – $100 = $74.9

Intermediate value = [P(41.8) + (1 – P)(16.2)] exp(-rf*dt) = $29.2

12.79
19.6
5.8
29.2
9.8
1.6
41.8
16.2
3.1
0.0
57.4
26.1
6.1
0.0
0.0
74.9
Max [$74.9, 0]
39.8
11.8
0.0
0.0
0.0

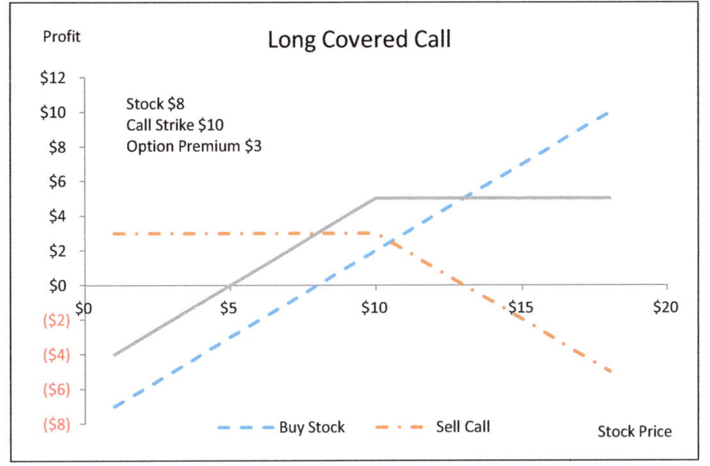
Long Covered Call
Profit
Stock $8
Call Strike $10
Option Premium $3
$12
$10
$8
$6
$4
$2
$0
($2)
($4)
($6)
($8)
$0
$5
$10
$15
$20
Buy Stock
Sell Call
Stock Price

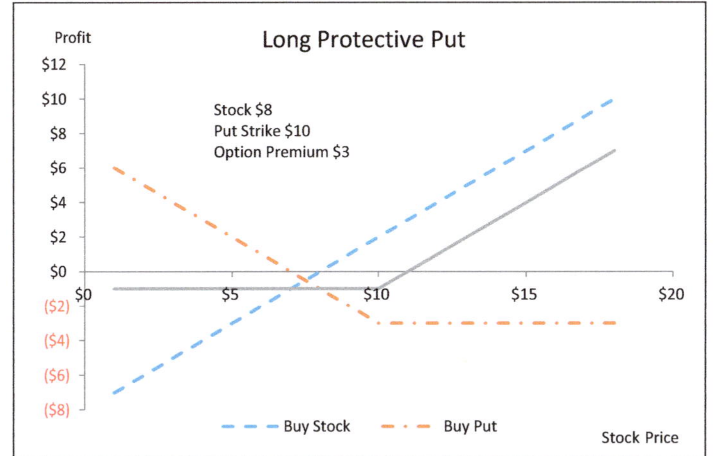
Long Protective Put
Profit
Stock $8
Put Strike $10
Option Premium $3
$12
$10
$8
$6
$4
$2
$0
($2)
($4)
($6)
($8)
$0
$5
$10
$15
$20
Buy Stock
Buy Put
Stock Price

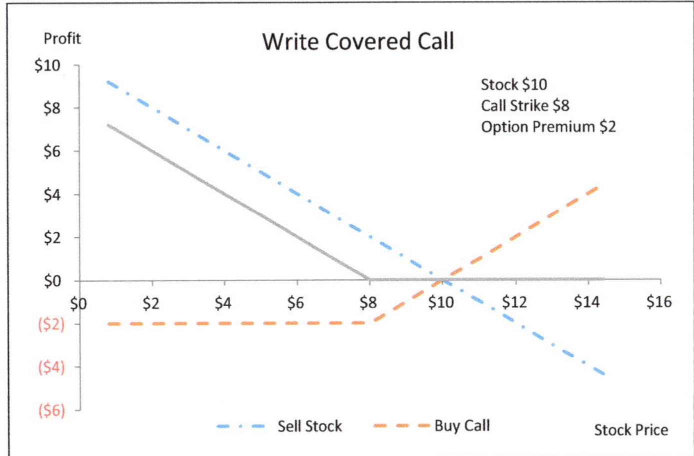
Write Covered Call
Profit
Stock $10
Call Strike $8
Option Premium $2
$10
$8
$6
$4
$2
$0
($2)
($4)
($6)
$0
$2
$4
$6
$8
$10
$12
$14
$16
Sell Stock
Buy Call
Stock Price

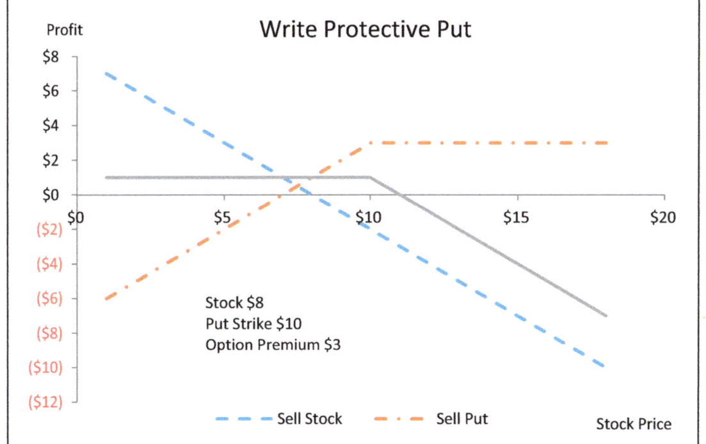
Write Protective Put
Profit
Stock $8
Put Strike $10
Option Premium $3
$8
$6
$4
$2
$0
($2)
($4)
($6)
($8)
($10)
($12)
$0
$5
$10
$15
$20
Sell Stock
Sell Put
Stock Price

Real Options
Valuation

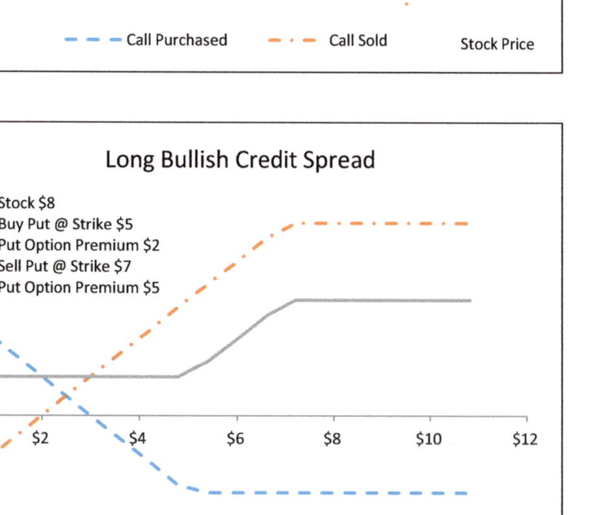
Long Bullish Debit Spread
Profit
Stock $8
Buy Call @ Strike $10
Call Option Premium $3
Sell Call @ Strike $12
Call Option Premium $2.5
$8
$6
$4
$2
$0
($2)
($4)
($6)
$0
$5
$10
$15
$20
$25
Call Purchased
Call Sold
Stock Price

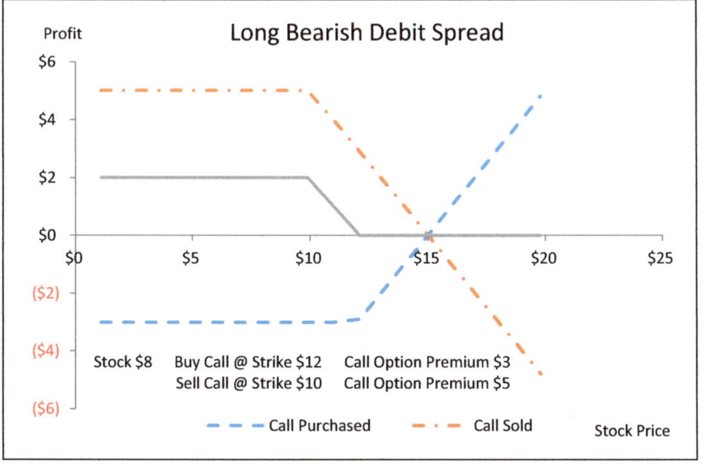

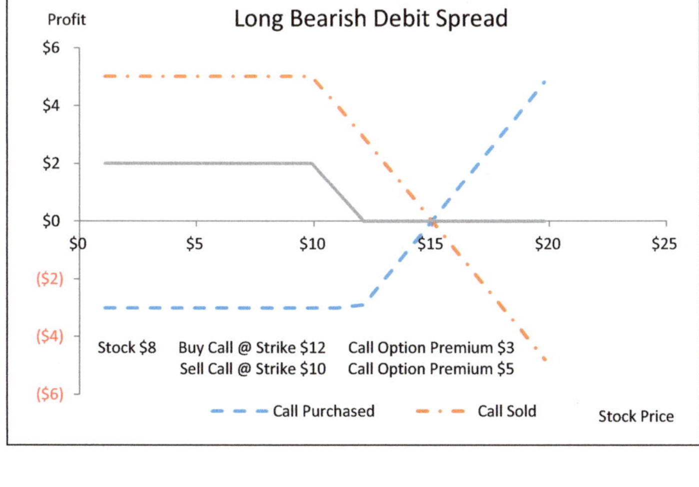
Long Bearish Debit Spread
Profit
$6
$4
$2
$0
($2)
($4)
($6)
$0
$5
$10
$15
$20
$25
Stock $8
Buy Call @ Strike $12
Sell Call @ Strike $10
Call Option Premium $3
Call Option Premium $5
Call Purchased
Call Sold
Stock Price

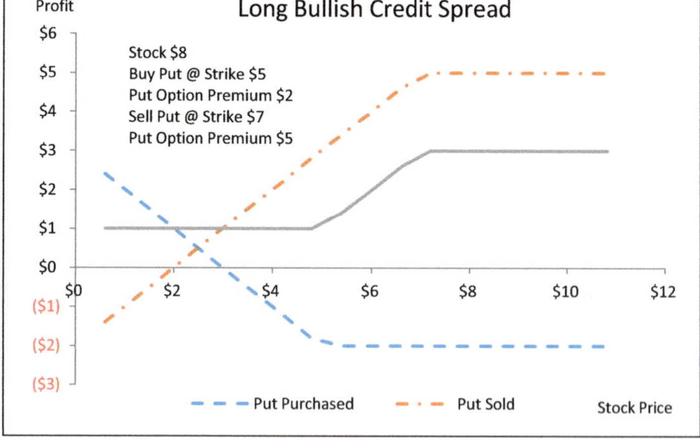
Long Bullish Credit Spread
Profit
Stock $8
Buy Put @ Strike $5
Put Option Premium $2
Sell Put @ Strike $7
Put Option Premium $5
$6
$5
$4
$3
$2
$1
$0
($1)
($2)
($3)
$0
$2
$4
$6
$8
$10
$12
Put Purchased
Put Sold
Stock Price

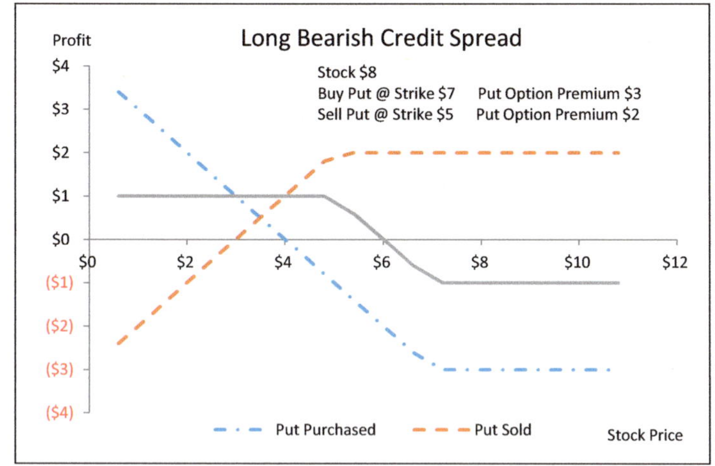
Long Bearish Credit Spread
Profit
Stock $8
Buy Put @ Strike $7
Sell Put @ Strike $5
Put Option Premium $3
Put Option Premium $2
$4
$3
$2
$1
$0
($1)
($2)
($3)
($4)
$0
$2
$4
$6
$8
$10
$12
Put Purchased
Put Sold
Stock Price

Real Options
Valuation

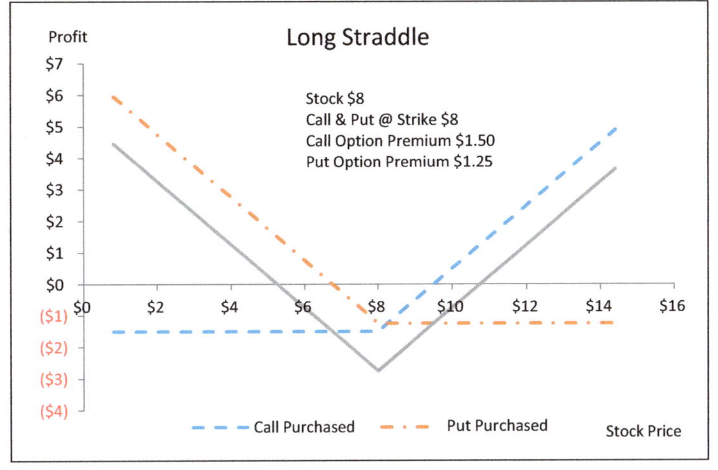
Long Straddle
Profit
Stock $8
Call & Put @ Strike $8
Call Option Premium $1.50
Put Option Premium $1.25
Call Purchased
Put Purchased
Stock Price

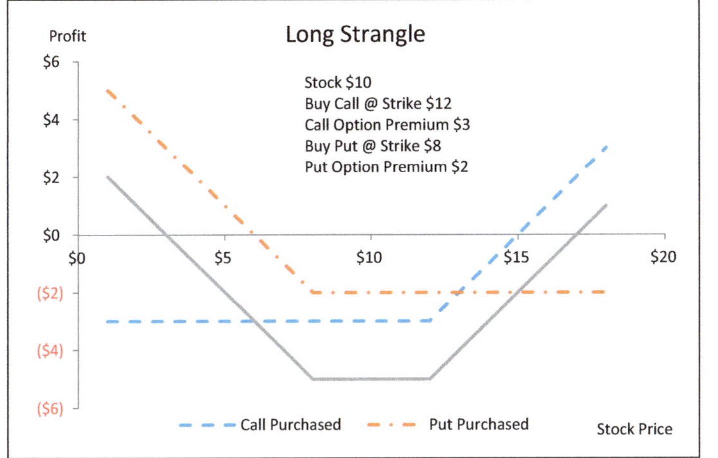
Long Strangle
Profit
Stock $10
Buy Call @ Strike $12
Call Option Premium $3
Buy Put @ Strike $8
Put Option Premium $2
Call Purchased
Put Purchased
Stock Price

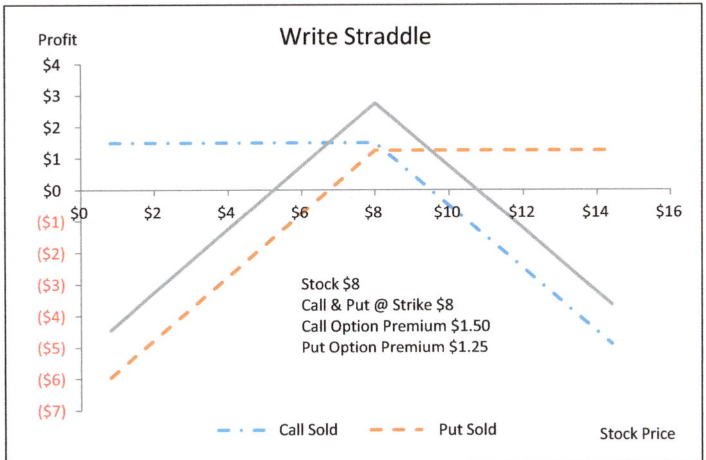
Write Straddle
Profit
Stock $8
Call & Put @ Strike $8
Call Option Premium $1.50
Put Option Premium $1.25
Call Sold
Put Sold
Stock Price

Write Strangle
Profit
Stock $10
Sell Call @ Strike $12
Call Option Premium $3
Sell Put @ Strike $8
Put Option Premium $2
Sold Purchased
Put Sold
Stock Price

Real Options Valuation

Futures

- Purposes of futures markets
  - Price discovery – revelation of future cash market prices, allowing people a good estimate of what prices will be, to make consumption and investment decisions.
  - Hedging – wheat farmers can lock in the prices of wheat for future delivery (anticipatory hedge); hedging is the prime reason for the development of the futures market.
  - Risk shifts – hedgers transfer risk to speculators.
- Exchanges and the four types of futures
  - Worldwide exchanges – following the opening of the Chicago Board of Trade, 1848
  - Agricultural and metallurgical contracts – oil, meat, livestock, forest products, textiles, foodstuffs, and minerals
  - Interest earning assets – interest rate futures started in the 1975
  - Foreign currencies – exists concurrent with the forward market (larger)
  - Indexes – stock index futures (no actual delivery, only by reverse transaction or cash)
- The futures market quotes long positions, short positions, and open interests.
- Exchanges are nonprofit associations of members, and memberships on the exchanges are called seats on the exchange. Only members have the right to trade securities on the exchange. Traders on the exchange are either speculators or hedgers. Short hedgers are firms who own the asset and long hedgers are firms requiring the assets. Futures are traded via organized exchanges and is the major difference between them and forward contracts, which have no physical location for market trades to take place.

Futures II

- Futures have standardized terms (quantity, quality, time, and manner of delivery) and forwards do not. The exchange also sets minimum fluctuation prices (called the tick size); for example, the basic price movement, or tick, for a 5,000-bushel of grain contract is $12.50 per contract. Contracts also have a maximum price fluctuation limit per day (changes over time); for example, wheat cannot move more than 20 cents from the close of the preceding day. These restrictive regulations do not reduce trade; they actually stimulate trade since uniformity promotes liquidity.
- Each exchange has a clearinghouse. It guarantees that traders in the futures market will honor their obligations. The clearinghouse does this by splitting each trade once it is made and acting as the opposite side of each position, that is, acting as a buyer to every seller and seller to every buyer. This action allows either side of the trade to reverse their positions at a future date without having to contact the initial trade's opposite party. Traders are worry free in the sense that they are able to reverse their positions at any time
- To safeguard the clearinghouse, the exchange requires traders to post a margin to settle their accounts on a daily basis. The purpose of this margin is to ensure that traders will perform their contractual obligations. The initial margin (usually the maximum daily fluctuation, in cash, bank letters of credit, or Treasury bills), maintenance margin (margin call if a deposit falls below this level), and variation margin (additional funds deposited) are required to be settled in cash only, in order to bring the account back above the maintenance margin. Margin deposits posted with a broker will be transmitted to the exchange's clearinghouse.
- Closing a Futures Position
    - A position can be settled via delivery of assets to a location or via a cash settlement.
    - A position can also be settled by making a reverse or offsetting trade. Since the other side of your position is held by the clearinghouse, if you make an exact opposite trade (maturity, quantity, and good) to your current position, the clearinghouse will net your positions, leaving you with a zero balance
    - A position can also be settled through an exchange for physicals. Here, you find a trader with an opposite position to yours and deliver the goods and settle up between yourselves off the floor of the exchange (the only exception to the Federal law requiring all trades to take place on the exchange floor in the pit).

Futures Valuation Assumptions

- The futures price is the price of a good today for delivery at some future date.
- The spot price is the good's price today, the cash price.
- The basis represents the difference between the spot price today and the futures price today. It is a function of time to maturity, financing cost, and storage cost.
- The spread is the pricing differential between two existing futures contracts, for example, September and December contracts. Spread and basis are relatively stable over time.
- Open, high, and low represent the opening futures price, the high for the day, and the low for the day.
- The settle is the price at which futures contracts are marked to market for the previous day. The settle is NOT necessarily the last trade price of the day. If the final minutes were highly volatile, the settlement committee will review the end-of-day trading patterns and determine a fair settlement price for the contract based on the day's trading activities.
- The change represents the change in the settlement price relative to the previous day's settlement price.
- The open interest is the number of contracts that are currently outstanding for a particular maturity date, and it fluctuates as contracts are bought and sold. As the term to maturity nears, open interest falls, offsetting trades close positions.
- A normal market implies a negative basis, that prices in the future are generally higher than spot prices. An inverted market is the opposite.
- The basis must converge to zero on the maturity date of the contract. At maturity, the futures contract becomes the spot asset. That is, the futures delivery of the underlying will occur on maturity date.
- The basis will be wider for more distant contracts
- The basis tends to be stable; the cost of carry arbitrage forces stability. Even if spots and futures prices fluctuate wildly, the basis is relatively tame.

Types of Futures

- A T-bill futures contract requires the delivery of a 90–92-day T-bill on the maturity date of the contract based on $1 million of par value. T-bill futures are essentially traded forward rates of interest. The valuation technique is essentially: $1 + {}_3f_4 = \frac{(1+R_4)^4}{(1+R_3)^3}$
- T-bond futures, unlike T-bills, pay periodic interest payments. The result is that you have to consider the present value of these cash flows.
- Stock Index Futures
  - All major stock index futures contracts are settled in cash since there is no physical exchange of goods available at maturity.
  - The contract size of most major US indices (S&P 500, NYSE) is $500 times the value of the index. If the S&P 500 is 950, the contract size is $500 x 950 = $475,000. After November 1997, the multiplier split to 250.
  - Most contracts trade on March, June, September, and December cycles.
  - The futures price for a generic stock index futures contract is

    $$F_{0,t} = S_0(1+C) - \sum_{i=1}^{N} D_i(1+r_i)$$

    where F, S, and C are the futures, spot, and cost of carry. D_i is the dividend on stock i and r is the interest earned on reinvesting the ith dividend until the future's maturity.
- Foreign Exchange Futures
  - Foreign exchange futures contracts are traded at the International Monetary Market, and each contract has a size based on the foreign currency.
  - British pound (62,500), Canadian dollar (100,000), French franc (250,000), Japanese yen (12,500,000), German mark (125,000), Swiss franc (125,000), and Australian dollar (100,000).
  - Settlement involves the transfer of the appropriate currency two days after the expiration date.
  - The price of a foreign currency futures contract is

    $$F = S\left(\frac{1+r_d}{1+r_f}\right)$$

    which is also the interest rate parity, where r is the interest rate for the domestic (d) and foreign (f) countries and S is the spot exchange rate (in $/FX).

Carrying Cost Complications in Futures

- In a perfect market, we have the cost of carry relationship $F_{0,t} = S_0(1 + C)$.
- In cash and carry arbitrage, you sell the futures and buy the spot at T transaction cost, and the futures price must be lower to make a profit. If $F_{0,t} < S_0(1 + C)(1 + T)$ it indicates that the spot price is higher than the futures price.
- In reverse cash and carry, buy futures, sell spot, and pay transaction costs T, which reduces the proceeds from your short sale where $F_{0,t} > S_0(1 + C)(1 - T)$.
- Put the two calculations above together and we have the transaction cost boundaries: $S_0(1 + C)(1 - T) < F_{0,t} < S_0(1 + C)(1 + T)$ where in the equation, the left side is the reverse cash and carry and the right side is cash and carry arbitrage.
- There are also differential lending and borrowing rates and the cost of carry C will differ:

  $S_0(1 + C_L)(1 - T) < F_{0,t} < S_0(1 + C_B)(1 + T)$
- Short sale restrictions only pertain to the left side where only a fraction of the proceeds can be used, *f*, making the final analysis $S_0(1 + fC_L)(1 - T) < F_{0,t} < S_0(1 + C_B)(1 + T)$
- Cost of carry models of futures contracts can be applied on contracts written on underlying assets that exhibit the following characteristics:
  - Ease of short selling
  - Large supply of the good
  - Nonseasonal production of the good
  - Nonseasonal consumption of the good
  - Ease of storage
- Interest rate futures, stock index futures, and currency futures all exhibit these characteristics and, hence, we can use the cost of carry methodology as well.

Real Options Valuation

Futures Valuation

- If the spot price for the September silver contract is \$4.65 while the settlement price for a futures contract deliverable in September is \$4.73 and \$4.80 for October:
  - The Basis = Current Cash Price – Futures Price
  - The basis is \$4.65 – \$4.73 = –\$0.08 indicating a normal market
  - The Spread = September Futures – October Futures = \$4.73 – \$4.80 = –\$0.07
- Suppose that the spot price of silver is \$4.65, the 1-year futures price is \$5.20, and the appropriate interest rate is 8%. Design a cash and carry arbitrage and compute your profits per troy ounce.
  - Our goal is to perform riskless arbitrage. Intuitively, the spot price looks too low relative to the futures price. So, buy the spot and sell the futures. However, riskless arbitrage means that you don't put any of your money down; so, borrow the required funds.
  - Borrow \$4.65 today and owe \$4.65(1.08) = \$5.02 in one year.
  - Buy one ounce of silver today at \$4.65.
  - Sell futures for delivery of one ounce in a year at \$5.20.
  - In one year, we deliver the silver on the futures and receive \$5.20.
  - Pay off the \$5.02 loan and pocket the \$0.18 difference.
  - If the futures price was less than \$5.02, then a reverse cash and carry arbitrage could take place by selling silver short today and lending the proceeds at 8% a year while at the same time entering into a futures contract to buy one ounce of silver in one year. In one year, accept delivery and repay the short sale. (Assume you have some silver to begin with.)
  - Assuming a perfect market with no transaction costs and no restrictions on writing contracts between two parties (i.e., short selling is allowed and is costless).
  - You can either buy the silver today or a futures contract today for delivery of silver in the future. The futures price will depend on some carrying costs between these two dates including Storage costs, Insurance, Transportation, Financing costs.
  - The futures price must then be constrained by $F0,t = S0(1 + C)$ where C is the cost of carry. After minor manipulation, we have $C = (F0,t ⍰ S0) – 1$.
  - Futures Prices in imperfect markets will need to incorporate transaction costs, bid/ask spreads, commissions, differential borrowing and lending rates, and restrictions to short sales, each of which has an effect on the perfect markets version of cost of carry model above.

Futures Valuation II

- Suppose you have the following interest rate and currency data on the US and British markets. Show if there is arbitrage opportunity.

1-year forward rate ($/pound)	= 1.58
Spot rate	= 1.60
US 1-year rate	= 6%
British 1-year rate	= 10%

- Using interest rate parity, we have F = 1.60[1.06 ÷ 1.10] = 1.54.

  Borrow $1 for 1-year at 6% and owe $1.06 in one year

  Exchange $1 for pounds at spot and get 1/1.60 = 0.625 pounds

  Lend pounds for 1-year at 10% and get 0.625(1.1) = 0.6875 pounds in one year

  Enter into a forward exchange agreement to exchange 0.6875 pounds for dollars at the 1.58 dollar per pound rate

- Wait one year, collect (0.6875)(1.58) = $1.08625 from your British lending activities and repay your $1.06 loan, resulting in a riskless profit of 2.625 cents.
- In the equation below, if the right side > left side, borrow $ and lend FX. If the left side > right side, borrow FX and lend US:

$$(1+r_d) = \frac{F}{S}(1+r_f)$$

Swaps

- Interest rate swaps (periodic cash flows in the same currency) and Currency swaps (not denominated in the same currency).
- Notional principal amount. In interest rate swaps, the principal amount is not exchanged; in currency swaps, the principal amount is exchanged at inception.
- Default risk is important since there are no daily mark to market procedures in swaps.
- Interest Rate Swap
  - Suppose you are a bank where your deposits represent liabilities and are short term. In other words, your deposit represents floating rate liabilities. Your assets are loans (auto, homes, personal etc.), which carry fixed rates of interest. You face the risk that when interest rate rises, your cash outflow will increase but cash inflow is fixed. If you remain unhedged, your cash outflows rise, and profits fall when interest rate rises. Hedging is done through an interest rate swap: receiving floating and paying fixed.
  - Your bank's assets have an average fixed rate of 10% with an average maturity of 5 years. Bank liabilities are composed of short-term deposits that are pegged to LIBOR. You hedge against the probability of rising interest rates by entering into an (plain vanilla) interest rate swap. A swap dealer has offered you the following quarterly swap: 8% fixed for LIBOR floating with a notional principal value of $50 million for 5 years. Diagram and compute the quarterly cash flows for the bank.

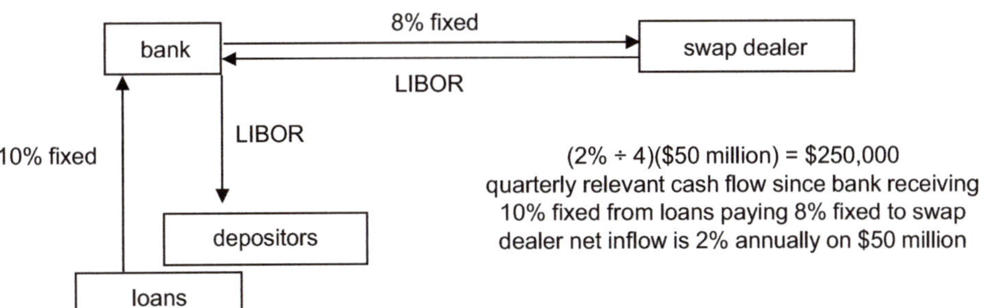
8% fixed
bank
swap dealer
LIBOR
LIBOR
10% fixed
depositors
loans
(2% ÷ 4)($50 million) = $250,000
quarterly relevant cash flow since bank receiving
10% fixed from loans paying 8% fixed to swap
dealer net inflow is 2% annually on $50 million

Swap market refinements

- Off market swaps – fixed rate is set other than the prevailing fixed rate.
- Amortizing swaps – notional value declines, forcing the fixed rate payments to reduce over the life of the swap.
- Seasonal swaps – notional principal value varies at each intervening settlement.
- Index amortizing swaps – notional principal changes in response to the behavior of an underlying market index.
- Forward swaps – cash flows begin at some prespecified future date.
- Basis swaps – two different floating rates are involved (LIBOR vs. Prime Rate).
- Equity and commodity swaps – cash flows are referenced to the performance of an underlying equity index or commodity.
- Swaptions – an interest rate swaption is an option to purchase an interest rate swap with prespecified terms on or before a specified date.

Real Options
Valuation

Swaps II

- Currency Swap. Firm A is a US-based firm that would like to borrow funds to finance a project in France. Firm B is a French firm that would like to borrow funds in the US. Firm A can borrow at 8% in the US and 10% in France, while Firm B can borrow at 8% in France and 10% in the US. These two counterparties have the incentive to come together and initiate a currency swap. Since both firms have the relative borrowing advantage in their home market but would like to borrow in the other, each firm should borrow in the market where they have the comparative advantage and swap those cash flows. Use the interest rates above and assume that the current exchange rate is $0.20/franc. Assume that the principal or notional value is $20 million. The swap is for 3 years. Outline and graph the resulting cash flows.
    - Initial borrowings: Firm A borrows $20 million at 8% in the US for 3 years, and firm B borrows FF100 million at 8% in France for 3 years.
    - Firm A sends $20 million to Firm B in exchange for FF100 million.
    - Firm A pays Firm B French francs fixed for 3 years at 8% equaling FF8 million.
    - Firm B pays Firm A US dollars fixed for 3 years at 8% equaling $1.6 million.
    - At the end of year 3, the principal or notional values are re-exchanged. Firm A sends FF100 million to Firm B in exchange for $20 million.

FF100 million termination A to B

Firm A

FF8 million

$1.6 million

Firm B

$20 million termination B to A

FF100 million to get started

Risks in Swap contracting

- Measurement risk – difficult in examining interest rate and exchange rate exposure, measuring the sensitivity is difficult.
- Basis risk – mismatch between the cash inflow and cash outflow.
- Creditworthiness – counterparty defaults on its obligation.
- Availability of a suitable counterparty.
- Mismatch risk – risk of the availability of a suitable counterparty on the side of the perspective dealer (middleman requires both sides to the swap).

Multinational Finance

- The current international monetary system is a floating-rate system. In this system, currency exchange rates are allowed to fluctuate in response to market conditions with a minimum of governmental intervention. Central banks, like the US Federal reserve and Germany's Bundesbank, do intervene in the currency markets to smooth out fluctuations, but it is impossible for a central bank to permanently prop up a weak currency. Also, governments do enter into agreements to try to keep currencies within predetermined ranges. However, if market forces move the exchange rate outside one of these ranges, there is little that the countries can do other than adjust the target range.
- Prior to 1971, the world operated on a fixed-exchange-rate system. The value of the US Dollar was linked to gold at the fixed price of $35 per ounce, and the values of other currencies were then tied to the dollar. For example, in 1964, the British pound was fixed at $2.80 for 1 pound, with a 1 percent permissible fluctuation around this rate. Thus, the British government had to regularly intervene in the foreign exchange market to keep the pound in the range of $2.77 to $2.83. When the pound fell, the bank of England had to buy pounds, offering either foreign currencies or gold in exchange. Conversely, if the pound reached the top of the range, the Bank of England would sell pounds. When a currency increases in value relative to another currency, it is said to appreciate. Under the fixed-exchange-rate system, strong currencies had to be revalued occasionally, which changed the tie to other currencies to a new, higher rate. Conversely, a currency that loses value is said to depreciate, and such currencies had to be devalued under the old, fixed-rate system.

Multinational Finance II

- A multinational firm is a firm that operates in two or more countries. The reasons for going international include seeking new markets, new materials, new technologies, new customers and market, production efficiency, diversity, avoidance of political and regulatory hurdles, and other strategic issues.
- Factors that distinguish management of a multinational versus a domestic firm: different currency denominations, economic and legal ramifications, language differences, cultural differences, role of governments, political risk, and others.
- Exchange-rate direct quotation is the amount of US $ required to buy 1 unit of a foreign currency, denoted as US$/UK£.
- As an example using fake countries and currencies, we have the direct quotation of US$1 being equivalent to 0.0075 Hispaniola Peseta and 0.0063 Portuguese Escudo. Exchange-rate indirect quotation is the amount of a foreign currency able to be purchased with US$1 and is the reciprocal of the direct quotation, so we have Hispaniola Peseta per U.S. Dollar is 133.3 and Polyasian Escudo per U.S. Dollar is 158.7.
- A cross rate is the exchange rate between any two currencies that do not involve US$. For instance:
  - Pesetas per Escudo = [Pesetas ÷ Dollar] x [Dollar ÷ Escudo] = 133.3 x 0.0063 = 0.840 Pesetas per Escudo
  - Escudos per Peseta = [Escudo ÷ Dollar] x [Dollar ÷ Peseta] = 158.7 x 0.0075 = 1.19 Escudos per Peseta
  - Note that the two cross rates are reciprocals of one another.
- Other issues facing multinationals include repatriation of earnings, when to do so and how to do so; political risk; exchange-rate risk; cash management; credit management; and other global legal issues.
- Issues to consider when going global include fixed exchange rate versus floating versus pegged exchange rates, trade deficit versus trade surplus, currency exchange devaluation versus revaluation, and foreign currency value depreciation versus appreciation.
- Exchange-rate risk is the risk that the value of a cash flow will decline due to a change in the exchange rates.
- Spot rates are the rates paid to buy currency for immediate delivery, for example, going to a bank or foreign currency exchange service for immediate exchange of a currency.

Triangular Arbitrage in Multinational Finance

- Triangular arbitrage will force prices to equilibrium.
    - Suppose we have in the market 0.800 Pesetas per Escudo quoted. How can we take advantage of this disequilibrium and what happens next? Since in the market, with 0.8 P/E, buy Pesetas since they are worth more. So, if we buy US$1 worth of Pesetas we get P133.3 while simultaneously selling Pesetas for Escudos, with 0.8 P/E, we get P133.3 x [E1 ÷ P0.8] = E166.625. Then sell these Escudos for US$ at a rate of US$1/E0.0063 and get E166.625 x 0.0063US$/E = $1.05.
    - Suppose we have in the market 1.5 Escudos per Peseta quoted. How can we also take advantage of this disequilibrium? Since in the market, with 1.5 E/P, Pesetas since they are worth more, so, buy US$1 worth of Pesetas or get P133.3 while simultaneously selling Pesetas for Escudos, with 0.8 P/E, we get P133.3 x [1.5 E/P] = E199.95. Then sell these Escudos for US$ at a rate of US$1/E0.0063 and get E199.95 x 0.0063US$/E = US$1.26.
- The Law of One Price or Purchasing Power Parity (PPP) states that the level of exchange rates adjusts so that identical goods cost the same amount in different countries. The two related concepts are Absolute PPP and Relative PPP. For example, if we use the PPP idea, we have $e_0 = P_h \div P_f$. If a bottle of Chardonnay costs $20 a bottle in the US. and assuming PPP holds, the same bottle of Chardonnay will cost $2 x [1E ÷ $0.0063] = E317.46.
- Forward rates are the rates paid to buy currency for delivery at some agreed upon future date of delivery. Forward currency transactions can be used to hedge some of the potential exchange-rate risks.
- The forward rate is said to be at a discount if the forward currency is less valuable than the spot rate. The forward rate is said to be selling at a premium if the forward rate is higher than the spot rate.
- Interest Rate Parity is a relationship that stipulates the following condition: $f_t \div e_0 = [1 + k_h] \div [1 + k_f]$, where f_t is the forward rate, e_0 is the spot rate, k_h is the home interest rate, and k_f is the foreign interest rate. The problem is that Interest Rate Parity does not hold in reality.
- Suppose a US investor wants to invest $1000 in a German bank that returns 10% interest a year. Suppose in order to avoid any foreign exchange-rate risk, the spot rate is 1.558 DM/$ and the 1 year forward rate is 1.5493 DM/$. What happens?
    - Convert $1000 into DM1558 and invest it in Germany. At the end of the year, you will have 1.10 (DM1558) = DM1713.80. Agree to exchange your DM1713.80 today in 1 year at a forward rate of 1.5493 DM/$. Hence, in 1 year you will get DM1713.80 x [$1 ÷ DM1.5493] = $1106 which is in essence, 10.6% return, not simply a 10% interest but also a 0.6% return from the foreign exchange market since the market believes that the mark will strengthen relative to the dollar. That's why DM/$ forward rate is selling at a discount!

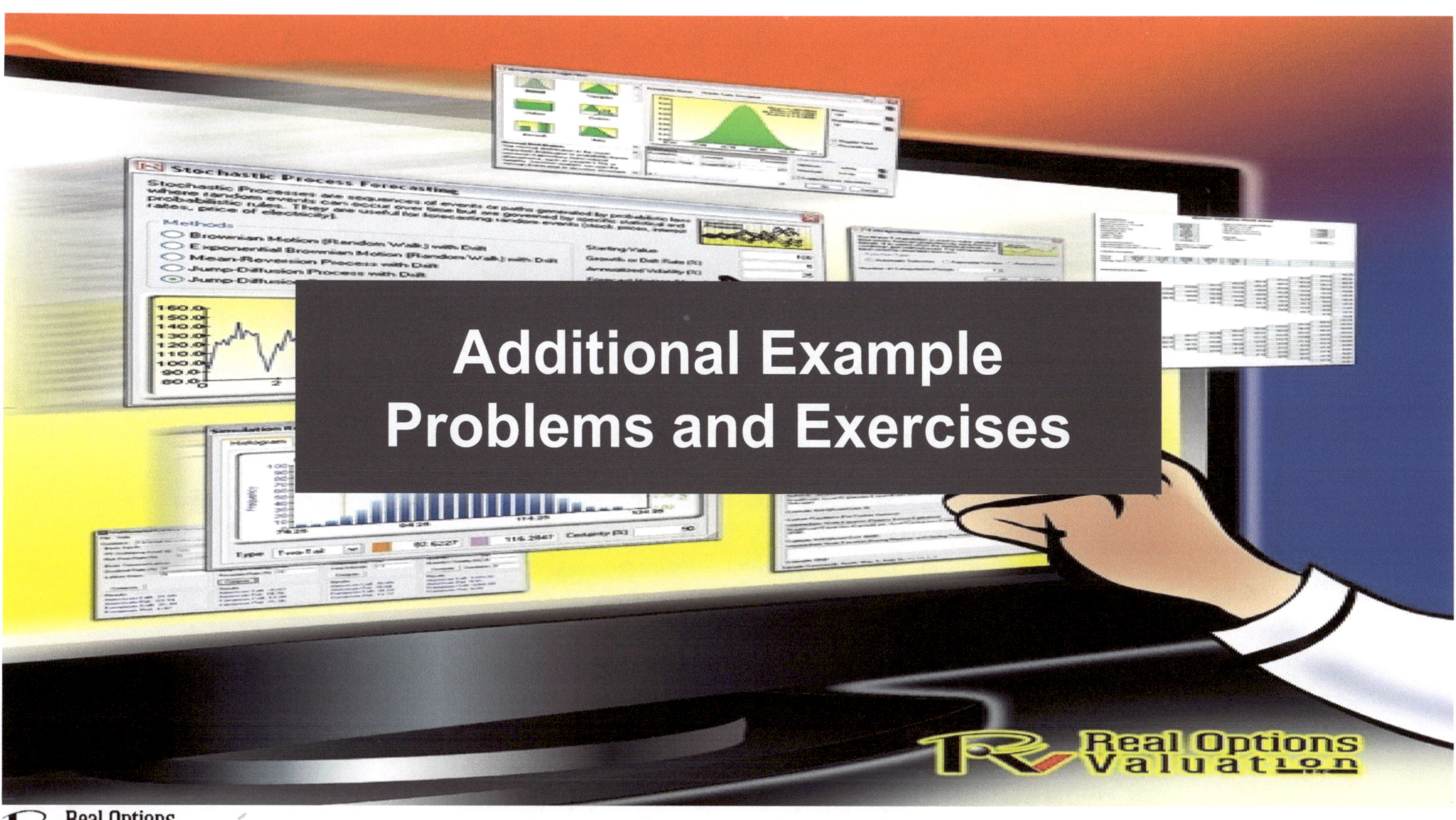
Stochastic Process Forecasting
Methods
Brownian Motion (Random Walk) with Drift
Exponential Brownian Motion (Random Walk) with Drift
Mean-Reversion Process with Drift
Jump-Diffusion Process with Drift
Additional Example
Problems and Exercises
Real Options
Valuation

Exercise: Financial Statement Analysis

If Net Income (NI) is $3M, Earnings Before Interest and Taxes (EBIT) is $6M, and Tax Rate is 40%, what is the Interest payment?

$3,000,000/(1 – 0.4) = $5,000,000 taxable income

$6,000,000 – $5,000,000 = $1,000,000 interest paid

EBIT – Interest – Taxes = NI

If Net Income is $3.1M and Depreciation expense is at $0.5M, what is the estimated net cash flow?

$3,100,000 net income + $500,000 depreciation = $3,600,000 net cash flow

Which of the following will increase the amount of cash on a company's balance sheet?

(+) $2 million cash inflow

(–) $3 million cash outflow

(–) negative cash flow and negative net income

(–) dividends paid

Exercise: Financial Statements Analysis II

Which do you choose assuming a personal tax rate of 36%: a corporate bond yielding 9% or a municipal bond yielding 7%? Assume no state taxes.

Given

Municipal bonds = 7%, no tax, 7% profit

Corporate bonds = 9%, tax at 36%

0.36(9%) = 3.24% taxes

After-tax equivalent for corporate bond = 5.76%

So, we choose municipal bonds.

Alternatively, the before tax equivalent yield = 7% ÷ (1 – 0.36) = 10.94% as compared to 9% on corporate bonds. So, you should choose the municipal bond.

NOTE: The formula used is called a before tax yield equivalent for a tax-free municipal bond. In other words, assuming that the muni is taxable, although in reality it is not, what would its yield be?

Equivalent Yield = [Tax Free Yield] ÷ [1 – Tax Rate]

Exercise: Financial Ratios Analysis

Given that Current Asset (CA) = \$3M, Current Ratio (CR) = \$1.5M, and Quick Ratio (QR) = 1.0, what are the Current Liabilities (CL) and Inventories (INV)?

1.5 = \$3M/CL

CL = \$3M/1.5 = \$2M

1.0 = [\$3M – INV]/\$2M

\$2M = \$3M – INV

INV = \$1M

Given that Days Sales Outstanding (DSO) = 40 days, Avg. Daily Sales = \$20,000, and we assume 360 days a year, what is the Accounts Receivable (AR)?

40 = AR/(\$20,000 x 360)/360 or

40 = AR/(\$20,000)

AR = \$800,000

Exercise: Financial Ratios Analysis II

Given that the Equity Multiplier = 2.4, what is the Debt Ratio (DR) of the company?

DR = 1 – [1/2.4]	Debt + Equity = Total Asset
DR = 1 – 0.4166	Equity Multiplier = Total Asset ÷ Equity
DR = 0.5833 = 58.33%	Debt Ratio = Debt ÷ Total Assets

Given that the Return on Asset (ROA) = 10%, Profit Margin (PM) = 2%, and Return on Equity (ROE) = 15%, what are the Total Asset Turnover (TAT) and Equity Multiplier (EM) of the company?

	ROA = PM x TAT and ROE = ROA x EM
0.10 = 0.02 x TAT	Return on Asset = Net Income ÷ Sales
TAT = 0.1/0.02 = 5.0	Profit Margin = Net Income ÷ Sales
	Return on Equity = Net Income ÷ Equity
0.15 = 0.1 x EM	Total Asset Turnover = Sales ÷ Assets
EM = 1.5	Equity Multiplier = Total Asset ÷ Equity

Exercise: Financial Ratios Analysis III

Given that the Sales/Total Assets = 1.5, Return on Asset (ROA) = 3%, and Return on Equity (ROE) = 5%, what are the Profit Margin (PM) and Debt Ratio (DR) of the company?

ROE = (Net Income/Sales) (Sales/Total Assets) (Total Assets/Common Equity)

ROE = PM x TAT x EM = PM(1.5)(5%/3%) = 5%

PM = 2

Note: ROE = NI/S x S/TA = NI/CE

Equity Multiplier = Total Assets/Common Equity or ROE/ROA = 1.667

DR = 1 – 1/EM = 1 – 1/1.667 = 0.40 or 40%

Note: NI/CE ÷ NI/TA = NI/CE x TA/NI = TA/CE = EM

Exercise: Financial Ratios Analysis IV

Given that the Current Asset (CA) = $1,312,500, Current Liability (CL) = $525,000, and Investments (INV) = $357,000, how much can short-term debt increase such that the Current Ratio (CR) is 2.0?

CR now = $1,312,500/$525,000 = 2.50. So, to be above 2.0,

2.0 = ($1,312,500 + X)/($525,000 + X)

X = $262,500

Given that the Quick Ratio (QR) = 1.4, Current Ratio (CR) = 3, Inventory Turnover (IT) = 6, Current Asset (CA) = $810,000, and Cash = $120,000, what are Annual Sales and DSO?

Given that CA ÷ CL = 3 and CA = $810,000, we get Current Liability (CL) = $270,000

Given that [CA – INV] ÷ CL = 1.4, we have [$810,000 – INV] ÷ $270,000 = 1.4

Solving yields INV = $432,000

Given IT = Sales ÷ INV = 6, we have Sales ÷ $432,000 = 6, and we get Sales = $2,592,000

AR = CA – INV – CASH = $810,000 – $432,000 – $120,000 = $258,000

DSO = AR ÷ [SALES ÷ 360] = $258,000 ÷ [$2,592,000 ÷ 360] = 35.8 ≈ 36 Days

Exercise: Financial Ratios Analysis V

Given that Debt = \$500,000, Interest Rate = 10%, Annual Sales = \$2M, Avg. Tax Rate = 30%, and Net Profit Margin (NPM) on sales = 5%, what is the Times Interest Earned (TIE)?

EBIT = 0.05(\$2,000,000)/0.7 + \$50,000 = \$193,000

EBIT from Net Income, add Taxes and Interest

Also, [EBIT – INTEREST] (1 – T) = NI = [EBIT – 0.1(\$500,000)](1 – 0.3)

Solving yields EBIT = \$193,000

TIE = EBIT/Interest charges = \$193,000/(0.1 x \$500,000) = 3.86

Initially, a portfolio is worth \$150,000 with twenty similar \$7,500 stocks and a portfolio beta of 1.12. You sell 1 stock worth \$7,500 with a beta of 1.0 and buy a new \$7,500 stock with beta of 1.75. What is the new beta of the portfolio?

The new beta will be the contribution. So, the weight is 1/20 and the difference in beta is 0.75.

Hence, 0.75 (1/20) yields 0.0375, and the new beta is 0.0375 + 1.12 = 1.16

Your \$2.0M portfolio with a 1.1 beta has 20 stocks worth \$100,000 each. You sell 1 stock with a beta of 0.9 and purchase another stock of similar value with a beta of 1.4. What is your new portfolio beta?

Weight = 1/20, difference in beta is 0.5, which means we have 0.5(1/20) = 0.025 on top of the original 1.1, yielding 1.125

Exercise: Financial Ratios Analysis VI

The previous Return on Equity (ROE) for a company is 3%. The new Debt Ratio is 60%, resulting in $300,000 worth of new Interest charges. Assume an unchanging EBIT of $1M, Sales Revenues projected to be $10M, and a Total Asset Turnover of 2, and that the company faces a 34% Tax Rate. What will the new ROE be assuming the new debt ratio takes effect?

ROE = Profit Margin x Total Asset Turnover x Equity Multiplier

ROE = [Net Income ÷ Sales] x [Sales ÷ Total Asset] x [Total Asset ÷ Equity]

Given TAT = 2 = Sales ÷ Total Asset and Sales = $10M, Total Asset = $5M

Given D/A = 60% so E/A = 40% and since Equity Multiplier EM = TA/E = 1 ÷ 0.4 = 2.5

Net Income = Sales – Cost (not given here) (=EBIT) – INT (=EBT) – Taxes (=NI)

Net Income from EBIT – INT – Taxes = $1M – $300,000 – 34% Taxes = $462,000

So, ROE = [$462,000 ÷ $10M] x [$10M ÷ $5M] x 2.5 = 23.1%

Exercise: Financial Ratios Analysis VII

Assets = $1,000,000 and Basic Earning Power (BEP) = 20%. Currently the company has no securities, hence all income is operating income. The company is thinking of possibly financing 50% of assets with debt at an 8% interest rate and 40% tax rate. What is the difference between the ROE of the levered and unlevered positions?

BEP = EBIT ÷ TA = 20% = EBIT ÷ $1,000,000, and we get EBIT = $200,000

Levered: EBIT – INT – Tax

$200,000 – (50%)(8%)($1,000,000) = $160,000 then $160,000 (1 – 40%) = $96,000

ROE Levered = NI ÷ CE = $96,000 ÷ [50% ($1,000,000)] = 19.2%

Unlevered with 100% equity, NI = EBIT (1 – Tax) = $200,000 (1 – 40%) = $120,000

ROE Unlevered = $120,000 ÷ (100%)($1,000,000) = 12.0%

Difference in ROE = 19.2% – 12.0% = 7.2%

Exercise: Securities Market Line (SML) or Capital Asset Pricing Model (CAPM)

CAPM: $k_i = k_{rf} + [k_m - k_{rf}]\beta_i$

Risk Premium for a Stock: $RP_i = (MRP)b_i$, where *MRP* is the market risk premium

Portfolio Beta: $\beta_p = w_1\beta_1 + w_2\beta_2 + \ldots + w_n\beta_n$

k_i = required return on stock *i*

k_{rf} = risk-free rate

$[k_m - k_{rf}]$ = market risk premium = market return – risk-free rate

b_i = the Beta relative risk coefficient for a particular stock

Exercise: Beta and Portfolio Risk

Exercise: A portfolio includes \$35,000 invested with a Beta 0.8 stock and \$40,000 invested with a Beta 1.4 stock. What is the overall Portfolio Beta?

β_P = *[35,000 ÷ (35,000 + 40,000)] 0.8 + [40,000 ÷ (35,000 + 40,000)] 1.4 = 1.12*

Exercise: Given that the risk-free rate is 6%, expected return on market is 13%, and Beta is 0.7, what is the stock's required rate of return?

Required rate of return is $k_i = k_{rf} + [k_m - k_{rf}]\beta_i$

$$k = 6\% + 0.7[13\% - 6\%] = 10.90\%$$

Exercise: Given that the risk-free rate is 5% and the risk premium on the market is 6%, what is the expected return on the market? What is the required rate of return on a Beta 1.2 stock?

$k_i = k_{rf} + [k_m - k_{rf}]\beta_i$= *5% + 1[6%] = 11%*
$If\ Beta = 1.2, k_i = k_{rf} + [k_m - k_{rf}]\beta_i = k_{rf} + [MRP]\beta_i$= *5% + [6%]1.2% = 12.2%*

Exercise: Optimal Capital Structure

Assume that EBIT is \$500,000 with 100,000 shares outstanding. The price of the stock at present is \$20. Assume also that the marginal tax rate is 40%, total assets equal total equity, and earnings equal dividends. Further, the firm must borrow in increments of \$250,000 and its maximum debt is \$1,000,000. The following schedule holds:

Amount Borrowed	k_d	k_S
\$0	0.0%	15.0%
\$250,000	10.0%	15.5%
\$500,000	11.0%	16.5%
\$750,000	13.0%	18.0%
\$1,000,000	16.0%	20.0%

Exercise: Optimal Capital Structure *Cont.*

Since $EPS = \frac{[EBIT-(k_d)D](1-T)}{Shares}$ we could calculate the EPS for $D = \$0$:

Shares outstanding = 100,000

$$EPS = \frac{[\$500{,}000 - (0)(0)](1 - 0.4)}{100{,}000} = \$3.00$$

$$TIE = \frac{EBIT}{Interest} = \frac{\$500{,}000}{0(\$0)} = \infty \text{ undefined}$$

Exercise: Optimal Capital Structure *Cont.*

D = \$250,000:

$$\text{Shares outstanding} = 100{,}000 - \frac{\$250{,}000}{\$20} = 87{,}500$$

$$EPS = \frac{[\$500{,}000-(0.1)(\$250{,}000)](1-0.4)}{87{,}500} = \$3.26$$

$$TIE = \frac{\$500{,}000}{0.1(\$250{,}000)} = 20$$

D = \$500,000:

$$\text{Shares outstanding} = 100{,}000 - \frac{\$500{,}000}{\$20} = 75{,}000$$

$$EPS = \frac{[\$500{,}000-(0.11)(\$500{,}000)](1-0.4)}{75{,}000} = \$3.56$$

$$TIE = \frac{\$500{,}000}{0.11(\$500{,}000)} = 9.1$$

Exercise: Optimal Capital Structure *Cont.*

D = \$750,000:

Shares outstanding = $100{,}000 - \frac{\$750{,}000}{\$20} = 62{,}500$

$EPS = \frac{[\$500{,}000-(0.13)(\$750{,}000)](1-0.4)}{62{,}500} = \$3.86$

$TIE = \frac{\$500{,}000}{0.13(\$750{,}000)} = 5.1$

D = \$1,000,000:

Shares outstanding = $100{,}000 - \frac{\$1{,}000{,}000}{\$20} = 50{,}000$

$EPS = \frac{[\$500{,}000-(0.16)(\$1{,}000{,}000)](1-0.4)}{50{,}000} = \$4.08$

$TIE = \frac{\$500{,}000}{0.16(\$1{,}000{,}000)} = 3.1$

Exercise: Optimal Capital Structure *Cont.*

Assuming that $DPS = EPS$, $g = 0$ and $P_0 = DPS/k_S$ then we have the following:

Debt Level	k_d	k_S	$DPS = EPS$	P_0	WACC
$0	10.0%	15.0%	$3.00	$20.00	15.0%
$250,000	10.0%	15.5%	$3.26	$21.03	14.3%
$500,000	11.0%	16.5%	$3.56	$21.58	14.0%
$750,000	13.0%	18.0%	$3.86	$21.44	14.2%
$1,000,000	16.0%	20.0%	$4.08	$20.40	14.8%

Note that the optimal capital structure is also the one with the lowest WACC and highest stock price (P_0). In the calculations above, we assume a $2M total equity ($20 per share for 100,000 outstanding shares) and a 40% marginal tax rate.

Exercise: Computing a Discount Rate (WACC)

WACC: Gemulla Corporation requires \$15M to fund its ongoing projects, of which \$9M will be generated internally with equity. Gemulla's common stock market price is \$120 a share with \$5 dividends at t_0 and expected to grow at 11% a year. Another part will be funded with the proceeds at \$96 per share from 9,375 shares of 12% \$100 par preferred stocks. The remainder will be financed with debt of 5,000 issues of 10-year \$1000 par bonds with a 15% coupon issued to net the firm \$1,020 each. Interest is paid annually and the tax rate is 30%. What is Gemulla's WACC?

DEBT:

Using the formula, $V_B = \sum_{t=1}^{n} \frac{I}{(1+k_d)^t} + \frac{M}{(1+k_d)^N}$

This means 1020 = $\sum_{t=1}^{n} \frac{150}{(1+k_d)^t} + \frac{1000}{(1+k_d)^{10}}$. Solving yields k_d = ***14.61%.***

Using a calculator, k_d = *14.61%.*

Using tables, *1020 = 150PVIFA*$_{Kd,10year}$ *+ 1000PVIF*$_{Kd,10year}$ *get* k_d *= 14.61%.*

So, $k_d - \tau k_d = k_d(1-\tau)$ = *14.61%(1–0.3)* = ***10.23%*** .

Exercise: Computing a Discount Rate (WACC) *Cont.*

PREFERRED STOCK:

$$k_p = \frac{D_p}{P_{net}} = 12 \div 96 = \mathbf{12.50\%}$$

COMMON EQUITY:

$$k_s = \frac{D_0(1+g)}{P_0(1-F)} + g = \frac{D_1}{P_{net}} + g = [5(1+0.11) \div 120] + 11\% = \mathbf{15.63\%}$$

WACC:

$w_{ce} = 9M \div 15M = 0.60$

$w_{ps} = [9375 \text{ shares x } \$96 \text{ per share}] \div 15M = 0.06$

$w_d = 1 - 0.60 - 0.06 = 0.34$

$$WACC = \omega_d k_d (1-\tau) + \omega_p k_p + \omega_e k_e$$

$WACC = 0.34(10.23\%) + 0.60(15.63\%) + 0.06(12.50\%) = \mathbf{13.61\%}$

Exercise: Using Discount Rates and Hurdle Rates

Cost of Debt. Currently outstanding semiannual coupon bond with a 12% coupon rate, 15 years to maturity, and a current price of $1,153.72 with a 40% marginal tax rate.

$$\$1{,}153.72 = S\$60 \div [1 + (k_d \div 2)]^t + \$1{,}000 \div [1 + (k_d \div 2)]^{30}$$

or $\$1{,}153.72 = \$60\ PVIFA_{kd/2,\ 30} + \$1{,}000\ PVIF_{kd/2,\ 30}$

or N = 30, PV = –1153.72, PMT = 60, FV = 1000 and solving for I,

we get $k_d/2 = 5\%$ and, hence, $k_d = 10\%$.

Therefore, the component after-tax cost of debt = 10%(1 – 0.40) = 6%.

Exercise: Using Discount Rates and Hurdle Rates *Cont.*

- **Cost of Preferred Stock.** Perpetual preferred stock sells for \$113.10 per share with a 10% dividend payout rate, a \$100 par value, and \$2 flotation cost for new issues.

$$k_p = \frac{D_p}{P_{net}} = 0.1(\$100) \div (\$113.10 - \$2.00) = 9.0\%$$

Note that flotation costs are included in the computation and no tax adjustments are made since preferred stock dividends are paid from after-tax income.

- **Cost of Common Stock (Three Methods Comparison).** Risk-free rate is 7%, market returns at 13%, Beta of 1.2, dividends paid at time zero of \$4.19, and price of a common stock at time zero of \$50. Assume a growth rate of 5% and a cost of debt at 10%.

CAPM: $k_s = k_{rf} + \beta_i(k_m - k_{rf}) = 7\% + 1.2(13\% - 7\%) = 14.2\%$

Discounted Cash Flow: $k_s = \frac{D_0(1+g)}{P_0} + g = [\$4.19(1.05) \div \$50] + 0.05 = 13.8\%$

Bond Yield Plus Risk Premium: $k_s = Bond\ Yield + Risk\ Premium$ = 10% + 4% = 14%

So, the average is 14%.

Exercise: Using Discount Rates and Hurdle Rates *Cont.*

- **Cost of Common Equity.** Assume new common stock are issued at a flotation cost of 15%.

  $k_s = \frac{D_0(1+g)}{P_0(1-F)} + g = \frac{D_1}{P_{net}} + g = [\$4.19\,(1.05) \div \$50\,(1-0.15)] + 0.05 = 15.4\%$

  Therefore, the flotation adjustment is 15.4% - 13.8% = 1.6%.

  Adding flotation adjustment to the estimated cost of retained earnings, we have

  $k_e = k_s + \textit{Flotation Cost}$ = 14.0% + 1.6% = 15.6%.

- **WACC.** The target capital structure includes 30% long-term debt, 10% preferred bonds, 60% common equity, and a $300,000 retained earnings.

  Using retained earnings:

  $$WACC_1 = \omega_d k_d(1-\tau) + \omega_p k_p + \omega_e k_e$$
  $$= 0.3(10\%)(0.6) + 0.1(9\%) + 0.6(14\%) = 11.1\%$$
  $$WACC_2 = \omega_d k_d(1-\tau) + \omega_p k_p + \omega_e k_e$$
  $$= 0.3(10\%)(0.6) + 0.1(9\%) + 0.6(15.6\%) = 12.1\%$$

Exercise: Using Discount Rates and Hurdle Rates *Cont.*

Retained Earnings Break Point

BP_{RE} = Retained Earnings ÷ Target Proportion of Equity = $300,000 ÷ 0.6 = $500,000

In raising $500,000 in new capital, for example, the firm would finance as follows:

Debt	0.3($500,000) = $150,000
Preferred	0.1($500,000) = $50,000
Retained Earnings	0.6($500,000) = $300,000

Exercise: Using Discount Rates and Hurdle Rates *Cont.*

Project A: $700,000 cost at a 17.0% rate of return
Project B: $500,000 cost at a 15.0% rate of return
Project C: $800,000 cost at a 11.5% rate of return
Based on the Marginal Cost of Capital and Investment Opportunity Schedules below, accept projects A and B because the rates of return are greater than Marginal Cost of Capital for those costs.

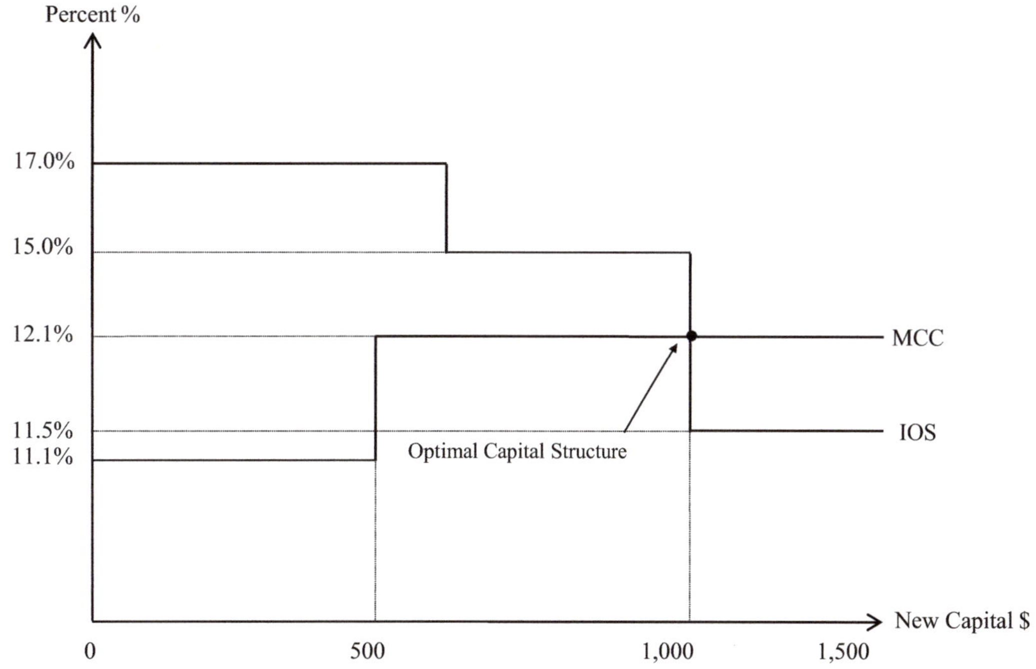

Exercise: Expected Rate of Interest

- Given that the *real* rate of interest is 3%, inflation is expected to be 2% this year and 4% during the next 2 years. Assume that there is no maturity risk premium. What is the yield on 2-year Treasury securities? What is the yield on 3-year Treasury securities?

Given $k = 3\%,\ p = 2\%\ yr.1,\ p = 4\%\ yr.2,\ MRP = 0$

$$k = k^* + IP + DRP + LP + MRP$$

2-year: $k = 3\% + (3\%) + 0 + 0 + 0 = \underline{6.00\%}$

3-year: $k = 3\% + (3.33\%) + 0 + 0 + 0 = \underline{6.34\%}$

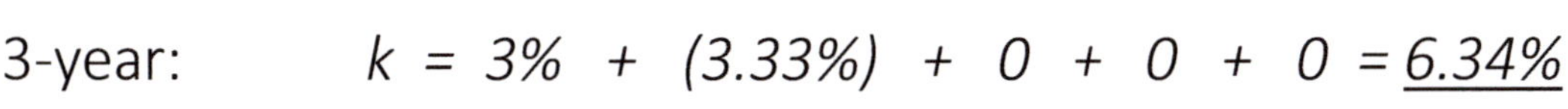

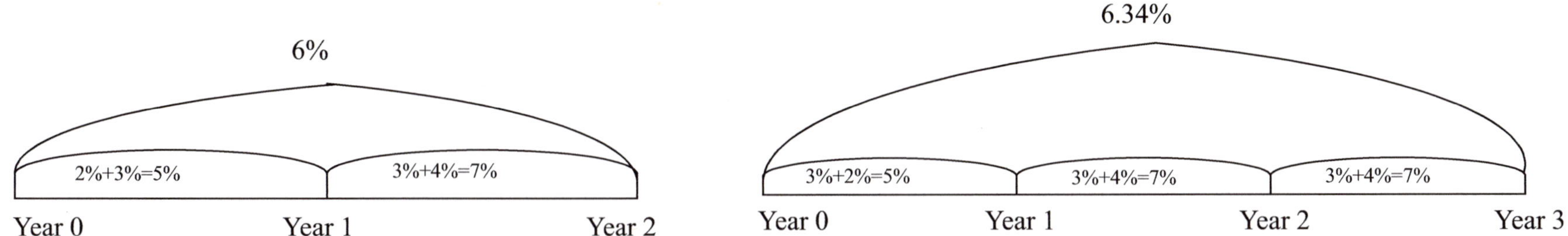

Exercise: Default Risk Premium

The Treasury Bond with a 10-year maturity is yielding 6% while a 10-year maturity corporate bond is yielding 8%. Assume a liquidity premium of 0.5%. What is the default risk premium on the corporate bond?

$$k = k^* + IP + DRP + LP + MRP$$

$$8\% = 6\% + 0 + DRP + 0.5\% + 0$$

$$8\% = 6.5\% + DRP$$

$$8\% - 6.5\% = DRP$$

$$\underline{1.5\%} = DRP$$

Exercise: Expected Rate of Interest

The 1-year Treasury Bill yields 5% and the market anticipated that 1 year from now, it will yield 6%. If the expectations theory is correct, what should be the yield today on a 2-year Treasury?

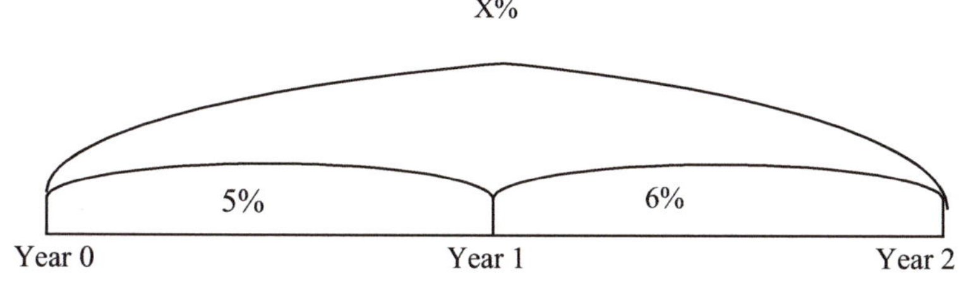

$$x = (5\% + 6\%) \div 2 = \underline{5.5\%}$$

Arbitrage: If actual X is 6%: Lend at 6% a year from money borrowed at 5.5% a year. If actual X is 5%: Borrow at 5% a year, deposit twice, and get 5.5% a year. Either way, arbitrage yields 0.5% a year. Free money pushes interest to equilibrate at 5.5%.

Exercise: Maturity Risk Premium

The real risk-free rate is 3% and inflation is expected to be 3% for the next 2 years. A 2-year Treasury Note yields 6.2%. What is the maturity risk premium?

$$k = k^* + IP + DRP + LP + MRP$$

$$6.2\% = (3\% + 3\%) + MRP$$

$$MRP = \underline{0.2\%}$$

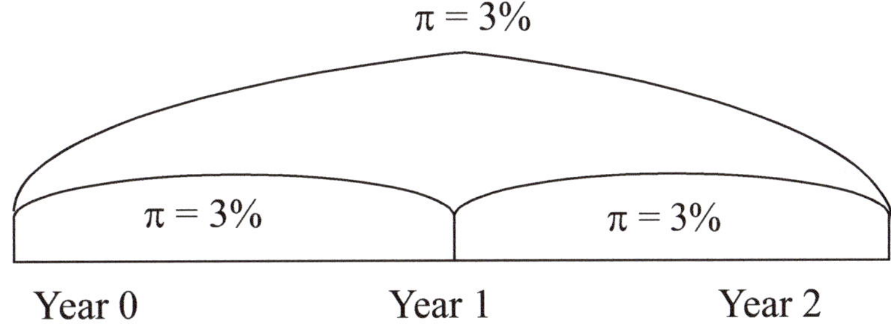

Exercise: Expected Rate of Interest

Interest rate on a 1-year Treasury Bill is 5.6% while a 2-year Treasury Note is yielding 6%. What does the market believe will be the yield on 1-year Treasuries 1 year from now assuming the expectations theory holds?

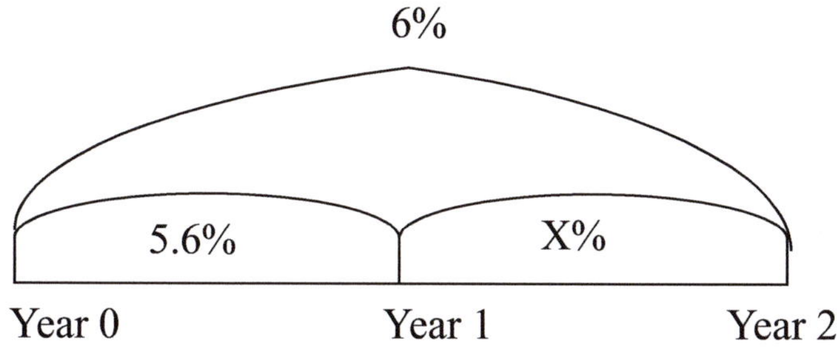

$$(5.6\% + x) \div 2 = 6\%$$

$$5.6\% + x = 2 \times 6\%$$

$$x = 12\% - 5.6\%$$

$$x = \underline{6.4\%}$$

Exercise: Exchange-Rate Examples I

If a US TV = $500 and a French TV = FF2,535., what is the spot rate between a Euro and Dollar?

$P_h = P_f(e_0)$

$\$500 = €2{,}535\ (e_0)$

$\$500/€2{,}535 = e_0$

$0.19724 = €1

€1 = $0.19724 or $1 = €5.07

If British pounds sell for $1.50 per pound, what should dollars sell in pounds per dollar?

Dollars should sell for $1/£1.50, or £0.6667 pounds per $1.

Suppose that €1 could be purchased for twenty cents US today, but if the € appreciated 10% tomorrow against the dollar, how many € would a dollar buy tomorrow?

The price of € is $0.20 today. A 10% appreciation will make it worth $0.22 tomorrow. A dollar will buy 1/0.22 = €4.5455 tomorrow.

Exercise: Exchange-Rate Examples II

Suppose the exchange rate between US dollars and Euros is €5.9 = $1, and the exchange rate between US dollars and pounds is £1 = $1.50. What is the exchange rate between € and £?

$$Cross\ Rate = \frac{Euro}{Dollars} \times \frac{Dollars}{Pound} = \frac{Euro}{Pound}$$

Cross Rate = 5.9 x 1.5 = € 8.85 per £1

Your company is headquartered in the US and all shareholders live in the US. Recently, you secured a loan through a Canadian bank for 5 million Canadian dollars to expand your plant in Toronto. At the time the loan was received, the spot rate was 75 cents US to a Canadian dollar. Recently, the spot exchange rate has changed to 70 cents US to a Canadian dollar. Has your company made a gain or loss?

The US dollar liability of the corporation falls from $0.75(5,000,000) = $3,750,000 to $0.70(5,000,000) = $3,500,000, corresponding to a gain of 250,000 US dollars for the corporation. However, the real economic situation might be somewhat different. For example, the loan is presumably a long-term loan. The exchange rate will surely change again before the loan is paid. What really matters, in an economic sense, is the expected present value of future interest and principal payments denominated in US dollars. There are also possible gains and losses on inventory and other assets of the firm.

Exercise: Leasing vs. Buying

A new machine costs $1,200,000 with a 4-year economic life but a 3-year MACRS class life. The tax rate is 40% and the cost of debt is 40%. Maintenance is $25,000 a year, payable at the beginning of each year. The residual value in year 4 is $125,000. Assuming that you lease the machine, the 4-year lease includes maintenance, and the lease payments are $340,000 a year payable at the beginning of each year.

Depreciable basis is $1,200,000

Year	MACRS Rate	Depreciation Expense	End-of-year book value
1	0.33	$396,000	$804,000
2	0.45	$540,000	$264,000
3	0.15	$180,000	$84,000
4	0.07	$84,000	$0
Total	1.00	$1,200,000	

Cost of owning the machine:

Year:	0	1	2	3	4
Cost of asset	(1,200,000)				
Depreciation tax savings		158,000	216,000	72,000	33,600
Maintenance	(15,000)	(15,000)	(15,000)	(15,000)	
Residual Value					75,000
Net Cash Flow	(1,215,000)	143,400	201,000	57,000	108,600

NPV of the cost of owning at 6% cost of debt is –$766,948.

Exercise: Leasing vs. Buying *Cont.*

Depreciation (T) is a tax-deductible expense, so it produces a tax savings.

Each maintenance payment is $25,000 but is tax deductible, so (1 – T)($25,000) = $15,000.

The ending book value is $0, so taxes must be paid on the full $125,000 salvage residual value, and the after-tax residual value is then (1 – 0.40) $125,000 = $75,000

Cost of leasing the machine:

Year:	0	1	2	3	4
Lease payments	–204,000	–204,000	–204,000	–204,000	

NPV cost of leasing at 6% cost of debt = –$749,294.

Each lease payment is $340,000 but is tax deductible, so (1 – T)($340,000) = $204,000.

Net Advantage to Leasing (NAL) = PV cost of owning – PV cost of leasing = $17,654.

Therefore, we conclude that leasing is preferable to owning the equipment.

Exercise: Warrants

Assume a 12% cost of debt and that the value of a warrant is \$1.50 each with 50 warrants issued per bond. The value of the package is $V_{package} = V_{bond} + V_{warrants} = \$1{,}000$

$$V_{warrants} = 50(\$1.50) = \$75$$

$$V_{bond} = \$925$$

The coupon rate needed to price the package at \$1,000 is

$$\$925 = I\ [PVIFA12\%, 20] + \$1000[PVIF12\%, 20]$$

$$I \approx \$110, \text{ which is an 11\% coupon rate}$$

Cost of warrants to the company:

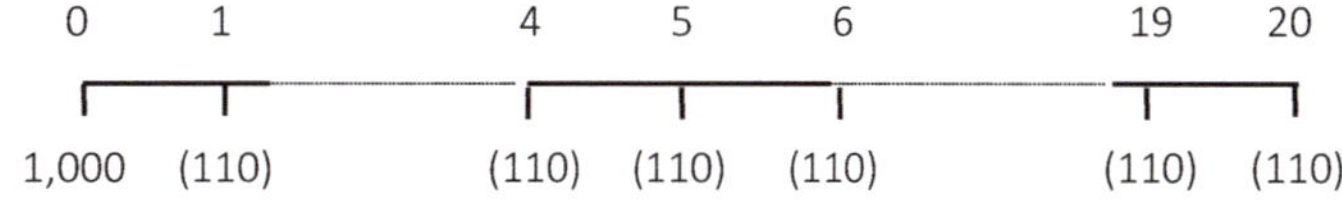

IRR = 12.93%

Warrants are expected to be exercised in 5 years when the stock price is \$17.50.

Exercise price = \$12.50.

At year 5, each bond brings in (\$17.50 – \$12.50) 50 = \$250 when the warrants are exercised.

Exercise: Convertible Bond

Assume a straight debt's kd is 12%, and a 20-year callable bond is issued with a 10% annual coupon. The convertible bond can be converted into 80 shares of common stock. Assume that the price of a common stock P0 is \$10, it pays a dividend D0 of \$0.74, and it is assumed to grow at an 8% rate.

Value of a convertible bond:

Conversion price = P_C = Par Value ÷ Conversion Rate = \$1,000 ÷ 80 = \$12.50

V pure bond = \$100[PVIFA12%, 20] + \$1,000[PVIF12%, 20] = \$850.61

Value of convertibility = \$1,000 – \$850.61 = \$149.39 or \$149.39/80 = \$1.87 per share

Conversion values: C_t = Conversion Rate (P_t) = $CR(P0)(1+g)^t$

$C_t = 80(\$10)(1.08)^t$

$C_0 = 80(\$10)(1.08)^0 = \$800$

$C_{10} = 80(\$10)(1.08)^{10} = \$1,727.14$

When will the issue be called? The company will force a conversion with a call when the conversion value = \$1,200. So, $C_t = 80(\$10)(1.08)^t = \$1,200$, and solving yields t ≈ 5 years. Alternatively, RATE = 0.08, PV = –800, PMT = 0, and FV = 1200, and solving yields NPER = 5 years.

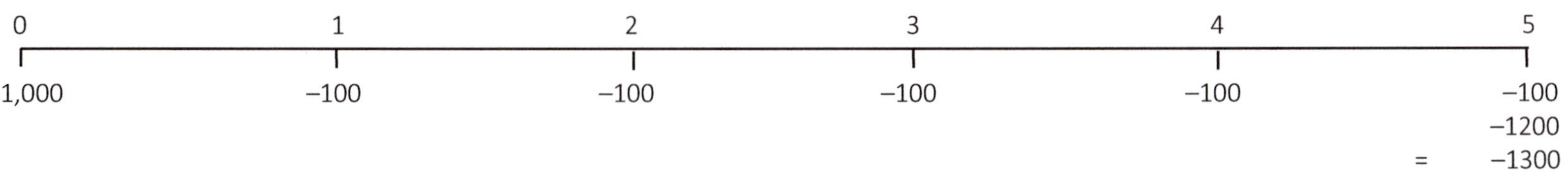

IRR = 13.08%. The cost falls between k_S of 16% and k_d of 12%.

Definitions, Key Concepts, Equations, and Formulae

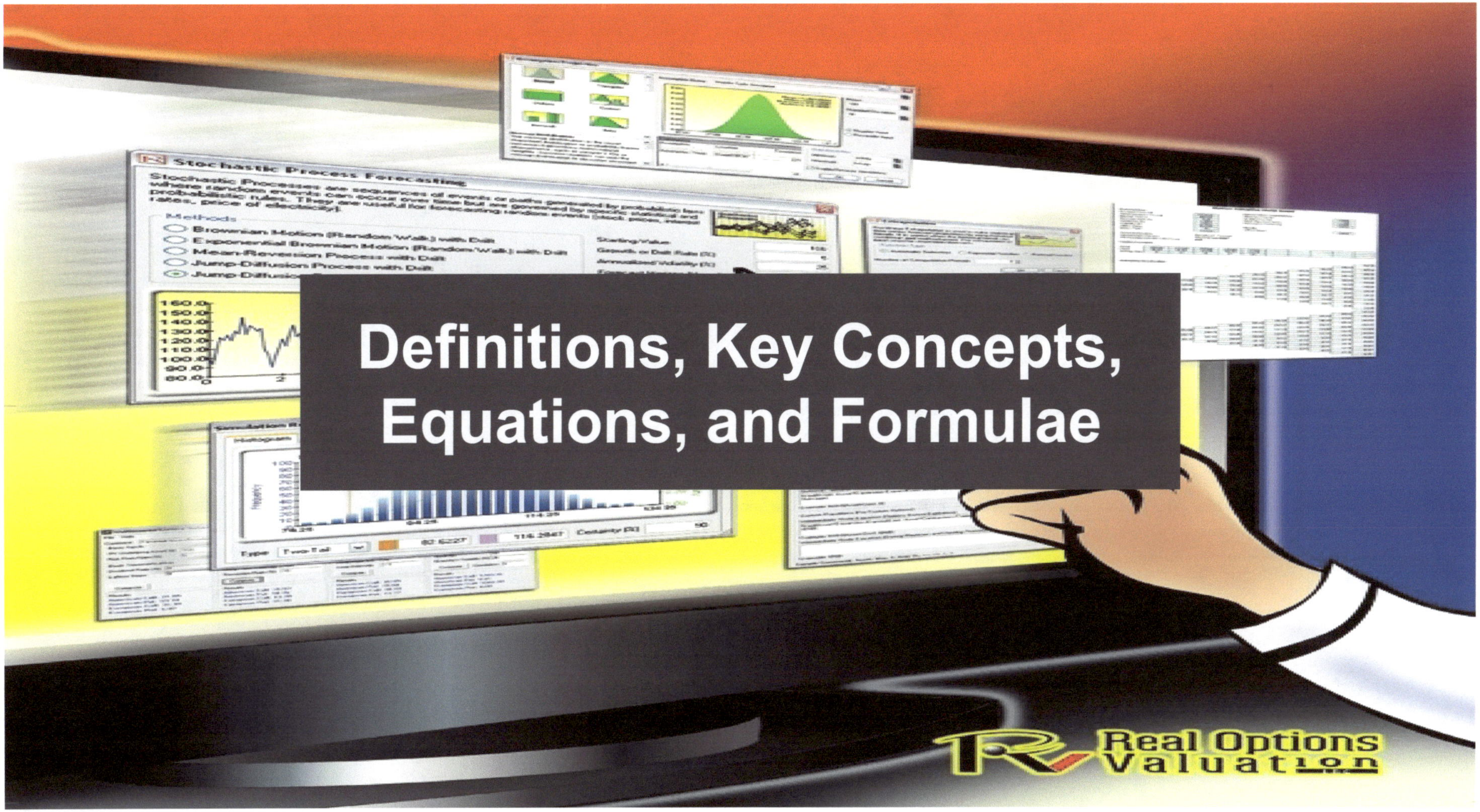

Real Options Valuation

PROJECT ECONOMICS ANALYSIS

CORPORATE LIFE CYCLE AND CAPITAL ALLOCATION

Definition. The primary objective of management should be to maximize stockholders' wealth, and this means maximizing the stock price. This objective further assumes a maximization of intrinsic or fundamental stock price with fair market value and an efficient market, as opposed to only market price maximization, which may be an incentive for short-term unethical gains. Maximizing intrinsic value will also maximize value to society as customers, investors, owners, and employees are part of the society, and maximization of value means higher efficiency, lower price, competitive products, new innovations, and so forth. Corporations sometimes face issues such as the Principal-Agent problem and raising capital (from raising debt to initial public offerings or IPOs). The most common forms of business corporations are:

Sole Proprietorship. Positives: cheap and easy to form, few regulations, no corporate taxes (taxed as personal income). Negatives: unlimited personal liability, limited to the life of the owner, hard to raise large sums of capital.

Partnership. Positives: cheap and easy to form. Negatives: unlimited liability, limited life, hard to transfer ownership, hard to raise large sums of capital.

Corporation. Positives: unlimited or infinite life, easy stock ownership transfer, limited liability. Negatives: double taxation, lots of technical and legal filings (taxes, bylaws, charters, board meetings).

Hybrids. Combinations of the above, including *Limited Partnership* where Limited Partners have limited liability and General Partners have unlimited liability; *Limited Liability Partnership (LLP/LLC)* with limited liability for all partners; *Professional Corporation (PC/PA),* which has corporate protection but is still exposed to professional malpractice liability (appropriate for attorneys, doctors, accountants); and *S Corporations,* which are similar to a regular corporation but owners are one or a few individuals and they choose to be taxed as a corporation.

TIME VALUE OF MONEY

Definition. A dollar is worth more today than a dollar to be received in the future. Because capital is productive over time, there is an opportunity cost to delayed payments. This simple intuition, known as the *time value of money,* is essential for, among other things, valuing stocks and bonds, determining whether to undertake a new corporate venture, acquisition, or investment, and deciding to buy or lease equipment.

Present Value. Present value refers to the current value of future cash flows. These future cash flows must be adjusted by an appropriate discount factor in order to account for the time value of money. The present value (PV) of a future value of the cash flow (FV) to be received in n periods assuming a simple discount rate of i is calculated as $PV_0 = \frac{FV_n}{(1+i)^n} = FV_n\left[\frac{1}{1+i}\right]^n$ for the typical discrete discounting approach, whereas for continuous discounting, we use $PV_0 = FV_n e^{-i(n)}$.

Future Value. Similarly, the future value (FV) of a current present value (PV) that is expected to return interest of i per period (simple compounding) over n periods is given as $FV_n = PV_0(1+i)^n$. The rule of 72 is a "back of the envelope" method for calculating the approximate number of years (n) it will take to double an investment given an expected return of (i) per year, assuming simple compounding where $= \frac{72}{i}$.

Annuity. An annuity is a series of fixed payments (PMT) to be received each period over a specified number of periods (n) and interest rate (i). The present value of an annuity is given as $PVA_0 = \sum_{t=1}^{n} \frac{PMT}{(1+i)^t} = PMT\left[\frac{1}{i} - \frac{1}{i(1+i)^n}\right]$.

Amortization Table. An analysis of a loan payoff table that breaks down the periodic fixed payment of an installment loan into its principal and interest components (the proportion going to interest payments decreases as principal is reduced over time, which means with the same periodic payments, the amount going to principal repayment increases over time) until the entire loan is paid off.

Perpetuity. A perpetuity is a series of fixed payments to be received each period for an infinite number of periods. The present value of a perpetuity is calculated as $PV_0 = \frac{PMT}{i}$. For a perpetuity with cash flows growing at a constant rate of g per period after CF_1, the cash flow at period 1, the present value of the perpetual stream is $PV_0 = \frac{CF_1}{i-g}$.

Cash Flow Series. The present value of a series of different cash flows to be received at different times (t) in the future is calculated as $PV_0 = \sum_{t=1}^{n} \frac{CF_t}{(1+i)^t} = \frac{CF_1}{(1+i)^1} + \frac{CF_2}{(1+i)^2} + \cdots + \frac{CF_n}{(1+i)^n}$.

Compounding Frequency. If the interest rate is compounded annually, then the effective interest rate is the quoted nominal rate. However, if more frequent compounding occurs (e.g., compounded monthly, daily, or continuously compounded) the actual or effective annual rate (EAR) equivalence would be higher than that quoted, where $EAR = \left(1+\frac{i}{p}\right)^{np} - 1$, and for the annualized equivalence, $n = 1$ in the preceding equation. In other words, we take the number of years and convert it into the total number of periods with $n \times p$, and the annual interest rate is now the periodic rate $\frac{i}{p}$.

FINANCIAL STATEMENTS ANALYSIS

Definition. The four basic statements contained in a firm's annual report are the balance sheet, the income statement, the statement of retained earnings, and the statement of cash flows. Investors use the information provided in these statements to form expectations about the future levels of earnings and dividends, and about the firm's riskiness.

Balance Sheet. The balance sheet shows assets on the left-hand side and liabilities and equity,or claims against assets (listed in order of liquidity) on the right-hand side (listed in the order in which they must be paid). Sometimes assets are shown at the top and claims at the bottom of the balance sheet. The balance sheet may be thought of as a snapshot of the firm's financial position at a particular point in time. The typical equation for a balance sheet is $Asset\text{–}Liabilities\text{–}Preferred\ Stock = Common\ Stockholder's\ Equity\ (Net\ Worth)$. The Common Equity section comprises common stock and retained earnings of the company.

Income Statement. The income statement reports the results of operations over a period of time, and it shows earnings per share as its "bottom line."

Statement of Retained Earnings. The statement of retained earnings, or statement of shareholder's equity, shows the change in retained earnings between balance sheet dates. Retained earnings represent a claim against assets, not assets per se.

Statement of Cash Flows. The statement of cash flows reports the effect of operating, investing, and financing activities on cash flows over an accounting period.

Free cash flow (FCF) is the amount of cash flow remaining after a company makes the asset investments necessary to support operations. In other words, FCF is the amount of cash flow available for distribution to investors, so the value of a company is directly related to its ability to generate free cash flow. It is defined as *NOPAT – Net Investment in Operating Capital*.

Market Value Added (MVA) represents the *Total Market Value of a Firm – Total Amount of Investor-supplied Capital*. If the market values of debt and preferred stock equal their values as reported on the financial statements, then MVA is the difference between the market value of a firm's stock and the amount of equity its shareholders have supplied.

Economic Value Added (EVA) is *After-tax Operating Profit – Total Dollar Cost of Capital*, including the cost of equity capital. EVA is an estimate of the value created by management (a measure of management performance) during the year, and it differs substantially from accounting profit because no charge for the use of equity capital is reflected in accounting profit.

ESTIMATING COST OF CAPITAL: WACC AND CAPM

Definition. Investors require a higher return for taking on additional risk. While certain risks associated with individual projects or companies can be eliminated through diversification (i.e., the creation of a broad portfolio of different projects or companies), there is an underlying market risk that cannot be diversified away. In the context of securities, the risk of a diversified portfolio is determined by the market risk of the securities in the portfolio.

WACC. In the most common form of this analysis, the company's future Free Cash Flows (FCF) are estimated and discounted at a rate that takes into account the capital structure of the firm (i.e., its mix of debt and equity) and the tax benefits associated with interest payments. This rate is known as the after-tax Weighted Average Cost of Capital (WACC), which is calculated based on the company's cost of debt (k_d), cost of preferred stocks (k_p), cost of equity (k_e), weight of the market value of outstanding debt (w_d), weight of the market value of preferred stocks (w_p), weight of the market value of equity (w_e), and marginal tax rate (t): $WACC = \omega_d k_d(1-\tau) + \omega_p k_p + \omega_e k_e$.

Cost of Debt. The after-tax cost of debt is used since interest paid on debt is tax deductible. We need to include this tax shield. If the company has issued debt in the past, the Yield to Maturity (YTM) or Yield to Call (YTC) can be used as an estimate of the cost of debt. A comparable company's debt YTM, YTC, or borrowing interest rate can also be used as a proxy of the marginal cost of debt if the company does not have any previously issued debt. The cost of debt after taxes is $k_d - \tau k_d = k_d(1-\tau)$.

Cost of Preferred Stock. The cost of preferred stock is $k_p = \frac{D}{P}$, which is similar to a perpetual stock valuation, and, usually, P_{NET} is the preferred stock price net of any flotation (F) costs where $P_{NET} = P_{PS}(1-F)$. No tax adjustments are made as preferred dividends paid are not tax deductible.

Cost of Equity. There are three ways to compute the cost of equity, typically raised by reinvested earnings (retained earnings or internal equity, and the cost is k_s) or raised through issuing new shares (external equity, and the cost is k_e). The three methods are CAPM, Discounted Cash Flow Model, and Risk Premium Over Bond Yield.

CAPM. The Capital Asset Pricing Model ($CAPM$) is a commonly used model that computes a security's expected rate of return (k_s). It is associated with the cost of capital and contribution to the risk of a portfolio (comprising the market as a whole and to the theoretical market portfolio). The model uses Beta (β), risk-free rate (k_{rf}), and expected return of the overall market k_m. That is, $CAPM: k_s = k_{rf} + \beta(k_m - k_{rf})$.

Discounted Cash Flow Approach. The DCF approach computes the cost of equity by using $k_e = \frac{D_0(1+g)}{P_0(1-F)} + g$, where g is the growth rate estimated by multiplying the retention rate (i.e., 1 – $Payout\ Rate$) with the return on equity.

Beta. A stock's Beta coefficient, β, is a measure of its market risk and measures the extent to which the stock's returns move relative to the market. β can be defined simply as the undiversifiable, systematic risk of a financial asset where a higher β means a higher risk, which, in turn, requires a higher expected return on the asset. An average stock (the market portfolio) has $\beta = 1.0$. A stock's β can be computed as the slope of a regression model with the stock's historical returns on the y-axis and the market's returns on the x-axis, for the same time period with the same periodic frequency.

INFLATION AND INTEREST RATES

Definition. Inflation premium (IP) and other associated risk such as maturity risk premium (MRP), liquidity premium (LP), and default risk premium (DRP) can be added into the discount rate to adjust for these associated risks. The risk-adjusted rate of return is, therefore, $k = k^*_{rf} + IP + DRP + LP + MRP$.

Inflation Premium. This is the premium added to the real risk-free rate of interest to compensate for the expected loss of purchasing power. The inflation premium is the average rate of inflation expected over the life of the security.

Default Risk Premium. Default risk is the risk that a borrower may not pay the interest and/or principal on a loan when it becomes due. If the issuer defaults, investors receive less than the promised return on the bond. Default risk is influenced by the financial strength of the issuer and also by the terms of the debt contract, especially whether collateral has been pledged to secure the debt. The greater the default risk, the higher the debt or bond's yield to maturity. A default risk premium (DRP) can be added to the real risk-free rate to compensate investors for the risk that a borrower may fail to pay the interest and/or principal on a loan when they become due. DRP can be computed multiple ways using advanced credit risk management models.

Liquidity Premium. A liquidity premium is added to the real risk-free rate of interest, in addition to other premiums, if a security is not liquid.

Maturity Risk Premium. This is the premium that must be added to the real risk-free rate of interest to compensate for interest rate risk, which depends on a debt or bond's maturity. Interest rate risk arises from the fact that bond prices decline when interest rates rise. Under these circumstances, selling a bond prior to maturity will result in a capital loss; the longer the term to maturity, the larger the loss.

PROJECT VALUATION: NPV, IRR, MIRR, ROI, PI, PAYBACK

NPV. The Net Present Value (NPV) is used to assess the present value of the project's expected future cash flows, discounted at the appropriate cost of capital. NPV is a direct measure of the value of the project to shareholders. The NPV of a project is the sum of the present values of all cash flows associated with the project over its life, assuming an appropriate discount rate. This includes any current investment associated with the project. The NPV method is used to determine whether a firm should undertake a project. In general, positive NPV projects (i.e., those with $NPV > 0$, assuming an appropriate discount rate) will increase shareholder wealth and therefore should be undertaken; negative NPV projects will decrease shareholder wealth and should be rejected. $NPV = \sum_{t=0}^{n} \frac{CF_t}{(1+k)^t} = CF_0 + \frac{CF_1}{(1+k)^1} + \frac{CF_2}{(1+k)^2} + \cdots + \frac{CF_N}{(1+k)^N}$ and the typical discount rate used is $k = WACC$.

IRR. The Internal Rate of Return (IRR) refers to the discount rate at which the NPV of a given project equals zero. Firms often use this value to determine whether to undertake a project: If the IRR exceeds the firm's cost of capital, the project is undertaken; if not, the project is rejected. In other words, we iteratively search for the IRR where $NPV = \sum_{t=0}^{n} \frac{CF_t}{(1+IRR)^t} = 0$.

Modified Internal Rate of Return (MIRR). The $MIRR$ approach assumes that cash flows from all projects are reinvested at the cost of capital ($WACC$), and not at the project's own IRR (this is assumed true in the traditional IRR approach). This reinvestment assumption makes the $MIRR$ a better indicator of a project's true profitability. The $MIRR$ can be obtained by solving $\sum_{t=0}^{n} \frac{COF_t}{(1+WACC)^t} = \sum_{t=0}^{n} \frac{CIF_t(1+WACC)^{N-t}}{(1+MIRR)^N}$ where COF_t are the cash outflows and CIF_t are the cash inflows at time t.

Profitability Index (PI). The profitability index (PI) is the ratio of the sum of the present value of cash flows to the initial cost of the project, which measures its relative profitability. A project is acceptable if $PI > 1$, and the higher the PI, the higher the project ranks:

$$PI = \frac{\sum_{t=1}^{n} \frac{CF_t}{(1+k)^t}}{CF_0}.$$

Return on Investment (ROI). ROI is mathematically very similar to PI. Whereas PI is a relative measure, ROI is an absolute measure. PI returns a ratio (the ratio is an absolute value, ignoring the negative investment cost) while ROI is usually described as a percentage; that is, we have $ROI = PI - 1$ or $ROI = \frac{Benefit - Cost}{Cost}$.

Payback Period. The Payback Period is the number of years it takes a firm to recover its project investment. Payback does not capture a project's entire cash flow stream (ignores CF beyond the payback date) and is thus not the preferred evaluation method. Note, however, that the payback does measure a project's liquidity, so many firms use it as a risk measure.

Discounted Payback. The discounted payback is similar to the payback period but uses the discounted cash flow in its analysis.

Note that the DCF analysis assumes that the firm maintains a constant ratio of debt to equity and has sufficient income each year to realize the tax benefits of interest payments. Mathematically, NPV, IRR, MIRR, ROI, and PI should provide similar rankings although conflicts may sometimes arise, and all methods should be considered as each provides a different set of relevant information.

EQUITY SECURITIES

Definition. Equity represents ownership in a corporation. There are two forms of equity: common stock and preferred stock. The smallest unit of equity is known as a share. Common stockholders (or shareholders) exercise control over a company by voting for its Board of Directors and, in certain cases, by voting directly on major corporate issues (e.g., mergers). These common stockholders are entitled to receive whatever assets or earnings are available from the business once its creditors have been paid. A company distributes its profits to shareholders through periodic dividend payments, typically on a quarterly basis. These dividend payments often grow as a company's earnings grow; however, a company can choose to reduce or even eliminate its dividend payments. Whereas interest payments are paid out of before-tax income, dividends are paid out of after-tax income; thus, interest payments are tax-advantaged, relative to dividends. Dividend Yield is computed as the ratio of dividend per share of common stock to the price per share. The Payout Ratio is defined as the dividend per share divided by the earnings per share.

Preferred Stock. Preferred stock is an equity security with certain features similar to debt. Like bonds, preferred stock typically offers a fixed dividend; however, payment on a preferred dividend can be withheld without threat of default. All preferred dividends must be paid before a company can pay a dividend to its common shareholders.

Liquidation Event. In the event of liquidation, holders of preferred shares line up behind debtholders but ahead of common shareholders. Preferred stock often has a conversion feature that allows shares to be converted into common shares. Preferred dividends, like common dividends, are paid out of after-tax income.

Valuation. The dividend discount model values an equity security based on the future dividends anticipated by holders of that security. These future dividends (Dt), which represent the cash flows associated with share ownership, are estimated and discounted at the appropriate cost of equity capital (k_s) to give the present value of the security or the theoretical price of the stock (P_0). That is, $P_0 = \sum_{t=1}^{\infty} \frac{D_t}{(1+k_s)^t} = \frac{D_1}{(1+k_s)^1} + \frac{D_2}{(1+k_s)^2} + \cdots + \frac{D_\infty}{(1+k_s)^\infty}$. If a constant growth rate (g) is assumed for these dividends, this model can be simplified using the familiar formula for a growing perpetuity: $P_0 = \frac{D_0(1+g)}{k_s - g} = \frac{D_1}{k_s - g}$.

DEBT SECURITIES

Definition. Companies periodically need funds to invest in projects and to cover working capital shortfalls. Typically, companies raise capital by issuing one of two types of corporate securities: debt (referred to as bonds or fixed income securities) and equity (referred to as stocks). When a company issues debt, it is essentially borrowing money with the promise that it will ultimately repay the amount borrowed (the principal) and make regular interest payments in the interim. The face value of each bond (typically $1,000) is referred to as the par value. Interest payments are often called coupon payments. These payments are typically made annually or semiannually. Bonds that repay the face value at a specified future time but do not make any intermediate coupon payments are known as zero-coupon bonds or strips. If the company fails to make its payments, it defaults on its debt and must turn over assets to repay the debtholders. A company's interest payments are deducted from its taxable (i.e., before-tax) income; this favorable tax status is referred to as a tax shield.

Debt Features. Debt securities are characterized by a number of features. Maturity refers to the period over which the bond is to be paid back. Seniority refers to the liquidation preference of the bond in the event of a default. Holders of subordinated debt must wait until the firm's more senior creditors have been paid before seeking claims on the company's assets. Assets are sometimes pledged as collateral against a loan; holders of a collateralized bond will have first claim on these assets in the event of a default. This type of security is also known as secured debt. Unsecured long-term loans are known as debentures. While interest payments are typically fixed at the time of issuance (e.g., 5% annually), some bonds offer a variable rate that can fluctuate based on another rate (e.g., prime rate or LIBOR plus 1%). These are referred to as floating-rate bonds.

Bonds. Debt securities are rated by several ratings agencies according to the likelihood of default. Standard & Poor's scale runs from AAA (least likely default) to C; Moody's scale runs from Aaa to C. The highest quality bonds are known as investment grade (AAA-BBB for S&P, Aaa-Baa for Moody's). Bonds with lower ratings are commonly referred to as junk or high-yield bonds. A convertible bond allows holders to exchange the bond for a specified number of shares of common stock in the firm at a prespecified conversion rate.

Valuation. Bonds are relatively easy to value using simple present value formulas. A bond is essentially a combination of an annuity (the coupon payments) and the discounted value of the face value to be paid back at maturity (the exception here is the floating-rate bond, which can have fluctuating coupon payments). For a nonfloating-rate bond (V_B) with a given face value paid at maturity (M), periodic coupon interest payment (I), discount rate (k_d), and total number of periods until maturity (N), the bond value is $V_B = \sum_{t=1}^{N} \frac{I}{(1+k_d)^t} + \frac{M}{(1+k_d)^N} = I\left[\frac{1}{k_d} - \frac{1}{k_d(1+k_d)^N}\right] + \frac{M}{(1+k_d)^N}$.

The current price of a bond is often used to determine its yield to maturity ("yield"). The yield refers to the discount rate at which the present value of the bond is equal to its current market price and represents the rate of return required by investors for this type of loan (essentially the bond's IRR). Note that for corporate securities, the yield is greater than the risk-free rate (i.e., the interest rate on risk-free bonds such as US Treasury Bonds); this is because all corporate securities carry some degree of default risk.

Duration. Duration is a measure of a bond's effective maturity. It is defined as the weighted average of the time until each payment, with weights proportional to the present value of each payment. Macaulay Bond Duration is $\sum_{i=1}^{n} \frac{PVCF_i(time)}{V_B}$ and the Modified Duration is $MD = \frac{Macaulay}{\left(1+\frac{YTM}{\#coupons}\right)}$. Duration can be a useful measure in understanding the sensitivity of a bond's price to changes in interest rates. This estimation method is only accurate for small, identical changes in interest rates at all maturities (parallel shifts, not twists/turns/smiles/frowns). The percentage change in a bond's price $\frac{\Delta P}{P} = \%\Delta P$ with respect to a given absolute change in interest rates Δi can be estimated using $\frac{\Delta P}{P} = \%\Delta P = -MD(\Delta i) + \frac{1}{2}C(\Delta i)^2$.

LEASE VERSUS BUY

Definition. There are at least two parties to every lease. The *lessor* is the owner of the leased property and receives *tax benefits of ownership through depreciation tax savings*. The *lessee* buys the right to use the property in exchange for lease or rental payments to the lessor, and in most cases *lease payments can be expensed for tax savings*.

Operating Lease. This lease provides for both financing and maintenance; the lessor maintains and services the equipment and the costs of maintenance are built into the lease payments; the lease is not fully amortized (rental payments do not cover the full cost of the asset over the life of the lease); the lease term is less than the useful life of the equipment; the lessor can recover the cost of the equipment through subsequent leases, renewals, and sale of the equipment; and the lease usually has a cancellation clause to protect the lessee from obsolescence, but it comes at an exit penalty.

Financial or Capital Lease. A lessor is usually a financial institution, a wealthy individual, or a specialized leasing company, and the lessor purchases the equipment from the manufacturer or distributor; the lessee simultaneously executes a contract to lease the equipment from the financial institution; the lease is fully amortized and not cancellable, including a rate of return equal to an interest rate the lessee would have paid on another secured loan with similar characteristics; maintenance is not covered in the lease agreement as the lessor is not the manufacturer but a financial intermediary; the lessee pays property taxes and insurance on the property or equipment; and the lessor receives a return net of property taxes and insurance payments (these leases are usually known as a "net, net lease").

Sale and Leaseback. The firm that owns an asset sells the property or equipment to another firm and simultaneously leases it back for a stated period under certain terms; the seller receives a lump sum of the sale price and in return pays periodic rental payments (this is an alternative to a mortgage); lease payments cover the purchase price to the lessor plus a return on investment. These leases are like a special type of financial lease.

Synthetic Lease. A special purpose entity (SPE) purchases the asset using borrowed funds that are guaranteed by the company. Then the SPE leases the asset back to the company in short-term renewable lease contracts. Such leases allow the company to not report the asset on its balance sheet and the asset does not have to be capitalized, allowing the obligation to be hidden from shareholders.

Lessee Evaluation. The lessee's analysis consists basically of a comparison of the PV of costs associated with leasing versus the PV of costs associated with owning. The difference in these costs is called the *Net Advantage to Leasing* (NAL).

Lessor Evaluation. The lessor evaluates the lease as an investment. If the lease's NPV is greater than zero, or if the IRR > lessor's opportunity cost, then the lease should be written.

DERIVATIVE SECURITIES

Definition. Derivatives are financial instruments whose value is wholly determined by the price of an underlying asset, often a financial security. Some of the most commonly used derivatives include forwards, futures, call options, and put options. Unlike debt or equity, derivative instruments are typically used to protect the company from certain risks (e.g., fluctuations in the price of commodity inputs or foreign currency) rather than to finance corporate projects. Other derivatives include swaps and exotic options.

Forwards. A forward contract is an agreement between two parties to buy/sell an underlying asset (e.g., commodity, stock, stock index, or foreign currency) at a prespecified price on a prespecified date. These agreements are typically privately arranged deals between two financially sophisticated entities (e.g., banks or corporations). Each contract specifies (1) the amount and quality of the good to be provided; (2) the delivery price; (3) the time of delivery; and (4) the delivery location. The party that has agreed to buy the underlying asset is said to have taken a long position; the party that has agreed to sell the underlying asset is said to have taken a short position.

Futures. Futures contracts are conceptually identical to forward contracts, except that they are more standardized agreements that can be traded on regulated exchanges (e.g., Chicago Board of Trade and the Chicago Mercantile Exchange). In addition, these contracts are priced each day, or marked to market. The price of a forward/futures contract ($F_{0,1}$) entered into at time t_0 to purchase a share of a nondividend-paying stock with current price S_0 at future time t_1 assuming a per-period continuously compounded risk-free rate of rf is calculated as $F_{0,1} = S_0 e^{rf(t_1 - t_0)}$.

Options. A call option gives its owner the right, but not the obligation, to buy an asset at a specified price (the exercise or strike price) on or before a specified date (the expiration date). Payoff to the holder of a call option at expiration is $S - X$ if $S > X$ and 0 if $S \leq X$, where S is the stock price at expiration and X is the exercise price. A call is in-the-money if the asset price is greater than the exercise price; it is out-of-the-money if the asset price is lower than the exercise price. A put option gives its owner the right, but not the obligation, to sell an asset at a specified price on or before a specified date. Payoff to the holder of a put option at expiration is $S - X$ if $S < X$ and 0 if $S \geq X$. A put is in-the-money if the asset price is lower than the exercise price; it is out-of-the-money if the asset price is greater than the exercise price. The holder of either a call or put option is said to have taken a long position; the seller of the call or put has taken a short position. The holder of a European option can exercise only when the contract expires; the holder American options can exercise at any time up to and including the expiration date.

Valuation. One common formula for estimating the value of options is the Black-Scholes option pricing model. For European options on nondividend-paying stocks, the inputs to this formula are the current stock price (S), the exercise price of the option (X), the time to expiration (T), the continuously compounded per-period risk-free interest rate (rf), and an estimate of the volatility of the underlying stock (S). The formula makes use of the cumulative normal distribution (F). The price of a call and put are:

$$Call = S\Phi\left(\frac{\ln\left(\frac{S}{X}\right)+\left(rf+\frac{\sigma^2}{2}\right)T}{\sigma\sqrt{T}}\right) - Xe^{rf(T)}\Phi\left(\frac{\ln\left(\frac{S}{X}\right)+\left(rf-\frac{\sigma^2}{2}\right)T}{\sigma\sqrt{T}}\right)$$

$$Put = Xe^{rf(T)}\Phi\left(-\frac{\ln\left(\frac{S}{X}\right)+\left(rf-\frac{\sigma^2}{2}\right)T}{\sigma\sqrt{T}}\right) - S\Phi\left(-\frac{\ln\left(\frac{S}{X}\right)+\left(rf+\frac{\sigma^2}{2}\right)T}{\sigma\sqrt{T}}\right)$$

Put-Call Parity. Put-call parity refers to the relationship between the price of a European put and a European call with the same exercise price and expiration date on the same underlying asset. Put-call parity for European options on a nondividend-paying stock, where C is the price of the call and P is the price of the put is $C - P = S_0 - Xe^{rf(T)}$.

RISK ANALYSIS: SENSITIVITY, SCENARIO, RISK SIMULATION

Definition. Risk can be defined as the chance that some unfavorable event will occur. The risk of an asset's cash flows can be considered on a stand-alone basis (each asset by itself) or in a portfolio context, where the investment is combined with other assets and its risk is reduced through diversification. Correlation among projects and assets will affect the portfolio's risk: Negative correlations between assets or projects will reduce the total portfolio risk. Most rational investors hold portfolios of assets, and they are more concerned with the overall riskiness of their portfolios than with individual assets.

The expected return on an investment is the mean value of its probability distribution of returns. The greater the probability that the actual return will be far below the expected return, the greater the stand-alone risk associated with an asset. The wider the spread of the forecast distribution, the higher the risk. The average investor is risk averse, which means that he or she must be compensated for holding risky assets. Therefore, riskier assets have higher required returns than less risky assets.

An asset's risk consists of *diversifiable risk*, which can be eliminated by diversification, plus market risk, which cannot be eliminated by diversification (*systematic risk*). The relevant risk of an individual asset is its contribution to the riskiness of a well-diversified portfolio, which is the asset's market risk. Since market risk cannot be eliminated by diversification, investors must be compensated for bearing it.

Measures of Risk. Some typical measures of risk include Probability of Occurrence, Standard Deviation, Variance, Semi-standard Deviation, Volatility, Beta, Coefficient of Variation, Value at Risk (VaR), Worst-Case Scenario, Range, Regret, and Risk-Adjusted Return on Capital.

Sensitivity Analysis. Sensitivity analysis is a technique that shows how much a project's NPV will change in response to a given change in an input variable such as sales, other things held constant.

Scenario Analysis. Scenario analysis is a risk analysis technique in which the best- and worst-case NPVs are compared with the project's expected NPV.

Decision Tree. Decision-tree analysis shows how different decisions in a project's life affect its value and are modeled using single-point estimates of various risk scenarios (probabilities of occurrence of certain events and their respective payoffs given certain events occur along a decision path).

Monte Carlo Risk Simulation. Monte Carlo simulation is a risk analysis technique that uses a computer to simulate future events and thus to estimate the profitability and riskiness of a project.

FINANCIAL CASH FLOW	OPERATIONAL CASH FLOW	CASH FLOW TO INVESTORS
+ Revenues	+ Revenues	+ Revenues
– Direct Cost of Goods Sold (COGS)	– Direct Cost of Goods Sold (COGS)	– Direct Cost of Goods Sold (COGS)
= GROSS PROFIT	= GROSS PROFIT	= GROSS PROFIT
– Indirect Expenses	– Indirect Expenses	– Indirect Expenses
= EBITDA	= EBITDA	= EBITDA
– Depreciation	– Depreciation	– Depreciation
– Amortization	– Amortization	– Amortization
= EBIT (OPER. INCOME)	= EBIT (OPER. INCOME)	= EBIT (OPER. INCOME)
– Interest		
= EBT		
– Tax	– Tax	– Tax
= Net Income (NI)	= NOPAT	= NOPAT
+ Depreciation	+ Depreciation	+ Depreciation
+ Amortization	+ Amortization	+ Amortization
+ Noncash Expenses	+ Noncash Expenses	– Total Gross Invested Oper. Capital
= Net Cash Flow (NCF)	= Operational Cash Flow (OCF)	= Free Cash Flow (FCF)
	– Interest (After Tax): [INT (1-T)]	
	= Net Cash Flow (NCF)	

Formula Sheet

Project or Company Value:

$$\frac{FCF_1}{(1+WACC)^1}+\frac{FCF_2}{(1+WACC)^2}+\ldots+\frac{FCF_N}{(1+WACC)^N}=\sum_{t=0}^{N}\frac{FCF_t}{(1+WACC)^t}$$

Future Value:

$$FV_n = PV_0(1+i)^n = PV_0[FVIF_{i,n}] \quad \text{Continuous: } FV_n = PV_0\, e^{in}$$

Present Value:

$$PV_0 = \frac{FV_n}{(1+i)^n} = FV_n\left[\frac{1}{1+i}\right]^n = FV_n[PVIF_{i,n}] \quad \text{Continuous: } PV_0 = FV_n\, e^{-in}$$

Future Value of an Annuity:

$$FVA_n = PMT\left[\sum_{t=1}^{n}(1+i)^{n-t}\right] = PMT\left[\frac{(1+i)^n}{i}-\frac{1}{i}\right] = PMT[FVIFA_{i,n}]$$

Present Value of an Annuity:

$$PVA_0 = \sum_{t=1}^{n}\frac{PMT}{(1+i)^t} = PMT\left(\frac{1}{i}-\frac{1}{i(1+i)^n}\right) = PMT[PVIFA_{i,n}]$$

Future Value of an Annuity Due:

$$FVA_n = PMT\left[\sum_{t=1}^{n}(1+i)^{n-t}\right](1+i) = PMT\left[\frac{(1+i)^n}{i}-\frac{1}{i}\right](1+i) = PMT[FVIFA_{i,n}](1+i)$$

Present Value of an Annuity Due:

$$PVA_0 = \left[\sum_{t=1}^{n}\frac{PMT}{(1+i)^t}\right](1+i) = PMT\left(\frac{1}{i}-\frac{1}{i(1+i)^n}\right)(1+i) = PMT[PVIFA_{i,n}](1+i)$$

Present Value of Perpetuity:

$$PV_0 = \frac{PMT}{i}$$

Sum of Present Values of Uneven Cash Flows:

$$\sum PV_0 = \sum_{t=1}^{n} CF_t\left[\frac{1}{1+i}\right]^t = \sum_{t=1}^{n} CF_t[PVIF_{i,t}]$$

Sum of Future Values of Uneven Cash Flows:

$$\sum FV_n = \sum_{t=1}^{n} CF_t[1+i]^{n-t} = \sum_{t=1}^{n} CF_t[FVIF_{i,n-t}]$$

Multiple Compounding Periods Adjustment to N and i:

$n \times p$ and $i \div p$

Effective Annual Rate:

$$EAR = \left[1+\frac{i}{p}\right]^p - 1$$

Net Present Value:

$$NPV = CF_0 + \frac{CF_1}{(1+k)^1}+\frac{CF_2}{(1+k)^2}+\ldots+\frac{CF_N}{(1+k)^N} = \sum_{t=0}^{N}\frac{CF_t}{(1+k)^t}$$

Internal Rate of Return:

$$NPV = \sum_{t=0}^{N}\frac{CF_t}{(1+IRR)^t} = 0$$

Modified IRR (MIRR):

$$\sum_{t=0}^{N}\frac{COF_t}{(1+WACC)^t} = \sum_{t=0}^{N}\frac{CIF_t(1+WACC)^{N-t}}{(1+MIRR)^N}$$

Weighted Average Cost of Capital:

$$WACC = \omega_d k_d(1-\tau)+\omega_p k_p+\omega_e k_e$$

Profitability Index and Return on Investment:

$$\frac{\sum_{t=1}^{N}\frac{CF_t}{(1+WACC)^t}}{CF_0} = \frac{PV\ Cash\ Flows}{Initial\ Cost} \qquad ROI = PI - 1 = \frac{\sum_{t=1}^{N}\frac{CF_t}{(1+WACC)^t}-CF_0}{CF_0} = \frac{Benefit - Cost}{Cost}$$

Cost of Debt:

$$k_d - \tau k_d = k_d(1-\tau)$$

Cost of Preferred Stock:

$$k_p = \frac{D_p}{P_{net}}$$

Cost of Common Equity (Capital Asset Pricing Model):

$$k_s = k_{rf} + \beta_i(k_m - k_{rf})$$

Cost of Common Equity (Discounted Cash Flow Model):

$$k_e = \frac{D_0(1+g)}{P_0(1-F)}+g = \frac{D_1}{P_{net}}+g \quad \text{and} \quad k_s = \frac{D_0(1+g)}{P_0}+g$$

Cost of Common Equity (Bond Yield):

$$k_s = Bond\ Yield + Risk\ Premium$$

Market Risk Premium:

$$MRP = k_m - k_{rf}$$

Growth Rate:

$$g = ROE(1-Payout) = ROE(Retention\ Rate)$$

Securities Market Line:

$$E[R_i] = R_{rf} + (E[R_m]-R_{rf})\frac{\rho_{i,m}\sigma_i\sigma_m}{\sigma_m^2} = R_{rf} + (E[R_m]-R_{rf})\frac{cov_{i,m}}{var_m}$$

Bond Valuation:

$$V_B = \sum_{t=1}^{n}\frac{I}{(1+k_d)^t}+\frac{M}{(1+k_d)^N} = I\left(\frac{1}{k_d}-\frac{1}{k_d(1+k_d)^N}\right)+\frac{M}{(1+k_d)^N}$$

Stock Valuation:

$$\hat{P}_0 = \frac{D_1}{(1+k_s)^1}+\frac{D_1}{(1+k_s)^2}+\ldots+\frac{D_1}{(1+k_s)^\infty} = \sum_{t=1}^{\infty}\frac{D_t}{(1+k_s)^t}$$

Horizon Value:

$$V_N = \frac{FCF_N(1+g)}{WACC - g}$$

Portfolio Returns:

$$R_P = \omega_A R_A + \omega_B R_B + \omega_C R_C + \omega_D R_D$$

Portfolio Risk:

$$\sigma_P = \sqrt{\sum_{i=1}^{n} \omega_i^2 \sigma_i^2 + \sum_{i=1}^{n} \sum_{j=1}^{m} 2\omega_i \omega_j \rho_{i,j} \sigma_i \sigma_j} \quad e.g.: \sigma_P = \sqrt{w_1^2\sigma_1^2 + w_2^2\sigma_2^2 + 2w_1w_2\rho_{1,2}\sigma_1\sigma_2}$$

Mean:

$$\bar{x} = \frac{\sum_{i=1}^{n} x_i}{n} \text{ (sample)} \quad \mu = \frac{\sum_{i=1}^{n} x_i}{n} \text{ (population)}$$

Expected Returns:

$$\hat{k} = P_1k_1 + P_2k_2 + P_3k_3 + \ldots + P_nk_n = \sum_{i=1}^{n} P_ik_i$$

Variance:

$$s^2 = \sum_{i=1}^{n} \frac{(x_i - \bar{x})^2}{n-1} \text{ (sample)} \quad \sigma^2 = \sum_{i=1}^{n} \frac{(x_i - \mu)^2}{N} \text{ (population)}$$

Population Variance (Using Expected Returns):

$$\sigma^2 = \sum_{i=1}^{n} [k_i - \hat{k}]^2 P_i$$

Standard Deviation:

$$s = \sqrt{\sum_{i=1}^{n} \frac{(x_i - \bar{x})^2}{n-1}} \text{ (sample)} \quad \sigma = \sqrt{\sum_{i=1}^{n} \frac{(x_i - \mu)^2}{N}} \text{ (population)}$$

Population Standard Deviation (Using Expected Returns):

$$\sigma = \sqrt{\sum_{i=1}^{n} [k_i - \hat{k}]^2 P_i}$$

Coefficient of Variation:

$$CV = \frac{\sigma}{\mu} = \frac{s}{\bar{x}} = \frac{\sigma}{\hat{k}}$$

Pearson's Skew:

$$\frac{3(\mu - MEDIAN)}{\sigma} = \frac{3(\bar{x} - MEDIAN)}{s}$$

Grouped Data:

$$\bar{x} = \frac{\sum [mf]}{\sum f} \text{ and } s = \sqrt{\frac{\sum [m - \bar{x}]^2 f}{\sum f - 1}}$$

Correlation, Covariance, and Beta:

$$\rho_{x,y} = \frac{\text{cov}(x,y)}{\sigma_x \sigma_y} \text{ and } \beta_i = \frac{\text{cov}(i,m)}{\sigma_m^2}$$

Portfolio Weighted Average Return:

$$\hat{k}_p = w_1k_1 + w_2k_2 + w_3k_3 + \ldots + w_nk_n$$

Portfolio Standard Deviation:

$$\sigma_p = \sqrt{w_1^2\sigma_1^2 + w_2^2\sigma_2^2 + 2w_1w_2\rho_{1,2}\sigma_1\sigma_2} = \sqrt{w_1^2\sigma_1^2 + w_2^2\sigma_2^2 + 2w_1w_2cov_{1,2}}$$

Portfolio Beta:

$$\beta_p = w_1\beta_1 + w_2\beta_2 + \ldots + w_n\beta_n$$

Risk-Adjusted Interest Rate:

$k = k^*_{RF} + IP + DRP + LP + MRP$

$k = k_{RF} + DRP + LP + MRP$

Earnings Before Interest, Taxes, Depreciation, and Amortization (EBITDA):

Revenue – Operating Expenses

Earnings Before Interest and Taxes (EBIT) or Operating Income:

EBITDA – Depreciation – Amortization

Net Operating Profit After Taxes (NOPAT) and Net Income (NI):

NOPAT = EBIT (1 – Tax Rate) and *NI = (EBIT – Interest)(1 – Tax)*

Net Cash Flow (NCF):

Net Income + Depreciation + Amortization

Operating Cash Flow – (Interest Charges)(1 – Tax Rate)

Operating Cash Flow (OCF):

(EBIT)(1 – Tax Rate) + Depreciation + Amortization

NOPAT + Depreciation + Amortization

Net Operating Working Capital (NOWC):

Current Assets – Current Liabilities

Current Assets:

Cash + Accounts Receivables + Inventories

Current Liabilities:

Accounts Payable + Accruals + Wages Payable

Net Operating Capital:

NOWC + Operating Long-Term Assets

Free Cash Flow (FCF):

NOPAT – Net Investment in Operating Capital

Operating Cash Flow – Gross Investment in Operating Capital

Return on Invested Capital (ROIC):

NOPAT ÷ Total Net Operating Capital

Net Investment in Operating Capital:

Change in Net Operating Capital Year Over Year

Gross Investment in Operating Capital:

Net Investment in Operating Capital + Depreciation + Amortization

Market Value Added (MVA):

Market Value of Stock – Equity Capital Supplied

(Shares Outstanding) (Stock Price) – Common Equity

Total Market Value – Investor Supplied Capital

MV Stock + MV Debt – Investor Supplied Capital

Economic Value Added (EVA):

NOPAT – After-Tax Cost of Capital

EBIT(1 –Tax Rate) – (Total Net Operating Capital)(WACC)

Total Net Operating Capital (ROIC – WACC)

Common Stockholders' Equity (Net Worth):

Assets – Liabilities – Preferred Stock

Earnings Per Share (EPS):

Net Income ÷ Common Shares Outstanding

Dividends Per Share (DPS):

Dividends ÷ Common Shares Outstanding

Book Value Per Share (BV):

Total Common Equity ÷ Common Shares Outstanding

Equivalent Pre-Tax Yield on Taxable Bond:

(Yield on Nontaxable Bond) ÷ (1 – Marginal Tax Rate)

Equivalent Yield on Nontaxable Bond:

(Pre-Tax Yield on Taxable Bond)(1 – Marginal Tax Rate)

After Tax Income:

(Before Tax Income)(1 – Effective Tax Rate)

Current Ratio (CR):

Current Assets ÷ Current Liabilities

Quick or Acid Test (QR):

(Current Assets – Inventories) ÷ Current Liabilities

Inventory Turnover (IT):

Sales ÷ Inventory

Days Sales Outstanding (DSO):

Receivables ÷ (Annual Sales ÷ 360)

Receivables ÷ Average Sales Per Day

Fixed Assets Turnover (FAT):

Sales ÷ Net Fixed Assets

Total Assets Turnover (TAT):

Sales ÷ Total Assets

Total Debt to Total Assets (DA):

Total Debt ÷ Total Assets

Times Interest Earned (TIE):

Earnings Before Interest and Taxes (EBIT) ÷ Interest Charge

Profit Margin on Sales (PM):

Net Income Available to Stockholders ÷ Sales

Basic Earning Power (BEP):

Earnings Before Interest and Taxes (EBIT) ÷ Total Assets

Price/Earnings (PE):

Price Per Share ÷ Earnings Per Share

Market to Book (MB):

Market Price Per Share ÷ Book Value Per Share

Equity Multiplier (EM):

Total Asset ÷ Total Equity

Debt Equity (DE):

Total Debt ÷ Total Equity

Debt Ratio (DR):

Total Debt ÷ Total Assets

1 – (1 ÷ Equity Multiplier)

Operating Profitability:

$NOPAT \div Sales$

Capital Requirements:

Operating Capital ÷ Sales

Return on Asset (ROA):

Net Income Available to Stockholders ÷ Total Assets

(Net Income ÷ Sales) x (Sales ÷ Total Assets)

Profit Margin x Total Asset Turnover

Return on Common Equity (ROE):

Net Income Available to Stockholders ÷ Common Equity

ROA x Equity Multiplier

(Net Income ÷ Total Assets) x (Total Assets ÷ Common Equity)

Profit Margin x Total Asset Turnover x Equity Multiplier

(Net Income ÷ Sales) x (Sales ÷ Assets) x (Assets ÷ Common Equity)

$$ROE = \frac{NI}{CE} = \frac{NI}{CE} x \frac{S}{S} x \frac{TA}{TA} = \frac{NI}{S} x \frac{TA}{CE} x \frac{S}{TA} = \frac{TA}{CE} x \frac{NI}{TA}$$

Call Option Value:

$$Call = S\Phi\left(\frac{\ln(S/X)+(rf+\sigma^2/2)T}{\sigma\sqrt{T}}\right) - Xe^{-rf(T)}\Phi\left(\frac{\ln(S/X)+(rf-\sigma^2/2)T}{\sigma\sqrt{T}}\right)$$

Put Option Value:

$$Put = Xe^{-rf(T)}\Phi\left(-\frac{\ln(S/X)+(rf-\sigma^2/2)T}{\sigma\sqrt{T}}\right) - S\Phi\left(-\frac{\ln(S/X)+(rf+\sigma^2/2)T}{\sigma\sqrt{T}}\right)$$

Put-Call Parity:

$$Call - Put = S - Xe^{-rf(T)}$$

Value of a Bond:

$$V_B = \sum_{t=1}^{N} \frac{INT_t}{(1+k_d)^t} + \frac{M}{(1+k_d)^N} = INT\left(\frac{1}{k_d} - \frac{1}{k_d(1+k_d)^N}\right) + \frac{M}{(1+k_d)^N} = INT[PVIFA_{Kd,N}] + M[PVIF_{Kd,N}]$$

Value of Callable Bond (Called at Time N):

$$V_{CB} = \sum_{t=1}^{N} \frac{INT_t}{(1+k_d)^t} + \frac{Call\ Price}{(1+k_d)^N}$$

Semiannual Coupon:

$$V_B = \sum_{t=1}^{2N} \frac{INT_t/2}{(1+\frac{k_d}{2})^t} + \frac{M}{(1+\frac{k_d}{2})^{2N}} = \frac{INT}{2}[PVIFA_{\frac{Kd}{2},2N}] + M[PVIF_{\frac{Kd}{2},2N}]$$

Yield to Maturity (YTM):

$$YTM = Current\ Yield + Capital\ Gains\ Yield$$

$$YTM \approx \frac{C + \frac{Par - Price}{Years}}{\frac{Par + Price}{2}}$$

Perpetuity:

$V_B = \frac{INT}{k_d}$ and Current Yield: $k_d = \frac{INT}{V_B}$

Macaulay Bond Duration:

$$\sum_{t=1}^{n} \frac{PVCF_t}{V_B} time$$

Modified Duration:

$$\frac{Macaulay}{\left(1+\frac{YTM}{\#coupons}\right)}$$

Convexity:

$\frac{d^2P}{di^2} = \frac{\sum_{t=1}^{n} \frac{CF}{(1+i)^t}(t^2+t)}{(1+i)^2}$ and $\Delta P/P: -MD[\Delta i] + \frac{1}{2} C[\Delta i]^2$

Zero Growth Stock (Perpetuity):

$\hat{P}_0 = \frac{D}{k_S}$ and $k_S = \frac{D}{P_0}$

Constant Growth (Gordon Growth Model):

$\hat{P}_0 = \frac{D_0(1+g)}{k_S - g} = \frac{D_1}{k_S - g}$ and $k_S = \frac{D_1}{P_0} + g$

Preferred Stock (Fixed Dividends):

$V_{PS} = \frac{D_{PS}}{k_{PS}}$ and $k_{PS} = \frac{D_{PS}}{P_{PS}}$

Arbitrage Pricing Theory:

$E(R_j): R_f + \lambda_{jk}(E(F_k) - R_f) + \lambda_{jg}(E(F_g) - R_f)$

Additional Funds Needed (AFN):

Required Asset Increase – Liabilities Increase – Retained Earnings Increase

$$AFN_1 = \frac{A}{S_0}\Delta S - \frac{L}{S_0}\Delta S - MS_1(1-d)$$

Single Period Interest Rate Parity:

$$\frac{Forward\ Exchange\ Rate}{Spot\ Exchange\ Rate} = \frac{f_t}{e_0} = \frac{1+k_h}{1+k_f}$$

Expected t-Year Forward Exchange Rate:

$f_t = e_0\left(\frac{1+k_h}{1+k_f}\right)^t$ and Spot Rate $e_0 = \frac{p_h}{p_f}$

www.ingramcontent.com/pod-product-compliance
Lightning Source LLC
Chambersburg PA
CBHW061134030426
42334CB00003B/39
* 9 7 8 1 7 3 4 9 9 0 7 8 2 *